# Children's Riddling

# Children's
# Riddling

## John Holmes McDowell

 INDIANA UNIVERSITY PRESS
BLOOMINGTON & LONDON

This book was brought to publication with the assistance of
a grant from the Mellon Foundation.

Manufactured in the United States of America

Library of Congress Cataloging in Publication Data
McDowell, John Holmes, 1946–
    Children's riddling.
    Bibliography: p.
    1. Riddles—History and criticism.   2. Folk-lore and
children.   I. Title.
PN6367.M3      398.6      78-19551
ISBN 0–253–15020–5      1 2 3 4 5 83 82 81 80 79

For Juan José,
a riddle incarnate

The essence of a riddle is, while speaking of actual
facts, to make impossible combinations.
Aristotle, *The Poetics* xxii

Words are a plastic material with which one can
do all kinds of things.
Freud, *Jokes and Their Relation to the Unconscious*

The place of riddles in folk thought is an
unexplored field in the topography, if one may
call it that, of popular literature.
Taylor, *English Riddles from Oral Tradition*

The riddle is a short form, which makes it a
perilous object of study; for it permits one to
imagine that an exhaustive analysis is possible.
Kongas-Maranda, "The Logic of Riddles"

# Contents

# PREFACE

The following chapters undertake a comprehensive study of a riddling tradition nurtured by chicano and anglo children in the city of Austin, Texas, during the early 1970s. The primary corpus of riddles and riddlelike performances consulted in these pages was gathered in natural riddling habitats from working-class chicano children residing in the East Austin *barrio*. A secondary, comparative corpus comes from a middle-class anglo constituency in the same city. In all, I was able to peruse on the order of one thousand riddle acts, though a good many of these were either flawed or variants of previously encountered material. The actual number of discrete riddles and riddlelike routines constituting our overall riddling corpus would come to about half of this figure. A sampling of each of the two corpora is provided in the appendix to this book, along with annotations indicating that we are dealing with a riddle inventory so widely distributed in time and space that it could be considered a general, North American juvenile riddling corpus.

One of the innovations of the present inquiry into children's riddling is that it comprehends the entire range of riddlelike productions commonly co-occurring in children's riddling sessions. In order to demarcate this domain with clarity I have had to introduce some new terminology and to build these terms into an unprecedented taxonomy of riddle types. The key concept is that of the *interrogative ludic routine,* an extrasentential verbal sequence founded on the interrogative system of the language, but adapting that system to purposes of play. Consideration of the entire realm of children's riddling shows that all interrogative ludic routines incorporate some degree of ludic transformation, minimally a reversal of the felicity conditions governing the formulation of appropriate questions within our sociolinguistic code; additionally, certain kinds of interrogative ludic routines encompass further transformations of familiar semiotic codes. The true riddle, for example, transforms either the linguistic code or the code of enthymemes, i.e., the set of reasonable calculations deriving from ordinary commerce with the world; while various catches and routines of victimization transform the actual conversational conventions governing the conduct of the riddle act (and other varieties of verbal encounters).

There are essentially five broad perspectives informing the commentary on this domain of expressive behavior. First, I take some pains to elucidate the describable character of children's riddling. Here I am concerned with the texture of riddling, i.e., the articulation of the sensory medium (acoustic space) into distinctive and palpable patterns; with the structure of riddling, i.e., the syntactic and underlying semantic organization of the linguistic code; and with the content of riddling, i.e., the presence of referents and attributes in riddling and the modes of transformation whereby these are rendered strange and interesting. In addition, some attention is given to the riddling session as a unit of discourse, with its own identifiable patterning of form and content.

A second perspective operating in the analysis centers on riddling as process, a socially constructed verbal edifice implying a riddling etiquette and a creative adaptation of this etiquette to individual needs and strategies. A third perspective focuses our attention on the process of riddle acquisition, by proposing an acquisition model integrating psychological, psychosocial, and linguistic development as reflected in the riddler's progress. Fourth, we take up the role played by riddling in the processes of socialization and enculturation, a notion with important extensions to other genres of folklore. Finally, we deal with the reflexivity of riddling, riddling being one of the many forms of culture devoted to the examination of culture. That is to say, culture is both the subject and object of riddling, since riddling *is* culture and riddling *explores* culture. In this light, riddling emerges as a cultural form given over to examination of the composition and boundaries of culture. A further extension of this perspective draws us into the dialectology of riddling, correlating observable differences in riddling production to underlying differences in cultural orientation between the two population groups, working-class chicano and middle-class anglo, represented in our riddling samples.

To summarize, then, the five principal concerns of the commentary founded on our collection of juvenile riddling production include:

a. the describable character of riddling (form and content);
b. riddling as social process;
c. the acquisition of riddling competence;
d. the social and cognitive functions of children's riddling;
e. the reflexivity of riddling.

It will be seen immediately that this cast of concerns distinguishes the present study from what has been referred to as the European-literary approach to riddles, which, according to Abrahams and Dundes, "has tended to emphasize questions of origins, diffusion, classification, and form" (1974:130). Nor have I found it necessary to characterize my materials, as Archer Taylor does for a large portion of his corpus, in unflattering terms like the following: "The riddles in this chapter . . . are colorless and uninteresting. . . . These insipid products are degenerations of formerly vivid and picturesque conceptions" (Taylor 1951:9). Instead, my preoccupation with the cognitive and social dimensions of human behavior leads me to accept the children's riddling production on its own terms and to emphasize questions of form and content, social process, acquisition, function, and reflexivity. I do not prescribe this approach as the only possible one, nor do I feel that the treatment given to these concerns is in any sense definitive. But I would suggest that the present examination of a single riddling tradition does identify a fruitful avenue of inquiry into the character of riddling—as a form of artistic expression, as a unit of social intercourse, and as a component of cultural systems.

The collecting phase of this project was funded by the Southwest Educational Development Laboratory through a grant from the National Institute of Education, and I would like to record here my appreciation for this support. Three previous publications adumbrate parts of the argument developed in these pages:

"Interrogative Routines in Mexican-American Children's Folklore," Working Papers in Sociolinguistics, no. 20 (1974). Sponsored by the Social Science Research Council. Produced by the Southwest Educational Development Laboratory.

"The Speech Play and Verbal Art of Chicano Children: An Ethnographic and Sociolinguistic Study." Dissertation, University of Texas (1975).

"Riddling and Enculturation: A Glance at the Cerebral Child," Working Papers in Sociolinguistics, no. 36 (1976). Sponsored by the Social Science Research Council. Produced by the Southwest Educational Development Laboratory.

Like the tokens of quotidia corralled in interrogative ludic routines, these adumbrations are themselves greatly transformed, and augmented with a good deal of new thinking as well.

My understanding of riddling has been enhanced by pleasurable conversation with many friends, among them Richard Bauman, Roger Janelli, Américo Paredes, Roger Abrahams, and Elliott Oring. I must thank assorted members of my family, and Professors Bauman and Kirshenblatt-Gimblett, for their attention to this study in manuscript form. To colleagues and students at Indiana University, and to former associates at the University of Texas, I record a heartfelt thanks for all the good talk on topics folkloric. And to my wife, Leonice Santamaría, *muchísimas gracias* for help rendered in collecting and transcribing the riddling materials.

# Children's
# Riddling

# Introduction 1

In the controversial thesis formulated by Philippe Ariès, the concept
of childhood as a discrete stage of life has entered only comparatively
recently into European consciousness: "Medieval art until about the
twelfth century did not know childhood or did not attempt to portray
it. It is hard to believe that this neglect was due to incompetence or
incapacity; it seems more probable that there was no place for childhood in the medieval world" (Ariès 1962:33). Modern North America is painfully cognizant of childhood, as evidenced in the enormous
amount of attention bestowed on this celebrated stage of life in popular and scholarly literature. Indeed, the minions of popular culture
have identified the child as an important and well-placed ally and
have found telling means of speaking to him, as any parent in our
society can attest. A most cursory glance over the cultural forms at
our disposal reveals not only a pervasive concept of childhood but
moreover a major cultural focus on the child. It is in the context of
the child's increasing celebrity that the comment by W. C. Fields, to
the effect that "anybody who hates children can't be all bad," acquires its special poignancy. As Philippe Ariès theorizes, we have
come full circle from the Middle Ages in our regard of children: "Our
world is obsessed by the physical, moral, and sexual problems of
childhood" (1962:411).

As every generation rewrites history, so too every generation re-
discovers its childhood, in accordance with current notions of human
nature and the social contract. Since children are scarcely able to
formulate scholarly disquisitions on the nature of childhood, it falls
upon their adult mentors to impose on childhood a set of characterizations answering to notably adult preoccupations. In the face of
powerful images such as the child as innocent ("trailing clouds of
glory . . ."), the child as father to the man, the child as simpleton,
and the child as rascal, the child incarnate recedes beyond our grasp

1

into a penumbra of cultural fantasy and stereotype. The existence and autonomy of childhood as a distinct stage of life is no longer at stake. The question looming as large as ever is: Who in fact are these humanoids occupying the ontological gap between birth and adolescence?

A basic precept informing the present inquiry into children's riddling is that the children must be allowed to speak for themselves. The child's world constitutes a delicate cultural system in its own right, fully deserving of the same objective and sensitive treatment accorded to exotic tribal societies. Our study is founded on a verbal corpus gathered in the crucible of peer-group interaction and supplemented by empirical observation of the children's daily routine as they move among their common habitats, the home, the street, and the school. In this manner we hope to capture something of the authentic flavor of childhood, entering into the child's consciousness and into his or her peer-group transactions. But we can hardly pretend to an entirely objective and authentic portrait of childhood. On the one hand, the present study necessarily repeats the process of rediscovery in the light of adult preoccupations. While I am not conscious of the total inventory of biases informing this study, I can readily point to two: first, the tendency to endow child cognition with all the force and validity we describe in adult cognition; and second, the tendency to find in the child's activity a teleology. The child I would fashion is a cerebral child, concerned with classification, taxonomy, and logical inference, and capable of turning his or her play arena into symposia on matters of interest or concern. This child is also engaged in activities significantly related to patterns of behavior composing the most mature set of cultural expressions. But whatever the bias I bring to this study, it must be facilitated and finally constrained by the empirical record provided in the verbal corpus and ethnographic observation.[1]

Moreover, the natural fragility of children's spontaneous behavior constitutes another limit to the authenticity of our portrait of childhood. The play of children among peers must remain partly inaccessible to adults. Most of this play occurs beyond the reach of the older generations. Seclusion from adult monitors is a prerequisite for some forms of play, notably play imbued with levels of exuberance and veracity incongruent with adult standards. Much of the child's verbal folklore paints adults as outsiders, indicating that children have at least a rudimentary sense of their position in the social hierarchy. We could speak of a stage-of-life consciousness, an almost political awareness of the power differential between children and adults. This consciousness appears in diverse forms: narratives depict mothers as witches, rhymes poke fun at adult liaisons such as teachers. Material of this kind belongs to the peer group, and communicating it to adults amounts to a betrayal.[2]

By the same token, adults are not always appreciative of the folk-loric materials communicated across the generation barrier. Verbal performances of great fascination to the child are routinely dismissed by adults as trivia or roguery. The divergent perspectives of child and adult restrict the possibility of genuine empathy in the cultiva-tion of verbal folklore. Naturally, we exempt from this generaliza-tion the genres of adult-to-child folklore, such as the nursery rhyme and fairy tale, where there is clearly a basis for aesthetic collabora-tion. But in large part, the child's repertoire of verbal folklore devel-ops under the stimulus of peer-group interaction, along lines foreign to adult expectations. Much of children's folklore circulates as an esoteric store of traditional routines, skills, and wisdom.

The fieldworker in pursuit of children's folklore thus stands at some remove from the culture in which it flows, the culture of child-hood (Goodman 1970). In popular and scholarly usage alike, chil-dren have been compared to "savages" and treated as an enclave of primitive society lodged within the most highly developed societies. The child's culture is portrayed as homogeneous, regulated by oral tradition, and unfettered by the constraints of moral propriety as these are understood by educated, urbanized adults. The equation of children and savages is still an active one, as the following passage from the Opies demonstrates: "The folklorist and anthropologist can, without travelling a mile from his door, examine a thriving unself-conscious culture . . . which is as unnoticed by the sophisticated world, and quite as little affected by it, as is the culture of some dwindling aboriginal tribe living out its helpless existence in the hinterlands of a native reserve" (Opie and Opie 1959:2). Like all analogies, this one partly reveals and partly distorts. But it has at least one major salutary effect, that of reminding us of the essential integrity of the child's world and the consequent need to approach the world of childhood with all due respect.

The child, then, is an appropriate object of ethnography. Adult investigators must leave behind notions of childishness by which they customarily view the world of children, just as ethnographers of other cultures must attempt to divest themselves of ethnocentrism derivative from their own cultural moorings. The ethnographer of children, therefore, develops field strategies likely to conserve the authenticity of children's natural behavior and subsequently guards against the intrusion of ageist stereotypes in making sense out of the ethnographic record. We shall examine below the strategy devised for collecting children's riddles, which essentially aimed at preserving intact the natural peer group as the social unit of interaction during the collecting process, thereby minimizing the impact of the adult observer. Other ancillary tactics included collection in natural habitats and the adoption of a participant-observer persona capable of being assimilated into the peer-group structure.

In regard to ageist bias entering in at the stage of analysis and interpretation, the primary safeguards have already been mentioned: first, the empirical approach subjecting all generalization to verification in the light of the data; and second, the tendency to find value and purpose in the materials of children's folklore.

## SAMPLE AND METHODOLOGY

There are two separate bodies of data for this study, a primary corpus collected by myself and Leonice Santamaría in East Austin, Texas, during the years 1974 and 1975, and a secondary corpus, providing comparative data, kindly made available to me by Professor Richard Bauman of the University of Texas, Austin, collected under his supervision by fieldworkers in the Texas Children's Folklore Project.[3]

The primary corpus derives from a sample of fifty chicano children of both sexes, ranging in age from four to eleven years. As table I indicates, the range from five to eight years is most amply represented.

TABLE I.    *Primary Research Sample*

| Age | 4 | 5 | 6 | 7 | 8 | 9 | 10 | 11 |
|---|---|---|---|---|---|---|---|---|
| Male | I | 5 | 5 | 5 | 5 | 3 | 0 | I |
| Female | I | 5 | 5 | 5 | 5 | 2 | I | I |

I make no claim to having exhausted the repertoires of the entire community, let alone of the children consulted for this project. But the repetition of material from one child to another as the collecting progressed led me to believe that I had acquired a fair sampling of the overall repertoire of children's riddling within this community.

The children in the primary sample live in East Austin, where socioeconomic level is uniformly working class, as indicated by the level of education of the parents, their occupations, and incomes. Educational levels rarely exceeded the early years of high school. Typical occupations given were custodians, construction workers, nurses' and teachers' aides, restaurant and hotel personnel, and unemployed. Family incomes in the area averaged just over 5,000 dollars annually, at great variance with the city average of over 9,000 dollars annually (1970 Census). These socioeconomic indicators will be treated in greater detail in chapter 8.

A variety of field techniques were employed in assembling the primary corpus, always with the intention of preserving intact the fragile universe of children's spontaneous play. In some instances, we were able to approach naturalistic collecting conditions, when the children were engaged in play and the familiar personage of the collector failed to disrupt the activity in progress. Frequently the folklorist became a focus of attention and was incorporated into the action. Since riddling does permit of a mixed constituency, adult and child, it would be inaccurate to label these occasions unnatural. In any event, we tried to maintain as low a profile as possible in order to allow the children's play to continue in its natural form. The typical session involved the interaction of folklorist and children. Usually the peer group remained intact as the social unit of interaction, though in some cases the interaction modulated in the direction of an interview format. Our goal was to preserve the natural quality of peer-group interaction, and this, to a considerable extent, we managed to do.

Collecting riddles in East Austin was always an adventure and frequently a treat. Children and adults alike received us with characteristic decency and curiosity. On more than one memorable occasion we found ourselves the beneficiaries of the generosity that flows so freely among the residents of East Austin. In a community where children play freely in their neighborhood peer groups, the observation and recording of this play did not constitute an insurmountable problem.

The secondary corpus is included for essentially comparative purposes. As I had no hand in its assembly, I feel less confident in utilizing it to the same extent that I have utilized the primary corpus. The secondary corpus was gathered from a group of twenty-five anglo, middle-class children, ages five to seven, resident in Austin during the autumn of 1976. Each child was interviewed individually and also recorded in the context of peer-group interaction. As we shall find in a later chapter, those children responsible for our secondary corpus occupy quite a different socioeconomic position from the children producing our primary corpus, and their riddling reflects this differential in socioeconomic status.

## THE CHILD'S HABITAT

The quest for children's riddles drew us into their daily rounds. While significant subcultural differences do exist, we can to a considerable extent describe a single pattern of activity and habitat for the great majority of contemporary North American children. The early years, up to age four or so, are spent primarily in the home and its environs, with excursions beyond this geographical and social nexus generally supervised by personnel associated with the home, i.e., parents or older siblings. Later, by the fifth or sixth year, the school environment becomes a part of the child's life. Around the same period, and with increasing regularity, the child begins to frequent neighborhood locations such as parks, stores, and a variety of play areas. For the sake of convenience we might gather these locations together under the label *street locations*. Other settings are only irregularly visited: a friend's or relative's house, a distant vacation spot, a parent's work place. There appears to be little misrepresentation in abstracting three principal settings from the continuous flow of children's meanderings as the essential constituents of the child's social and geographical habitat: the home, the street, and the school. As we shall see, these settings are related in interesting ways, each one fostering specific forms of behavior.

## THE HOME

The home is of course the locus of activity of the family. The family is the exclusive agent of socialization in the early years and remains a critical factor in this process throughout childhood and adolescence. We identify within the family nexus the major communicative network available to the young child. The child interacts first with the mother and later with the father, other siblings, and additional relatives living at home, such as grandparents. These communicative formats condition subsequent patterns of communication encountered as the individual matures and takes his place in adult society. Brian Sutton-Smith (1977) views the mother-infant paradigm as the model for all future communicative networks in which the child will participate. Here the infant receives and refines the fundamental attitudes of attending and performing. Likewise, the sibling peer group ranks as an extremely consequential arena of interaction, precursor of and preparation for all future peer groups. In the home environment the child experiences the initial stimuli that are incorporated into later expressive behavior and moreover begins to construct and transmit stylized interpretations of his experience.

The concept of home entails connotations of identity, security, and authority. The home is the most intimate realm of the child's cosmology, providing a sense of self as a unit within a stable social environment. Presiding over the home are the awesome parental figures, who administer mercy and justice in ways often inscrutable to their progeny. Yet the home is also the environment fostering the most intense of affective relationships. These broad characterizations apply equally to our two communities, though as we shall see in chapter eight, many specific contrasts emerge as the analysis becomes more narrowly focused.

The street as a social node has some standing in the sociological literature. William Foote Whyte noted in a seminal study that "the nuclei of most gangs can be traced back to early childhood, when living close together provided the first opportunities for social contacts" (Whyte 1943:255). Implicit in the treatment of the street as a social environment is the elaboration of appropriate kinds of behavior, generically street behavior. In particular, it has been stressed that many communities promote differential behavior in the home and on the street.

Roger Abrahams organizes his study of black speech repertoires around this dichotomy of street and home. Speech behavior differs from home to street: "Talking is considerably more restricted in the house in regard to the subjects of discussion, the vocabulary used, the amount of noise generally permitted . . . and the communication relationships pursued in that ambience" (Abrahams 1974:6). The speech behavior of children is especially curtailed: "The value on silence in the home (on the part of children only) is just one facet of an elaborate system of deference which includes learning proper modes of address, how and when to act in the presence of adults, and how and where to look (mutely) when being addressed by an older person" (Abrahams 1974:9). The home is the locus of socialization into this complex and rigid system of speech decorum. By contrast, street talking is characterized by the features of casualness and spontaneity, a release from the constraints in effect around the home (Abrahams 1974:52).

The home as a social environment evinces the notable traits of the presence of parental authority, which must appear virtually absolute to the young child, and a set of social relationships, which are intimate, continuous, and enduring. When the child steps out into the street, he finds himself in quite another situation. Parental authority is left behind; adult supervision is at best intermittent. A child comes into contact with other children standing beyond the pale of the family matrix. As Jane Jacobs has it, streets "bring together people who do not know each other in an intimate, private fashion, and in most cases do not care to know each other in that fashion" (Jacobs 1961:55). No doubt intimate relationships can and do develop out of street acquaintances, but the quality of interaction on the street gains its distinctive flavor from the casual nature of street relations. To the young child just emerging from the family environment, street relationships involve contact with a social unit definitely perceived as "them," i.e., as outsiders, strangers, *forasteros*.

The street is not, of course, an undifferentiated plain. Children develop a manner of sacred geography, attaching special significance to sites and locations within their ken. In typical neighborhoods a range of unique nodes articulate the street expanse: the corner grocery, the shopping center, places to secure goods and meet friends; the park, an open area perfect for unbridled play, often entirely free from adult supervision; the woods or creek, a secluded area of pastoral fascination; the houses of friends or relatives, temporary bases in the uncertain street world; and schools, complicated sites involving juxtaposition of home and street. Each of these nodes has its own character and modifies street behavior accordingly. Still, across the entire range a form of behavior obtains that is recognizably in contrast to home behavior.

The street is the province of the peer group. Street behavior tends to be assertive, aggressive, rowdy, and belligerent in various shades and intensities depending on personality and circumstance. The child is released from his best behavior, a role imposed from without by adult monitors. On the street, children are prone to grapple with their peers for status, in a world devoid of prearranged social hierarchies. Moving into the street involves a transition to a world of adventure, risk, challenge, and one that opens up possibilities of triumph and glory, as well as defeat and ignominy. In short, the street is a world of negotiable status, comparatively uninhibited activity, and casual, spontaneous interaction.

Even as I write these words about the street I feel uneasy lest I be caught indulging in a modern form of romanticism. The street that I have described is the street that I knew as a child and the street that I observed in East Austin. Yet as Shipman (1972) warns, the child's access to this world of relatively uninhibited play is seriously in jeopardy, as the brokers of adult society further and further invade the child's domain and organize his time for him. Many of the anglo children included in this study would feel uneasy in a street environment as I have described it, simply because they have had little exposure to the world of the street. The child who spends summers away at camp and school days in school and then in any number of supervised activities (such as piano lessons, dancing lessons, and the rest) will acquire little of the street sense I have alluded to. Here again we discover a major difference in the lives of the two portions of our sample, and we will connect this difference to palpable differences in each group's cultivation of the oral tradition.

### THE SCHOOL

The school is a special setting involving the not always harmonious intersection of home and street. Parental authority is present by proxy, delegated to the teaching staff. However, unlike at home, this authority is clearly perceived to be less than absolute. Even with the acceptance of corporal punishment in Austin, and the occasional occurrence of abuses, the children nonetheless understand that obedience can be negotiated in school to a far greater extent than at home. Still, the presence of authority, though perhaps somewhat muted, tends to bring out the familiar syndrome of the child on his best behavior. The lack of affective identification with school personnel, however, renders mock obedience legitimate.

The classroom and other areas directly supervised by adults preserve this analogy with the home. But school also displays another forum, that of unsupervised play on the adjacent playground. While adult supervision may not be entirely absent even here, it is distant enough to permit the resurgence of street behavior, as many a weary teacher can attest. Playground behavior resurrects much of the pattern familiar from street behavior: status negotiation, casual, spontaneous interaction, comparatively uninhibited play. Even off the playground, these social ingredients are only partially contained by the efforts of adult authority. Street behavior is waiting to erupt at all times, not only on the playground, but also in the classroom when the teacher leaves momentarily, in the hallways, in restrooms, wherever the watchful eye of authority is absent or lax.

This uneasy tension of social environments tends to produce exaggerated forms of both street and home behavior. The fortunate teacher who manages to establish affective rapport with students may well elicit from the children behavior largely congruent with home patterns. In other classroom situations, and beyond the view of authority, children may engage in extreme forms of street behavior, such as fighting, taunting, and even vandalism. The crucial factor determining which type of behavior predominates is the degree of affective identification the child feels toward the school. Here again, the two portions of our sample, the working-class chicano kids and the middle-class anglo kids, exhibit a characteristically different pattern. The latter group is more likely to develop positive attitudes toward the school as an institution. These children are raised with positive expectations about school. The arrangements of the school environment, and the kinds of tasks proposed, are compatible with these children's prior socialization. Basil Bernstein, after a thorough consideration of pertinent details, concludes that the middle-class child adapts readily to the school environment, affirming that "there is no serious clash of expectations between the school and the middle-class child" (Bernstein 1970:230).

The situation of the chicano child is generally, though not always, rather different. Chicano children sometimes pick up negative attitudes toward school from parents and older siblings. Moreover, the school remains an alien institution, one that forces the child to repress much of his social identity. It only need be mentioned, by way of demonstration of this point, that as recently as ten years ago it was against the law to speak Spanish on the school grounds of the state of Texas, subject to corporal punishment. The chicano children I observed in East Austin were solidly aligned against the authority of school personnel, be they chicano or anglo. Incidents of cooperation often turned out to be mock collaboration. The school environment is probably a locus of tension in any community, but in the instance of East Austin there can be little doubt that external political and cultural circumstances exacerbate the situation.

## CHILD FOLKLORE

As the child moves within and between home, street, and school, he finds himself continuously immersed in communicative events, demanding from him appropriate kinds of responses, and allowing him periodic opportunities to express himself under the attentive or not so attentive gaze of parents, siblings, and peer-group associates. One of the many communicative resources he witnesses in his own culture and gradually develops and annexes to his own repertoire is that of traditional speech genres such as stories, jokes, riddles, and ditties. Working with children teaches one that these artistic verbal performances of children are savored in their own right as appealing kinds of linguistic concoctions, though the children clearly employ them as well in particular kinds of circumstances as instruments of social policy, either direct or indirect means toward the child's chosen end, be it status enhancement, censure of a troublesome individual, support of a friend, etc. The traditional verbal genres, as the Opies comment, are both "expressions of exuberance" and quite often "essential to the regulation of their games and their relationships to each other" (Opie and Opie 1959:17). There is every reason to believe that these two analytically separable functions often dovetail in actual circumstances.

The Opies elaborate: "The schoolchild, in his primitive community, conducts his business with his fellows by ritual declaration. His affidavits, promissory notes, claims, deeds of conveyance, receipts, and notices of resignation are verbal, and are sealed by the utterance of ancient words which are recognized and considered binding by the whole community" (Opie and Opie 1959:121). For instance, who can forget the magical efficacy of ready-made formulas like "Finders keepers, losers weepers," which makes the claim of ownership of a found item in perhaps the most powerful verbal fashion?

The ring of words chained in a metrical and rhyming pattern, of words not issuing merely from the moment at hand, but belonging to the collective treasury of shared wisdom, is virtually invincible. Roger Abrahams makes the point well in characterizing expressive folklore as "the approved and tested rhetoric of a community," which is designed "to influence action and attitude by allying wisdom with pleasure" (Abrahams 1971:17,19).

To this cultural storehouse the children gradually acquire access. Brian Sutton-Smith views the mother-infant diad as the child's initial exposure to social interaction of this kind. In the first two or three years of life, the mother models various kinds of cooing and gurgling behavior to the child, who first learns to attend to the mother's stimulus, then to imitate it, and finally to embark on patterned verbal emissions similar to the modeled material, but uniquely stamped by the child's own creative impulse. Sutton-Smith refers to the mother's modeling as frame, and the child's imitation and eventual improvisation as form. We then have an escalating alternation of frame and form as the mother and child continuously expand their repertoire of shared routines of verbal interaction (cf. Sutton-Smith 1977).[4]

As the child moves into sibling and other peer groups, the intensive, monolithic presence of the mother diminishes, and the irregular but still occasionally intense presence of child associates comes into play. It is in this social crucible that the child develops his incipient capacity to ask or pose a riddle, to tell a story, to recite a rhyme, and to receive appropriately any of these verbal performances. We might inquire at this point, what precisely is the nature of the verbal material associated together under the label *folklore?* Certainly all of the child's verbalizations cannot be considered folklore. Where does folklore begin and leave off?

While a hard and fast definition of folklore is probably neither possible nor desirable, we will find it useful to characterize verbal folklore as the result of the intersection of tradition and circumstance. We prescribe, therefore, two essential elements: tradition, a preexisting store of techniques, skills, and wisdom, selectively manifest in the competencies of individuals; and circumstance, a particular socially and culturally delimited event calling that preexisting knowledge into play. Each of these key terms requires further explication. By tradition I do not mean to stipulate some item with a pedigree of three or two or any other number of generations of currency. Traditions of this extended duration do exist, as we find with the old English and Scottish ballads still on the lips of Kentucky mountain folk. But other traditions are more short-lived. The marginal case would be a particular way of accomplishing some common task that is shared by only a few people for only a very brief period of time. Certain kinds of graffiti games in which an initial entry sets up a pattern developed by several different hands over the period of a day or two could be used as an example here. Traditions may be short-lived or long-lived, but the essential ingredient is that of shared knowledge within a given community. Urban North Americans are well acquainted with cycles of joke types, such as the mommy-mommy jokes, the Tom Swifties, the moron jokes, and so on. These are verbal traditions that remain current over the period of a year or two and then decline.

Another qualification of the term "tradition" is useful here. A particular item of folklore, let's say a riddle worded in a specific fashion, may be traditional even if it has never been performed in quite the same wording before. A proverb may be traditional even if it is innovative, as long as it conforms to the traditional patterns of proverb form and content. We immediately perceive the traditional aura of neo-proverbs like the following:

> Dope will get you through periods of time with no money
> better than money will get you through periods of time with
> no dope.

Modern coinings on traditional models derive from what we might refer to as a traditional competence. That is to say, the capacity to form appropriately and to recognize appropriately formed proverbs is traditional: proverb competence is itself a kind of shared knowledge carried through time. We will find it useful at times to allot a given performed item its place in traditional competence irrespective of the traditionality of the particular item itself.

Of circumstance we would simply observe that it entails the fortuitous convocation of a particular set of individuals, each with unique talents and purposes. Circumstance is the crucible that extracts from tradition and traditional competence the specific items performed at any given occasion. Human beings are not automatons, at least not in their social intercourse. They respond ingeniously and creatively to the circumstances they encounter, as Kenneth Burke notes, often seeking to shape those circumstances through the labels they impose on them (Burke 1941:1–3). Analysis of conversations and of extended performance genres such as the epic shows that conversants and performers alike constantly attend to momentary alterations in the tone of circumstance, and modify their behavior accordingly (Lord 1960, Sudnow 1972). Recognizing circumstance as one of our essential ingredients for the production of folklore forces us to attend to the emergent character of verbal folklore. Folkloric performances are not preordained in terms of specific content and sequence, but instead take shape in the crucible of tradition and circumstance (cf. Bauman 1975).

We have in mind then a tentative definition or characterization of the verbal materials known as folklore, or at least a sense of the forces responsible for generating and continuously regenerating folkloric performances. What can be said in general terms of the quality of these performances themselves? The array of forms of verbal folklore is vast indeed, and one hesitates to frame even a tentative formulation of a common quality to epic, ballad, tale, proverb, riddle, and the rest. Yet one insistent characteristic comes to mind: performances in all these genres tend to exhibit what I would call an accessible rhetoric. That is, the manner or style of presentation, the verbal register if you like, tends to be palpable or readily accessible. This quality marks these genres off from much of written literature, in which the author may indulge in stylistic subterfuge, and from much of ordinary conversation, which could be said to lack altogether a consistent or determined rhetoric.[5]

We should keep in mind throughout this study that the materials bound in these pages are native to another habitat, the oral channel of communication. The genres of verbal folklore are tailored to the conditions obtaining in oral communication. The oral channel is a powerful medium quite different in nature from the written channel. The spoken word perishes as a physical, sensuous presence almost immediately following articulation. The mind is the library of spoken messages, yet is entirely different from the libraries housing the frozen texts of written communication. In the oral medium there is no equivalent to the absolute retrievability attendant upon written communications. For this reason, the rhetoric of oral literature must be readily accessible.

Consider, for example, the role of repetition in oral communication. Oral literatures are possessed of a high degree of repetition and redundancy, much higher than levels normally associated with written literature. The systematic patterning of repetition with respect to oral and written literatures underlies the method developed by Milman Parry and Albert Lord for distinguishing oral and literary texts among our inherited classics (Lord 1960). Yet the repetition found in orally composed and performed texts does not fare well on the written page. In writing, the repetition appears to be just that, repetitive. In oral performance, with the resonance of the spoken words enveloping one in an ocean of live sound, the repetition takes on quite a different character. It can, of course, become highly evocative, as it does in the Latin Catholic Mass, to cite one example.

An accessible rhetoric, then, tends toward redundancy of form and content. Performers and audiences alike depend on a finite universe of stylistic effects and referential excursion, the former to encode and the latter to decode complex messages in the absence of fixed scripts. Patterns of meter and rhyme, framing devices, and limited referential universes contribute to the establishment of a predictable frame facilitating communication in the oral-aural network. These elements of redundancy constitute the traditional aesthetic treasury of the communities in which they occur. Their function thus transcends the facilitation of complex messages in the oral format. The accessible rhetoric confers on spoken language an affective force detectable even in our own visually oriented society. For children, the manipulation of phonetic patterns constitutes a game of virtually endless satisfaction. But there is plenty of evidence that adults too, though in more demure fashion, are susceptible to patterned spoken language. Note for example the patterning of language in television advertisements, or the palaver of preacher and politician. Even in unmarked conversation, it is arguable that people speak as much poetry as prose.

Walter Ong has delved deeply into the phenomenological differences between the various channels of perception. Ong attributes to sound a very special place in the sensorium and mentions the following characteristics:

1) sound is more real or existential than other sense objects, despite the fact that it is also more evanescent.

2) sound situates man in the middle of actuality and simultaneity; because of its association with sound, acoustic space involves presence far more than does visual space. (Ong 1967:111–30)

We see then that sound places the human recipient within a sensuous universe that is alive, active, enveloping. The force of spoken language has been well documented in reference to tribal societies. As an example, I could cite Bronislaw Malinowski, writing of the Kula in the Trobriand Islands:

The belief in the efficacy of a formula results in various peculiarities of the language in which it is couched, both as regards meaning and sound. The native is deeply convinced of this mysterious, intrinsic power of certain words; words which are believed to have their virtue in their own right, so to speak; having come into existence from primeval times and exercising their influence directly. (Malinowski 1922:449)

What is perhaps less understood is the efficacy of spoken language in modern societies, whose reliance on written forms of communication has partly removed their citizens from the oral-aural universe. In any case, it should be kept in mind throughout the present study that the representatives of oral literature frozen unnaturally in these pages must be understood, in fact perceived, as denizens of another, quite different medium, that of face-to-face, oral communication.

In my fieldwork with children's verbal folklore, I have encountered four major generic domains: stories, rhymes and songs, taunts, and riddles. Each domain equips the child with a tool suitable for coping with the recurrent aspects of the child's lot. Stories allow the children to reformulate past or imagined experiences, casting them in a form more approachable or resonant with community prototypes. Rhymes and songs allow for the celebration of treasured experience, and often for the mocking of adult conceptions of decorum, in what I have called elsewhere miniature rites of reversal (McDowell 1975). Taunts allow for the expression of aggression in verbal form, which may avert open hostility or serve as a precursor to it. Riddles allow children to explore the fabric of language and of culture, to poke about in the cognitive system they are busily assimilating.

Riddles, then, occupy a rather unique position amidst this constellation of children's verbal performances, being inherently reflective or contemplative creatures of imagination. The riddle is an instrument designed to scrutinize the cognitive underpinnings of culture (so we shall argue in a later chapter). Yet to speak of the riddle per se is to beg at the outset a number of interesting questions. What precisely is a riddle? The narrowest construction of the term would entail restricting the riddle to its purest form, the true riddle. Archer Taylor defines as true riddles "questions that suggest an object foreign to the answer and confound the hearer by giving a solution that is both obviously correct and entirely unexpected" (Taylor 1952: 285). Central to this construction of the term is the presence of the block element, that deliberate grain of confusion or ambiguity identified by Robert Petsch (1899), later adapted to the structural formulations of Alan Dundes and Robert Georges (1963), and more recently attaining the following representation in the work of Roger Abrahams:

> Techniques by which the image (or Gestalt) presented in the riddle question is impaired:
>
> 1. opposition—Gestalt is impaired because the component parts of the presented image do not harmonize.
>
> 2. incomplete detail—not enough information is given for the proper Gestalt to be made.
>
> 3. too much detail—the important traits are buried in the midst of inconsequential detail, thus "scrambling" Gestalt.
>
> 4. false Gestalt—details are provided that lead to an ability to provide a referent, and thus call for an answer, but the answer is wrong. (Abrahams 1968)

The problem with this construction of the riddle is that a good many verbal routines found in riddling sessions and displaying riddling form either fail to encompass a block element or present a puzzle that cannot be resolved on the basis of information conveyed in the riddle question. In the former case, the description is rendered in the most transparent manner, calling into play a deliberate collaboration of riddler and riddlee. In the latter case, the riddler unexpectedly shifts the terms of the engagement by playing fast and easy with the legitimate expectations the riddlee brings to the encounter. These sorts of variations on the theme of the true riddle crop up frequently in riddling sessions. Formally, they follow the technique of the true riddle. Are we then to call them riddles and recognize as bona fide members of the genre all verbal routines occurring in riddling sessions and evincing the linguistic form of the riddle?

Consider these observations from an article written jointly by Abrahams and Dundes:

> Riddles are by their very nature conventional, as are all genres of oral literature. These conventions are important because they provide the framework by which they are recognized and remembered. Each riddle announces itself as being of a certain type by its conventional phrasing. This conventional frame creates a pattern of expectation on the part of the hearers, allowing them to hazard a guess at the answer, since the range of possible answers is limited by the riddle's conventional mode of proposition. Further, a riddle of one type when proposed in a riddling session will tend to elicit others in the same class often using the same formula. But these conventions, in keeping with the intent of the riddler to confuse the riddlees, may be used to set up the pattern of expectation and then to frustrate it. (Abrahams and Dundes 1972:139–40)

The intent to confuse, which reigns supreme in most riddling sessions, is thus the ultimate source of riddle diversification. In the next chapter, we take up this matter of riddle diversity. I will propose and discuss the concept of the interrogative ludic routine, a riddle-like conversational event, which bends the question-answer paradigm to playful ends.

# Interrogative Ludic Routines 2

Scholarship on the riddle, particularly on European traditions and their derivatives, stands in essential agreement on one crucial point: the riddle in its characteristic form entails the pairing of a question and its answer. Elli Kongas-Maranda makes the point in this fashion: "The riddle is a structural unit, which necessarily consists of two parts, the riddle image and the riddle answer. In a riddling situation, these two parts are 'recited' by two different parties" (Kongas-Maranda 1971:193). The riddle image, as she calls it, elsewhere referred to as the riddle proposition (Scott 1969), typically takes on the interrogative form of the language in which it is posed. In English, we find riddles evincing the familiar markings of interrogatives, primarily the fronted question word and the auxiliary to the main verb. When this interrogative form is not manifest, we nonetheless understand the riddle image or proposition to have the force of a question.

While the question form is the most common linguistic dressing given the riddle in North American riddling, there are several other forms occurring frequently enough. A good many riddles take the form of simple propositions:

A riddle a riddle a hole in the middle.

It's a little circle in your stomach.

In the former example, the word *riddle* is of course an unmistakable tip-off, and the listener knows that a search for the appropriate referent is called for. Riddles of the latter sort occur in the midst of riddling sessions, and the discourse context enables the listener to perceive them as riddles. Moreover, even these unrevealing items are marked as peculiar sorts of propositions, oddly incomplete and in need of attention, as we shall see in a later chapter. Riddles are frequently posed in a form combining proposition and interrogation, as in this instance:

It's in a hole, what do you call it, in the zoo?

Here the interrogative may be embedded or conjoined with a riddle image in the form of a proposition.

Another sanctioned manner of riddle proposition is in the form of a short narrative. Many of the more elaborate and poetically styled riddles, especially dear to literary students of the genre, assume the form of a short narrative segment. Here is an example taken from Archer Taylor's exhaustive collection:

> White bird featherless
> Flew from Paradise,
> Perched upon the castle wall;
> Up came Lord John landless,
> Took it up handless,
> And rode away horseless
> To the King's white hall.
> —Snow    (Taylor 1951, #368)

Children also exploit the narrative form in posing riddles, and we will examine some of these in due time.

## SPEECH ACTS

We notice, then, that the riddle may take on a variety of expository forms, but in any event it has the force of a question, invariably precipitating the search for an appropriate answer. We might summarize by saying that riddle images or propositions are either questions or understood questions. This observation invites us to consider the nature of questions, since the English interrogative system would appear to be the linguistic substratum of riddles in the English language. Two well-trodden paths of inquiry into English interrogatives are available to us, and in the course of this study we shall have occasion to take a few steps down each of them. On the one hand, we have the formal description of linguistic structures, subsumed under labels such as generative or transformational linguistics, often associated with the name of Noam Chomsky. On the other, we have the excursions of the ordinary language philosophers and the sociolinguists into the social disposition of language. These two approaches, while sometimes viewed as being in conflict, are perhaps better understood as complementing one another. The former gives us a grasp on formal structures of language, and the latter explores the implementation of formal structures in social intercourse. As we initiate our examination of the riddle, we are perhaps best advised to look first to the latter group, since the riddle is by definition a social unit of discourse, inherently interactional in character.[1]

The key unit in the study of the social disposition of language is the speech act. As John Searle argues:

> The reason for concentrating on the study of speech acts is simply this: all linguistic communication involves linguistic acts. The unit of linguistic communication is not, as has generally been supposed, the symbol, word, or sentence, or even the token of the symbol, word, or sentence, but rather the production or issuance of the symbol or word or sentence in the performance of the speech act. (Searle 1969:16)

The speech act is the minimal unit of discourse, allowing for the accomplishment of a single conversational move. A partial inventory of conversational moves would include requesting information, making a promise, stating a fact, suggesting a solution, insulting a miscreant, and so on. These may be capsulized in the form of the verb associated with the speech act. An inventory of English verbs denoting speech acts would be large indeed, running into the thousands, according to J. Austin (1975:150). Consider the following set: state, argue, assert, promise, betray, lament, warn, apologize, ascribe, scold, command, reprimand. Among speech acts, we encounter, to be sure, transactions especially pertinent to the present inquiry: questioning, asking, requesting, inquiring, interrogating. As our list of speech acts expands, it becomes apparent that these are the instruments whereby the business of conversation is done. The speech act is the basic functional unit of social discourse, and it is through this instrumentality that people negotiate verbal transactions in society.

Note that the speech act is a functional rather than a formal unit, defined by the character of the social transaction it brings about, not by any necessary linguistic structure. Nonetheless, there are specific linguistic structures commonly associated with specific speech acts. For example, the speech act of commanding frequently, perhaps typically, takes the form of the imperative in English. Thus commands typically evince an understood second person singular subject, and a main verb in the infinitive form. If you wish, this could be thought of as the unmarked form of the command. But since our criteria in reference to speech acts are functional rather than formal, we would have to include other manifestations in the set of commands:

> Close the door.

> Would you close the door.

> I wish you would close the door.

> The door.

In actual social environments, any of these locutions could have the force of a command, even though only the first entry takes the characteristic imperative form. The test lies in the understandings brought into the interaction by its participants; their initiatives and responses will determine the actual business transacted during the encounter. The same variety of form is found in the speech act of questioning. Consider the following set:

> Were you at the scene of the crime?

> You were at the scene of the crime.

> Don't tell me you weren't at the scene of the crime.

Each member of this set could function in a specific situation as an interrogation, even though linguistically we have a question, a statement or proposition, and an imperative. The question is in some sense the privileged member of the set, the most common, typical, or unmarked form.

When our attention is placed firmly on the speech act, we are likely to judge not so much the truth or falsehood of any given instance but rather the propriety of its realization. It makes little sense to ask whether a question, promise, or apology is true or false; our concern would be rather, is it successfully executed? Here we turn to J. Austin's notion of felicity conditions. Austin holds that speech acts have no meaning, in the sense of propositional meaning, and are therefore not subject to evaluation in terms of truth and falsehood. They are, however, subject to another sort of evaluation, in terms of their felicity as tokens of the acts they purport to be. He tentatively identifies the following set of felicity conditions:

(A. 1) There must exist an accepted conventional procedure having a certain conventional effect, that procedure to include the uttering of certain words by certain persons in certain circumstances, and further,

(A. 2) the particular persons and circumstances in a given case must be appropriate for the invocation of the particular procedure invoked.

(B. 1) The procedure must be executed by all participants both correctly and

(B. 2) completely.

(C. 1) Where, as often, the procedure is designed for use by persons having certain thoughts or feelings, or for the inauguration of certain consequential conduct on the part of any participant, then a person participating in and so invoking the procedure must in fact have those thoughts or feelings, and the participants must intend so to conduct themselves, and further

(C. 2) must actually so conduct themselves subsequently. (Austin 1975:14–15)

In short, Austin shows that for a given speech act to be felicitous, each of six conditions must obtain: first, there must exist a recognized convention for accomplishing a speech act of its kind, with attendant rules governing participants, the language to be used, and circumstances; second, these preordained conventions must all be properly met; third and fourth, it must be correctly and completely executed; fifth and sixth, the participants must be sincere in their expressed intention to perform the speech act. If any one of these conditions is not met, the resulting speech act will be in some sense infelicitous, hence flawed with respect to the most normative case.[2]

Charles Fillmore has looked into the felicity conditions for the imperative sentence *Please shut the door* and suggests the following set:

(i) The speaker and the addressee of this sentence are in some kind of relationship which allows the speaker to make requests of the addressee.

(ii) The addressee is in a position where he is capable of shutting the door.

(iii) There is some particular door which the speaker has in mind and which he has reason to assume the addressee can identify without any further descriptive aid on the speaker's part.

(iv) The door in question is, at the time of the utterance, open.

(v) The speaker wants that door to become closed. (Fillmore 1971)

It will be seen that items i–iv relate back to Austin's points A. 1 and 2, while Fillmore's final proviso derives from Austin's point C. Clearly the violation of any of these provisos would render the request *Please shut the door* a bit odd. For example, the request would be infelicitous if the door were already closed (point iv above), or if the speaker had no social license to make requests of his addressee (i), or if the speaker desired the door to remain open (v).

What would an analysis of this kind tell us about questions? Geoffrey Leech proposes the following set of felicity conditions for questions:

(a) There is a piece of information (X) of which the questioner is ignorant.

(b) The questioner wants to know (X).

(c) The questioner believes that the addressee knows (X).

(d) The questioner is in a position to elicit (X) from the questionee. (Leech 1974:344)

Again, we find that the failure of any of these conditions to obtain creates a flawed or infelicitous questioning. If the questioner already knows the answer, then there is no authentic motivation of the speech act. We will see that apparent questions, that is, locutions displaying the interrogative markings, to which the questioner knows the answer are actually different sorts of speech acts. One example would be the rhetorical question, certainly an odd form of interrogation, in actual force more akin to an assertion. If the questioner does not really want to know the answer to his question (point b above), then once again we have no motivation for the question. A question asked in this spirit would be peculiarly hollow. The questioner must believe that his addressee might know the answer (c above). If he knows otherwise, there would hardly be any point to the question. And finally, the speaker must be allowed to ask questions of his addressee (d above). Cultures often establish availabilities and unavailabilities between members. In our own North American society, there are certain matters children are not entitled to question adults about, and I suppose the reverse is true as well. A question violating these availabilities would be infelicitous.

The question, then, as a speech act, entails in its most felicitous form certain availabilities of questioner and questionee, certain capacities on the part of questionee, and certain assumptions and intentions on the part of the questioner. With these conditions met, a felicitous questioning may be executed. This speech act is, of course, absolutely basic to social intercourse, as a means of transferring information from one member of society to another. Children are exposed to the speech act of interrogation very early in life, effectively at the mother's breast. In the early years, while they are acquiring the syntax of their language, they are also penetrating the mysteries of felicitous questioning. The question is so essential to our operation as adults that we take it entirely for granted. But in itself, the system of interrogation is tremendously complex, and there is no reason to believe that it is immediately apparent to children. Children must learn to hearken to the linguistic markings of questions, and also to the comparable force of locutions not marked as questions but achieving the same results. Children learn to respond to questions correctly, and eventually to produce felicitous questions of their own. In order to accomplish this they must attend to the conditions specified above making for felicitous questions. Their indoctrination into the interrogative system is pursued intensively over a period of years by adult and sibling monitors. Felicitous questioning is modeled and exhorted during this period of indoctrination.

## RIDDLES AS SPEECH ACTS

We now have some understanding of the linguistic and sociolinguistic substratum of riddling. We must now apply this understanding to riddling itself. What is the connection between interrogation and riddling? In order to make an effective response, it will be necessary to undertake a brief excursion into the theory of art and celebration. Roger Abrahams has recently articulated a theory of enactments, which "stylize and epitomize the everyday."[3] The argument runs as follows:

My drawing on enactment, then, is my attempt to find a term which includes performances, games, rituals, festivities, etc., in short, any cultural event in which community members come together to participate, employ the deepest and most complex multivocal and polyvalent signs and symbols in their repertoire of expression, thus entering into a potentially significant experience. (Abrahams, in press)

We are thus ushered into a realm of experience based on everyday routines and practices, yet somehow distanced from them. The common denominator of this diverse collection of events is the exploitation of everyday experiences for purposes of producing commentary on the everyday. There is the notion that enactments are transcendent —of ordinary experience, which they interpret, and of ordinary consciousness, which they heighten. In short, enactments are possessed of a high degree of cultural density; they are a focusing of signs and symbols into statements of particular conceptual and affective force.

How is the departure from the everyday brought to pass?

There are two obvious ways of departing from the everyday expressive codes: intensification (like ceremonial formalization), or by playful inversion. The former stylizes the serious dimension of everyday behaviors; the latter selectively up-ends these serious goal-oriented or teleological patterns. The serious apparently serves the social order, the ludicrous comments upon society and its orders, and not always very kindly. The ludicrous could hardly exist without the serious, whose very patterns it inverts. (Abrahams, in press)

There are two alternative routes to the transcendence of ordinary experience. Either we reproduce in stylized form the patterns of the everyday, as we find in public ceremonial, or we reverse these same orders, creating a ludic structure that is a transformation of ordinary structure. The domain of enactments branches into these two distinct categories, contrasted in terms of technique and affect.

Let us return at this point to the riddle. We have explored briefly the speech act that is the everyday substratum of the riddle, interrogation; and we have touched on a formula for transforming the everyday into powerful, heightened statement, the enactment. Conjoining these two perspectives yields the riddle as a ludic transformation of interrogation. We select the ludic alternative here, since riddles are famous as devices of confusion, ambiguation, and inversion. Riddles, then, are ludic or playful devices built out of interrogative availabilities in the host language and culture. Riddles seize on one of the most basic of conversational resources and turn it to purposes of diversion, play, and, since antistructure ultimately comments on structure, to purposes of transcendent enlightenment as well. One link is still missing in our argument. The reader will inquire, in what sense do riddles transform questions? Where is the inversion?

Let us recall the felicity conditions for the speech act of questioning. Riddles violate these conditions at every turn, thus showing themselves to be particularly infelicitous questions. Point a: "There is a piece of information (X) of which the questioner is ignorant." In riddling we find just the opposite to be the case. If the riddler is ignorant of the answer to the riddle, we have a sorry state of affairs indeed, since the children recognize the riddler/as the sole and final judge of the appropriate answer. In fact, for a felicitous riddle to be performed, we must specify quite the opposite of point a: "There is a piece of information (Y) of which the riddler is uniquely possessed."

Point b: "The questioner wants to know (X)." For questions, this is the sincerity clause. In the case of riddles, however, it has no force whatsoever. Since the riddler is already uniquely possessed of the answer to the riddle, he cannot possibly be said to want to know the answer. Instead, it is the riddlees who must in reality desire the answer to the riddle in order for felicitous riddling to take place.

Thus the target of the sincerity clause is displaced in riddles. Again, point b is inverted for riddling: "The riddlee wants to know (Y)." Point c: "The questioner believes that the addressee knows (X)." We find just the contrary state of affairs with riddles. Except in extraordinary cases, children are loath to pose a riddle if they feel that members of the riddling audience are already familiar with the answer. On occasion, when the correct answer is known and expounded by the riddlee, the riddler denies the proposed answer and holds out for an acceptable surrogate. In fact, the felicity condition for riddles corresponding to point c above reverses the direction of belief: "The riddlee believes that the riddler knows (Y)."

Point d: "The questioner is in a position to elicit (X) from the questionee." Here we have the only overlap of felicity conditions between questioning and riddling. In riddling too the participants must stand within the sanctioned network of availability in order for the interaction to be executed in a felicitous manner. There are restrictions in many societies on who may pose riddles to whom. For example, take the following description of riddling availabilities among the Mbeere of Kenya: "Riddling is associated with children in Mbeere; while adults of all ages participate in posing riddles with children, adults do not frequently exchange riddles alone together" (Glazer and Gorfain 1976: 191). In Mbeere, then, a riddle posed among adults could in the proper circumstances be infelicitous, at least so one would suppose. Similar calculations might be made concerning our own society, which tends to confine most riddling to situations presenced by children. In any event, the concept of availability applies equally to questioning and riddling. This is not to say that the two availabilities need be coterminous; in fact they appear to carve out rather different social segments.

Despite this apparent overlap in felicity conditions, point d does not very happily map onto riddling. The riddler does not elicit (Y) from the riddlee so much as countenance riddlee's attempts to divine (Y). The power of elicitation runs in the opposite direction; it is the riddlee who has the power to elicit (Y) from the riddler. Otherwise, the riddling contract would dissolve, and riddles could be posed and left unsolved by the riddler. As veterans of riddling sessions, we can immediately perceive the wrongness of this state of affairs. The riddler may dally in delivering the solution (Y), but he is under an obligation to provide (Y) ultimately. Here is one procedure involving danger to younger, less accomplished riddlers, who are often caught posing a riddle to which they know no answer, thereby incurring the wrath of the more experienced participants.

The availabilities of participants in riddling are thus not identical to those of questioning. We might state them for riddling as follows:

Riddler must countenance riddlee's attempts to divine (Y).

The riddlee is in a position to elicit (Y) from the riddler.

Thus we find that on this point also, the pattern obtaining in reference to questions is reversed in the case of riddling. The total set of contrasts is summarized below:

### Questions: Felicity Conditions

a. There is a piece of information (X) of which the questioner is ignorant.
b. The questioner wants to know (X).
c. The questioner believes that the addressee knows (X).
d. The questioner is in a position to elicit (X) from the questionee.

### Riddles: Felicity Conditions

1. There is a piece of information (Y) of which the riddler is uniquely possessed.
2. The riddlee wants to know (Y).
3. The riddlee believes that the riddler knows (Y).
4. Riddler countenances riddlee's attempts to divine (Y).
5. The riddlee is in a position to elicit (Y) from the riddler.

We see that the two sets of felicity conditions stand in a relationship of inversion. On the basis of this evidence we can surely conclude that the riddle does constitute a transformation by inversion of the question. The riddle, then, is an enactment of the kind using playful inversion as a vehicle for transcending its foundation in everyday expressivity, the speech act of interrogation.

## INTERROGATIVE LUDIC ROUTINES

Having established the riddle as a playful inversion of interrogation, we are now in a position to introduce terminology that will help us sort out the diversity of riddlelike performances occurring in riddling sessions. For the broad range of locutions sharing the surface structure of the riddle, I suggest the term *interrogative ludic routines*. By interrogative I intend precisely the speech act of interrogation as we have discussed it in this chapter. Routine is used here following Dell Hymes (1971:58) to designate sequential organizations beyond the sentence. And the word ludic, from the Latin root meaning play, keys the departure of these routines from the plane of everyday reality via the device of playful inversion. Interrogative ludic routines are enactments based on interrogation, but inverting the customary procedures of that speech act. The term riddle, or riddle proper, will henceforth designate only those interrogative ludic routines incorporating an identifiable block element.

Interrogative ludic routines may be dispersed in a variety of discourse environments. They are found in ballads, narratives, speeches, advertisements. They may alternate with narrative segments as in the case of Yoruba storytelling (Abodunde 1977). But their most common haunt is the riddling session. The posing of a riddle creates a field, or a set of conditions favorable to the posing of related items (Labov 1972). Among children in North America, interrogative ludic routines often cluster into riddling sessions incorporating the performance of a wide range of verbal expressions. Many of these, like jokes, narratives, and catches, are largely external to the present study. For example, the knock-knock joke commonly co-occurs with riddles and other interrogative ludic routines in riddling sessions. This form establishes a mock scenario of visitation, with set parts for the participants culminating in a final linguistic sleight of hand. But the knock-knock is not an interrogative ludic routine: the addressee does not undertake to divine the chicanery perpetuated in the knock-knock, but merely responds to the speaker's initiative with the foreordained locutions. The knock-knock then, while ludic in intent and incorporating interrogatives, is not an interrogative ludic routine, though it is a closely related peripheral form. In the following chapters, however, we shall find our hands full in accounting for the most common types of interrogative ludic routines.

I would cite two reasons for the diversity of forms elaborated from a single model, the riddle. First, the purpose of the riddle is to confuse. As Abrahams and Dundes (1972) have noted, one means of bringing about confusion is tampering with listener expectation. A riddling item that follows the familiar protocol, but then derives its referent through a novel cognitive process, is likely indeed to snare the riddlee in its deception. Under continuous elaboration in the hands of the folk, a good deal of diversity in riddling strategy has developed, much of which is found in the form of catch riddles or parody riddles. But another explanation for diversity exists, though it has been rather neglected in the literature on riddling. Riddling is one of the performance genres that thrive on participation in concert of persons in different age brackets. In many parts of the world, riddles are characteristic of adult-to-child interaction. Even when adults are largely (though not entirely) removed from the picture, as in our own society, riddling typically brings together children of different age levels. The youngest of this set are often beginning riddlers, just gaining a feel for the genre. The older children in the group may well be seasoned veterans of riddling, possessing developed repertoires. There is something in riddling for the novice as well as for the veteran: the former enjoys an opportunity to delve more deeply into the mysteries of these puzzling questions, while providing for the latter an appreciative audience. But the riddling competence of five-, six-, seven-, and eight-year-olds is strikingly diverse. Each age level indulges in a characteristic form of riddling, thus contributing to the overall diversity of riddling in riddling sessions.

Brian Sutton-Smith (1976) has labelled the efforts of young riddlers "preriddles." For these children, he notes, the riddle appears to be a puzzling question with an arbitrary answer. In their attempts to produce riddles, these younger children are constrained to three possibilities: (1) to reproduce, often without comprehension, riddles they have heard from older children or adults, (2) to create puzzling questions and give them arbitrary answers, or (3) to create questions in the manner of riddle questions and provide them with reasonable answers. But children at the early stages of riddling, age five or so, do not comprehend the operation of the block element, the legitimate means of introducing confusion. That the first alternative is frequently pursued is shown by interviews with children regarding their comprehension of riddles they have heard or performed. The following dialogue between child and interviewer is symptomatic:[4]

I: Yeah, how about that one that's "What's black and white and red all over?"
C: A newspaper.
I: Yeah, the thing is: how is a newspaper red?
C: I don't know.
I: That one doesn't make sense to you?
C: No . . . cause a newspaper isn't red . . . and blue . . . it's black and white.

The invention of outlandish questions and referents is another alternative, and we find the younger set performing with great hilarity items like the following:

What has two trees, two eyes, and lies in the dark?    *Light bug.*
Who holds up the train?    *Batman.*

Some of these charming productions are recognizable as flawed versions of items in current circulation:

Why do ducks fly backwards?    *They crack up.*
What happens when ducks fly upside down?    *They quack up.*
Why is a barn so noisy?    *Cause of the animals inside.*
Why is a barn so noisy?    *Cause the cows have horns.*

In a later chapter we will examine in more detail this valiant but flawed output of the riddling novitiate. But at present we turn our attention to the third option available to the newcomer, the invention of questions with readily identifiable answers.

## DESCRIPTIVE ROUTINES

Children of all ages, but especially beginners, perform in riddling sessions a large number of routines that incorporate no block element and evidently are not intended to confuse. These routines appear to be succinct renditions of familiar environmental props. The riddle image or proposition describes in more or less detail one or more attributes of an object. There appears to be little deliberate confusion in the description. The other children then set about naming the object rendered in the description. The only distortion derives from the incomplete language skills of the children, and the inevitable difficulty of recognizing a whole from the enumeration of its parts. This group of interrogative ludic routines, following the riddling prototype but lacking the ludic transformation of the block element, will be referred to as "descriptive routines."

The descriptive routine, an exercise in transparent definition, blends almost imperceptibly into a riddle form involving deception based on noncriterial definition, producing what Abrahams (1968) calls a "scrambled Gestalt." It is not always possible to sort these two out, especially as a child's attempt at transparent definition may easily approach an adult's notion of noncriterial definition. In a routine like:

What's brown and it's round and it's made out of sticks?

one can be fairly certain that the child has sought a criterial definition of a bird nest. But what should we do with the following routine?

What's up in the sky and lives in the sky?    *God.*

Is this a descriptive routine, exhibiting the child's best effort to depict the referent, or is it a riddle proper, involving the tactics of noncriterial definition? In making assignations to one category or another, I have taken into account the child's apparent intention, the response of the audience, and the overall ethos of the interaction. Yet I cannot deny Barbara Kirshenblatt-Gimblett's suggestion (personal communication) that some of these marginal cases may indeed represent the child's first taste of a block element.

The majority of descriptive routines focus on the physical attributes of objects, their size, extension, form, anatomy, color: the basic elements of empirical reality, primarily as visually perceived. In these routines the children display and exercise what we might think of as a scientific language, i.e., a concise and precise terminology integrating a range of perceptual data. These routines are of a naturalistic bent, representing the empirical observations of the children and their growing capacity to discuss their environment in socially appropriate terms. Here is a sample of descriptive routines performed by the chicano children:

> What's red?    *A rose.*
>
> What has five sides and lives in the sea?    *A starfish.*
>
> What's square and it gots a point on the top?    *A house.*
>
> What gots a lot of colors when it rains?    *A rainbow.*
>
> It's in a circle, gots little sticks, and they got something planted.
> *A tree.*

The referents of descriptive routines tend to be the familiar tokens of childhood, objects regularly encountered in the children's daily orbit. Here we find an analogy to Archer Taylor's observation that "the themes of riddles are found almost exclusively in the vicinity of the farmer's house" (1952:4).

Another group of descriptive routines focuses on instrumentality and causation. Here the object is described in relation to its uses or according to its participation in cause-effect relationships.

*Instrumentality*

> How come you have to wear your pants?    *So your underwear won't show.*
>
> What do you need feet for?    *To walk.*
>
> How come they need fence the house?    *So the dog won't go.*
>
> Why do you need a moustache? *So you won't be a* bolillo.
> (*bolillo* equals gringo)

*Causality*

> How come the rabbit eat a lot?    *Cause he wants to get fat.*
>
> How come you want to buy something to eat?    *Cause you're thirsty.*
>
> How come a rabbit goes into a hole?    *Cause she eats a lot of carrots.*

These routines too represent a further probing into reality, an exploration of the capacity of language to render common empirical observations in a socially communicable fashion. Whether the child focuses on the description of attributes, instrumentalities, or causality, he is pursuing the capacity of language for transparent description.

Descriptive routines enable the riddling novice to participate in the role of riddler, and they enable seasoned riddlers to extend the session when the stock of known riddles is temporarily exhausted. Acceptable routines may be manufactured from thin air, or more precisely, from the discourse and larger context. A good many incorporate objects present at the scene of riddling:

What is brown?   *Your hair.*

What's big, big, big?   *Her head.*

Who grows a beard?   *Santa Claus and you.*

While the descriptive routine conserves much that is characteristic of riddling, it departs from the model in two ways. First, as we have seen, from the point of view of cognition, descriptive routines incorporate no block element. Partly as a consequence of this fact, they differ in another respect. Descriptive routines establish an arena of collaboration rather than one of competition. Riddling is generally described as an agonistic form, but descriptive routines display the children in a most cooperative mood. Divination of the correct referent provides confirmation of the scientific language the children are trying out, and is thus seen as desirable in this context.

We might return at this point to Ward Goodenough's formulation of culture (1963:258). He views culture as a mental system responsible for "the ways in which people have organized their experience of the real world," for the formulation of "propositions and beliefs by which they explain events and design tactics for accomplishing their purposes." He speaks of a "series of recipes for accomplishing particular ends." Without insisting too much at this point, it is not difficult to connect to this formulation of culture the work getting done in descriptive routines. In a later chapter we will develop this argument.

Before moving on to the next category of interrogative ludic routine, I should note that the descriptive routine is far from being a free form. While it avoids certain of the constraints of riddles, it nonetheless has an aesthetic character all its own, and excellence may be pursued in this domain as in the domain of riddles proper. The following exchange between a younger child, the first to speak, and his older friend, helps clarify both the distinctive character of the descriptive routine, and the pursuit of excellence in this form:

> —Oh, what's red and white, what's red and white,
>  and doesn't do nothing, and has a stick down its
>  side, and the red and white thing is against the
>  stick?
> —I don't know.
> —Flag.
> —To a pole, red white and blue stuck on to a big
>  pole.

In this exchange, we see that the invention of adequate descriptive routines is not always a simple task. The younger child creates a routine that is meant to be transparent in the manner of descriptive routines, but because of the difficulty of spontaneously formulating a transparent description, comes out rather opaque instead. The older child then proposes a more adequate version, in which the misleading element "doesn't do nothing" is eliminated, the inappropriate term "stick" is replaced by "pole," and the missing element, the color blue, is inserted. Through these editorial corrections, the older child imposes a descriptive routine that satisfies the canons of the form.

The second broad category of interrogative ludic routine is the riddle proper. The riddle proper, corresponding to certain parody forms and true riddles, occurs frequently in children's riddling, and is greatly appreciated, especially by the older children. But there is little evidence that the majority of children perceive the true riddle as having any special priority in their riddling inventories. True riddles are an important part of most sessions, but other types of interrogative ludic routines are equally valued by the children.

The riddle proper differs from the descriptive routine by virtue of the presence of a block element, or a deliberate technique of obfuscation. In the formulation presented by Roger Abrahams (1968), the riddle promotes a false or misleading gestalt through the citation of misleading, incomplete, or overly complete information. In cognitive terms, the riddle proper involves the use of language to conceal rather than to reveal, as was the case for the descriptive routine. Obfuscation animating proper riddles may derive from primarily linguistic incongruity, or from incongruity lying outside the province of the linguistic code. The sources of ambiguity brought into the riddle proper will be treated at length below.

The riddle proper establishes an agonistic arena. The riddler seeks to stump the riddlee, while the latter attempts to provide a solution even when the conventional solution does not come readily to mind. As the riddling session progresses, individual children take turns occupying the roles of riddler and riddlee, so that the one who was stumped anticipates the opportunity to become himself the stumper. Riddles proper precipitate a round of friendly competition quite unlike the marked cooperation noted in the case of descriptive routines. An arena of true competition depends on two factors: first, the routine must genuinely embrace a block element, making it difficult of solution; and second, the routine must conform to certain ground rules, making it capable of solution. The riddle proper is a true test of ingenuity, ideally capable of solution. Certain conversational ground rules remain operative, thereby restricting the riddler's license in manufacturing confusion and acting to guarantee the validity of the contest. In one subset of riddles proper, as we shall see below, the riddler ups the ante by dragging even the background rules of conversation into the deception.

The riddle proper, then, establishes a competitive arena. In cognitive terms, it manages a ludic transformation of everyday orders, codes, and understandings. Riddles proper and descriptive routines are easily contrasted in each of these dimensions. What binds them together as varieties of the same species is their common exploitation of interrogation, and their co-occurrence in riddling sessions. Riddles proper explore the wrinkles in language and conceptual codes; descriptive routines center on the regularities of these codes. If the riddle flirts with chaos, as Abrahams (1968) suggests, then the descriptive routine is wedded to order.

As we have noted in the foregoing discussion, the governing impulse of the riddle proper, which is to deceive, leads to the creation of parody forms sounding like riddles but escalating beyond the riddle's normal scope of deception. Some of these routines engage in victimization of riddlee, in flagrant cases actually subjecting riddlee to physical abuse. This domain of riddling was identified by Archer Taylor (1952:287) as built on "whimsical questions," or questions requiring "the possession of a special bit of information." On inspection it can be seen that the greater part of this set of parody forms utilizes the device of selectively violating the fabric of social convention providing for harmonious communication among individuals in society. Erving Goffman describes a number of territories of the self that are susceptible to contamination by, among other things, words. In Goffman's poetic terms: "When individuals come into one another's immediate presence, territories of the self bring to the scene a vast filigree of trip wires which individuals are uniquely equipped to trip over" (Goffman 1972:106). Since violation of these territories is disruptive of normal commerce between individuals, society provides codes of etiquette aimed at avoiding interpersonal conflict. Goffman cites "brief rituals one individual pays for and to another, attesting to civility and good will on the performer's part, and to the recipient's possession of a small patrimony of sacredness" (1972: 106).

It is precisely toward these background rules of etiquette that the parody forms of riddling are directed. Routines of victimization countenance infractions such as lying without compunction, breaking frames without warning, openly contradicting self and other, making unsavory allegations concerning other, and in some cases actually punishing other with physical violence. In essence, the victimization occurs as riddlee is maneuvered into the position of a straight man, subject to the ludic extravagance of the complementary persona, the clown. In the insulated forum of the riddling session, these tactics are tolerated. In other conversational settings they could, of course, prove quite disruptive. Here are some examples of the subset of riddles proper leaning toward victimization of riddlee:

> You got two shoes and one sock. What do you need?  *Another sock.* (Riddler administers a punch to riddlee)
>
> What's green and has wheels?  *Grass, I lied about the wheels.*
>
> Why do jays walk all the time?  *They don't.*
>
> How come the leaves are falling off the trees?  *Because they saw your face and they screamed.*

In these and many other parody forms, riddlee no longer can count on the appearance or constancy of any move made by riddler.[5]

Richard Bauman (1977) proposes the term "solicitational routine" for the entire set of ludic routines derivative from the basic conversational move of solicitation. A solicitation is "a speech act, the function of which is to elicit a verbal or physical (kinesic) response" (Sinclair and Coulthard 1975:16). It is immediately apparent that the domain of activity we are concerned with in this study is a subset of this larger category of solicitational routines. Incorporating this observation, I present below an encapsulation of the territory we have mapped out in this chapter.

*Solicitational ludic routine:* a large category of play activity based on the conversational act of solicitation.

*Interrogative ludic routine:* one type of solicitational ludic routine; specifically, those routines based on the speech act of interrogation, but turning this speech act to playful intent.

*Descriptive routine:* one type of interrogative ludic routine; specifically, those members of the latter category engaging in transparent description and precipitating a cooperative ethos among interactants.

*Riddle proper:* another type of interrogative ludic routine; specifically, those members of the latter category incorporating a block element and precipitating a competitive ethos among interactants.

*True riddle:* one type of riddle proper, involving a true test of wit, which restricts its tactics of obfuscation to linguistic and conceptual incongruity.

*Routine of victimization:* another type of riddle proper, which countenances the selective violation of the very fabric of social intercourse in the interests of deception.

Finally, we could design a taxonomy for this group of categories (fig. 1).

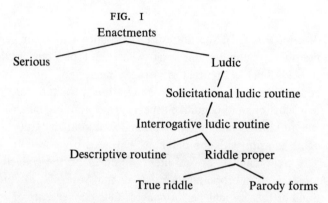

FIG. I

Enactments

Serious                    Ludic

Solicitational ludic routine

Interrogative ludic routine

Descriptive routine          Riddle proper

True riddle          Parody forms

Having worked out in this chapter a theoretical handle on the riddle and a topography of the territory covered in this study, we move on in subsequent chapters to a consideration of specific features of the interrogative ludic routine.

# Texture 3

A brief survey of the literature on riddles and other genres of oral literature convinces one that whatever topics are well or poorly treated, there is one that is virtually neglected: the texture, or aural composition, of genres of oral literature. Structure and content, social function, and cognitive aspects are commonly taken into account. But folklorists and others working with oral materials very seldom come to grips with the palpable, sensuous organization they display. The great majority of oral literature on file in the collections of folklorists and anthropologists exists in the form of pale prose translations of the original performances. Our conventions of transcription are so geared to capturing the referential content of language that we tend to neglect the array of sound qualities and modulations wrought on the medium of oral performance.

Franz Boas observed long ago: "The form of modern prose is largely determined by the fact that it is read, not spoken, while primitive prose is based on the art of oral delivery and is, therefore, more closely related to modern oratory than to the printed literary style" (Boas 1925, quoted in Tedlock 1971:125). In fact, looking closely at speech, we find that even in our contemporary societies people retain a greater sensitivity to the organization of sound than one would suspect. The argument could be made that even informal genres of speech should be transcribed as poetry, in order to bring out metrical and phonological patterning, rather than as prose. Dennis Tedlock (1971) has convincingly made the case for treating "oral narrative as dramatic poetry."

Consider the impact of a few simple transcriptional innovations, the placement of softly spoken words in parentheses and the indication of pauses by line breaks, in the following passage of Zuni narrative, embedded within conventional opening and closing formulas:

Son'ahchi!
(The little baby came out.)
("Where is the little baby crying?" they said.)
(He was nursed, the little boy was nursed by the deer.)
("I will go to Kichina Village, for he is without clothing, naked.")
(When she got back to her children they were all sleeping.)
"He saw a herd of deer!
But a little boy was among them!"
"Perhaps we will catch him."
Then his deer mother told him everything!
"That is what she did to you, she just dropped you."
(The boy became
very unhappy.)
And all the people who had come killed the deer, killed the deer, killed
    the deer.
(And his uncle, dismounting
caught him.)
"That is what you did and you are my real mother!"
(He put the quiver on and went out.)
(There he died.)
This was lived long ago! Lee - - - - - - semkonikya!

(Tedlock 1971:125–26)

These simple innovations breathe a life into this narrative that is entirely lacking in prose transcriptions. One senses the presence of a flesh and blood narrator, the rapt attention of an enthralled audience. In short, the narrative is grounded in its true habitat, the setting of oral performance.

Transcriptions incorporating as much flavor as possible of the style of poetic oral performance should become mandatory. Yet the issue I would raise goes beyond that of mere transcription. The abundance of prose transcriptions is but a symptom of the larger neglect of the aural composition of oral literature. Improvement of transcription techniques would be an excellent first step, but thorough analyses of the structuring of the oral medium of each genre are ultimately called for. To this end, I propose to use the concept of texture to investigate the patterning of sound in riddling. By texture is intended the aural, sensuous, palpable contours and rhythms of speech. Major parameters include pacing, articulation, intonation, meter, phonological patterning, and related paralinguistic and expressive features. Texture resides in those facets of speech which are not narrowly semantic or syntactic (though it may be centrally implicated in either of these) yet serve to identify to the ear the presence of a recognizable speech genre. Texture allows us to perceive that a riddle, for example, is being performed, even if we are unable to make out the exact words spoken.[1]

I would hypothesize that every performance genre normally evinces one or more characteristic textural formations. In some genres, the texture is highly marked, as in tongue twisters with their steady isochronic meter and saturation of like phonetic output. Folksong, likewise, is distinctive in texture, notably for its systematic exploitation of pitch contour, but also in other respects (cf. List 1963). Other genres are less determined in reference to texture. The riddle, for example, betrays a characteristic aural composition that can be readily perceived if listened for, but the texture of the riddle hardly forces itself upon the consciousness of the listener. The point is that every genre of oral communication displays characteristic textural patterns that must be sought in the paralinguistic and expressive features pertinent to the analysis of that particular genre. Whether the texture is aurally subtle or conspicuous, it must accompany the performance of any genre of oral literature.

The riddle stands midway between genres with highly audible textures, such as folksong, rhymes, and the like, and genres like those of ordinary conversation, which are only marginally endowed with perceptible textural patterning. Let's take a look at the texture of a tongue twister, a genre of oral literature notoriously endowed with textural patterning.

Peter Piper picked a peck of pickled peppers.

Our attention is immediately drawn to the regular metrical character of our sample. We perceive the pulsation of an isochronic meter, with firm stresses evenly spaced throughout the line. While a great deal of English oral poetry is not readily analyzable into poetic feet, we do find this tongue twister exhibiting a succession of six trochaic feet.[2] (A slash / indicates stress, a dot the lack of stress.)

Peter Piper picked a peck of pickled peppers.
/   •   / •   /   •   /   •   /   •   /   •

Equally insistent to the ear is the alternation of like phonemes.

```
/p iy t r   p ay p r   p i k t   ə   pe k   əv   pikld   pep rz/
  p    t    p     p    p  kt        p  k         p k d   p p
    iy          ay        i              e             i        e
```

Two sets of phonemes are involved. The voiceless stops alternate in complicated fashion, with the bilabial member always occurring word initial. Matching these alternations with our poetic feet, we find the following pattern:

(1) p–t   (2) p–p   (3) p–kt   (4) p–k   (5) p–k   (6) p–p

We see that the pattern is highly unpredictable, even though only a few closely related phonemes go into its making. On this pattern we must superimpose another, the vowel gradation and alternation of like vowels.

(1) iy   (2) ay   (3) i   (4) e   (5) i   (6) e

This pattern is out of phase with the consonant pattern. In the first four poetic feet we get a progression of different vowels, while the final four feet are seen retrospectively as alternating pairs of vowels. The mesh of systems is extremely complex here, and the repetition of like phonemes contributes to the difficulty of successful vocal production. In reference to both metrical and phonological patterning, we can conclude that our sample tongue twister is indeed highly determined texturally. Using ordinary conversation as a baseline, we would never expect to find fourteen voiceless stops over such a short continuum of speech. The factors analyzed here lend the tongue twister a very distinctive texture. We might suppose that tongue twisters generally evince a texture characterized by a steady isochronic meter and a high density of like phonemic output organized into patterns of considerable intricacy, though only an extensive study could establish the point.

## RIDDLING TEXTURE

The riddle evinces some of these same characteristics, though in lesser degree, and other diagnostic textural features as well. The riddle too is a highly organized segment of sound. Beginning with the more global observations, we note that riddling entails the alternation of turns at speaking among two or more participants. The riddle proposition or image is enunciated, and the next turn at speaking is reserved for the riddlee, who retains a number of options at this point. Riddlee may produce an answer, request a restatement or clue, or surrender his turn at speaking to the riddler. Depending on which of these options is used, the riddler then regains the floor and responds appropriately. The smallest complete riddling unit is closed when riddler provides the elusive answer, or confirms a correct answer from the audience. A possible epilogue would be the commentary that sometimes accompanies the completion of the riddle.

In a later chapter we will take up the moves of riddler and riddlee during the negotiation of actual riddling sessions. At the present moment we will describe the most general structure of interchange, since the texture of riddling certainly derives in part from the alternation of different voices. Thomas Burns (1976) has drawn up a rather elaborate chart outlining the characteristic sequence of moves in what he refers to as the riddle act, a sequence that he apparently feels has cross-cultural validity. He isolates them as follows:

  I. Riddle act initiation
  II. Riddler's statement
  III. Riddlee's initial response to statement
  IV. Riddler-riddlee interaction in the contemplation period
  V. Riddle answer sequence    (Burns 1976:154–55)

Within each of these moves a variety of optional developments are listed as well.

The remarkable fact signalled by the list of moves is the uniformity of procedure in riddling traditions around the world. Riddling establishes a highly determined, quasi-ritualistic conversational sequence. Many societies designate formulas for realizing the moves of riddling.

In English we recall the traditional *riddle me,* a formula standing in the riddle act initiation slot. A comparable formula among the Dusun would be *raite dogox,* meaning, "Who will answer me?" according to Thomas Williams (1963), spoken by adult males in a whining voice characteristic of taunts among children and women. Thus riddling displays the formal redundancy essential to the formation of accessible rhetoric. Within the riddle act itself, a predictable series of moves takes shape through the use of a more or less formulaic language. Moreover, riddle acts are strung together through the operation of a few basic rules, such as those governing access to the role of riddler. Within larger sequences of riddle acts, each individual act is understood to be discrete; there is no necessary carry-over from one riddle to another.

The anatomy of a riddling session thus consists in an aggregate of discrete riddle acts, or interrogative ludic routines, themselves formulated in terms of highly determined moves and language. As far as texture is concerned, we note the alternation of speaking turns between the voice of riddler and riddlee within the routine itself, and the permanence or instability of any given speaker as riddler or riddlee from one routine to the next. Let us narrow the focus now and examine the texture of the principal move in the routine, what Burns calls the riddler's statement, equivalent to what I have termed the riddle image or proposition. In English-language riddling this move commonly takes the form of a question. Linguistically, these riddle questions are marked as peculiar in two ways. While they exhibit the common syntactic form of the WH question, they fail to exhibit the characteristic intonation of questions in English, and they tend to use highly paraphrastic constructions, especially evident in the retention of deletable conjunctions and articles. The paraphrastic construction is related to riddle metrics, which we will take up shortly. But for the moment, let's look at intonation in riddles.

English interrogatives generally employ one of two intonational patterns. The yes-no question exhibits the rising intonation one most readily thinks of in connection with questions. But a good many questions, and notably the question word, or WH question, do not end in this rising intonation. Questions of this kind may utilize instead a fall-rise pattern, attached to a focal word in the question (Bolinger 1965). Dwight Bolinger (1965), Ray Jackendoff (1972), and Emily Pope (1975) assign two intonational patterns to WH questions. The A pitch accent corresponds to falling intonation; the B pitch accent to a fall-rise pattern. As Ray Jackendoff (1972) notes, "in both accents, the focus syllable has a high pitch." Emily Pope draws the following conclusion: "Falling intonation correlates with assertiveness, new information, and finality, and rising intonation correlates with lack of assertiveness, old information, and non-finality" (Pope 1975:71). The actual disposition of these two patterns across the vast range of question types is a complicated matter, but in general terms we can conclude that questions in English, and to be more precise, focal words within English questions, are marked by either a rising intonation, a falling intonation, or a fall-rise pattern. How do riddle questions deploy this system?

The extraordinary thing about riddle intonation is that it is suppressed. Riddles tend to be delivered in a monotone, a steady unfluctuating intonation that drops off at the end of the question. A careful listening may distinguish particular words marked by subtle rising or falling intonation, but the tendency, at least in the performance of true riddles, is to eliminate or suppress normal question intonation. On this point descriptive routines and riddles proper stand in conflict: the former are far more likely to display conventional question intonation. But the true riddle, unlike any other question form in the English language, is likely to be recited in an intonational monotone.

This suppression of normal intonation derives from the riddler's reticence. As we have seen, standard question intonation identifies one or more focal words in the question, much in the way that intonation is used in declarative sentences to distinguish topic and comment. The identification of the focal word in a riddle question could provide riddlee with a powerful clue. Since the riddling arena is competitive, at least when true riddles are exchanged, the riddler seeks to minimize the clues communicated to riddlee. Suppression of normal intonation appears to be an essential element of the riddler's strategy.[3]

Let us look at a concrete example, the familiar newspaper riddle.

In my crude diagrams, a rising line indicates rising intonation; a falling line, falling intonation; and the squiggle, the fall-rise pattern. Consider the following possibilities:

1. What's black and white and red all over

2. What's black and white and red all over

3. What's black and white and red all over

4. What's black and white and red all over

In the first example, the inference is that someone has already referred in present discourse to something having the property of being black, white, and red all over, and the questioner is merely requesting the name of the object so characterized. Recall that the fall-rise pattern correlates to a focal word, in many cases the topic or new information of the sentence. In the first example above, the questioner seeks the referent of the description, the description itself being old information.

The second example keys a different sort of expectation. The questioner marks the word "black" as the focal word, since the fall-rise intonation centers on this word. The implication is that something has been described as being black, white, and red, and the questioner fails to find the adjective "black" appropriate in this case; or possibly, the questioner wishes to assert his awareness of an object that is white and red, but requests the name of an object that is in addition black. In any case, the word "black" functions as new information here, and the remainder of the description is relegated by the intonation to the status of old information.

The third example might well occur in a riddling session, but not as the initial performance of the riddle question. Here the word "red" is singled out for attention. Since this is in fact the pivotal word in the riddle, the riddler would not wish to draw attention to it by marking it as focal. However, if asked for a clue by mystified riddlee, he might well deliver this keyed version of the riddle. Or if, upon delivering one answer to the riddle, a newspaper, he still met with uncomprehending stares, he might provide explication in this fashion. But this keyed performance of the riddle, which identifies through intonation the critical word in the deception, would be avoided at all costs by astute riddlers performing their initial statement of the riddle.

In fact, the safest intonation for true riddles is the one diagrammed in example 4 above. Here nothing is revealed. The riddler suppresses that conventional fall-rise pattern in the interests of concealing vital clues. In the true riddle, words are not marked through intonation as they are in other sorts of questions. In conformance with the riddler's intent to deceive, a neutral pattern of intonation attends the performance of the riddle. The relationship of topic and comment, of new and old information, and of focus and periphery is indicated when one looks at riddle question and answer in combination.

A newspaper

A newspaper is black and white and read all over

The riddle answer is marked as focus, or topic, and the description as comment. This analysis of intonation demonstrates that the riddle question and answer are components of an integral unit that is provisionally split for the purpose of sowing confusion.

Descriptive routines depart from this pattern. In descriptive routines the object is to reveal through language, and thus the conventional markers of question intonation are present and properly deployed.

What is black and you can wear them

What has lots of windows and they can fly

These two routines are representative of descriptive routines. In each case the fall-rise pattern of intonation marks the focal words, drawing the addressee's attention to the significant junctures in the question. The ethos in descriptive routines is cooperation, and thus the suppression of intonation markers would be out of place. Here, as on other points of comparison, we find that our major categories of interrogative ludic routines stand in contrast to one another.

Returning to the matter of texture, we observe that the true riddle operates as an anomalous question, displaying the surface markings of WH questions, but suppressing the normal pattern of intonation associated with them. Descriptive routines, on the other hand, conform more closely to conventional patterns. The riddle question of true riddles, is, then, a most distinctive segment of sound, pressing on the ear as a question, yet deviant in this important regard. Here is one of the indelible textural markings of riddles. Any time one hears a question posed in monotone, the association with riddles is likely to arise.

I have noted that riddles are likewise notable for certain paraphrastic constructions, in particular the tendency to retain conjunctions and articles that would normally be deleted. In our sample riddle question, we find "black and white and red" rather than the usual linkage, "black, white and red." To what purpose is this conjunction retained? Is riddle texture once again subservient to riddle intent, the intent to confuse, as in the case of intonation? While the inclusion of the deletable "and" may appear to be akin to the neutrality exercised in the domain of intonation, I suspect another factor is at stake. Some riddles are poetry, clearly organized according to the prosodic constraints of poetic genres. But even those riddles which are not manifest poetry often incorporate a good deal of poetic effect. No doubt this patterning of sound lends them a kind of density conducive to their perseverance in oral tradition. Another important aspect of riddle texture is this patterning of sound in accordance with poetic impulses.

In order to approach this poetic quality of the ordinary riddle, let us explore two avenues: metrics and alliteration. We will leave aside for the moment those riddles which are thoroughly poetic artifacts, like this one:

A riddle a riddle a hole in the middle.

Instead, we focus on riddles that are not poetry but that, as we shall see, tend to exhibit poetic textures. What about our old friend, the newspaper riddle? Consider its metrics:

What's black and white and red all over?
·    /    ·    /    ·    /    ·    /·

This humble exemplar is readily scanned as a line of iambic tetrameter. Even the improvisations of children often exhibit metrical patterning:

What's brown and it's round and it's made out of sticks?
   •      /    •   •   /    •   •   /    •   •    /

Here we have four feet again, all anapests save the first one. Thus the paraphrastic constructions we have remarked work to good purpose in preserving the metric flow of riddles. The elimination of deletable conjunctions, articles, and pronouns, would in most cases disturb the delicate balance of stressed and unstressed syllables.

The metrics of children's riddles, however, are not always resolved into such neat and tidy packages of poetic feet. More often, we are confronted with strong and steady points of stress separated by an irregular number of slack syllables. Meter of this kind is found throughout many genres of English oral poetry, and typifies the folk meters of ballads, nursury rhymes, and hymns (Malof 1970). These meters are termed isochronic, since they partition off the poetic line into equal temporal units, articulated by the stressed syllables. In isochronic meter, the quantity of syllables between stresses is free, provided only that each stress comes at the proper time interval from the previous stress. Isochronic meter thus establishes a steady rhythmic pulse, with an evenly spaced succession of strong downbeats. A good many children's riddles display isochronic meter in exemplary form; others merely show tendencies toward isochronic meter; and some, no metrical pattern at all.

When isochronic meter is present, the stressed syllables usually belong to key substantives or adjectives in the description.

What's *red* and it's *round?*
     /              /

What's *black* and *white* and *red* all *over?*
      /        /         /        /

Why did the *moron* throw the *clock* out the *window?*
          /              /              /

In each case, ranging from the simplest innovations of children to

items drawn from oral tradition, the stressed syllables coincide with
the nouns and adjectives of greatest pith in the riddle proposition.
Here again, as in the case of intonation, neutrality is preserved. The
riddler gives equal articulatory stress to all components, and thus
refuses to mark the key component in any fashion. The texture of
riddles serves the riddler's inscrutability; conventional means of signalling key elements within sentences—intonation and stress—are
meticulously avoided.

Phonological patterning is another characteristic feature of children's riddling, as it is of virtually all children's language play (Sanches and Kirshenblatt-Gimblett 1976). The projection of like sounds
onto the spoken string is, of course, a basic resource of all verbal art
(cf. Jakobson 1960). Children tend to revel in this form of sound
patterning in particularly uninhibited fashion, not infrequently to the
entire neglect of the semantic component of language. Jump ropers
are privy to mysterious sound concoctions such as:

> Acca bacca soda cracker
> Acca bacca boo.

As children mature, their verbal play develops an increasing balance
between the patterning of sound and meaning (Sanches and Kirshenblatt-Gimblett 1976, Brady 1975, Freud/Strachey 1960).

Riddling too is invested with alliteration and assonance, though
to a lesser degree than in some of the other genres of children's verbal
play. As in the instance of isochronic meters, we are involved in a
sliding scale here: a good many riddles are conspicuously patterned,
and others only marginally so. Most of them provide at least a
snatch or two of phonetic redundancy. One common method entails
the verbatim repetition of words and phrases, creating a kind of
parallelism:

> White *from the outside,* green *from the inside.*

> What's up *in the sky* and lives *in the sky?*

In these structures we find the kernel of what Roman Jakobson
(1966) has termed the fundamental constitutive device of poetry,
parallelism.

Full rhyme is common in those riddles that are unmistakable poetic structures, but even riddles masquerading as prose exhibit patterns of near-rhyme:

What's *brown* and it's *round* and it's *made* out of sticks?

Even more subtle an effect is achieved in routines that do not manifest rhyme as such, but display intricate patterns of related phonemes projected linearly onto the riddle proposition:

What has five sides and lives in the sea?

To illustrate the complexity of the pattern, we will need a phonetic transcription.

| /wut | hæ z | fayv | saydz | æ nd | livz | in | ðə | siy/ |
|------|------|------|-------|------|------|-----|-----|------|
|      | z    | f v  | s z   |      | vz   |     | ð   | s    |

This single line contains nine instances of fricative phonemes, /s,f,v, z,ð/.

| Fricatives | labio-dental | dental-alveolar | |
|------------|--------------|-----------------|---|
| − voiced   | f            | θ               | s |
| + voiced   | v            | ð               | z |

Syntagmatically disposed, the sequence plays voicing against the lack of voicing at the same point of articulation, and nearby points of articulation against one another while the manner of articulation is held constant. In short, a group of like phonemes, defined simply as + continuent and + anterior in the system of Chomsky and Halle (1968), is projected into an intricate pattern of contiguities in this child's interrogative ludic routine. The patterning of sound is so intense here that we are reminded of our preliminary analysis of the tongue twister.

It is worth pausing at this juncture to note that in this routine we encounter an apt illustration of Roman Jakobson's mechanism of verbal art. Jakobson proclaims, in a by now classic passage, that "the poetic function projects the principle of equivalence from the axis of selection to the axis of combination" (Jakobson 1960:358). In the child's routine

What has five sides and lives in the sea?

we find a selective set of phonemes, those having the features + continuent and + anterior, disposed in the following combinatory pattern: z, f, v, s, z, v, z, ð, s. This children's routine, like many others, contains in rudimentary form the mechanisms responsible for the creation of poetic effect. Naturally more could be said about the patterning of sound in even this routine, but there is no need to belabor the point.

## POETICS OF CHAOS

The texture of interrogative ludic routines can be described at several levels. The riddling session evolves through a succession of riddle acts, or interrogative ludic routines, usually initiated by a succession of riddlers. The routines themselves are highly patterned into a sequence of characteristic moves, each move likewise highly formulaic in content. The principal move of the routine, the riddle proposition or question, has a distinctive texture of its own. Riddle questions suppress or neutralize conventional question intonation, in such a manner as to dispense with the customary marking of focal words in sentences. Riddle descriptions are also constructed along poetic lines, whether they be poetry or not, evident in the tendency toward isochronic meter as well as in the phonetic patterns of rhyme, alliteration, and assonance.

A question lacking these textural effects is not likely to be heard as a riddle. My research indicates that children at an early age, as early as four years, respond to riddling texture long before they have mastered the nuances of metaphor, the key element in riddle semantics. Younger children, who are unable to produce a sensible riddle, still are quite capable of imitating the texture of riddles in their flawed performances. Children who know how to riddle are still seduced into creating semantically anomalous routines like the following:

What's big big big like the fig in the dog?

This misfired routine, which had no solution, meets with all three specifications of riddling texture. In performance the intonation was neutralized; hints of isochronic meter are present, especially in the regularity of the final two downbeats; and we find repetition of morphs and phonemes, and the play of like phonemes, in this instance especially the voiced stops. Riddling texture, it appears, is somewhat detachable from other aspects of riddling competence.

Riddling thus comes upon us with its own inimitable structuring and arranging of the phonetic environment. Riddling sessions are conversations, preserving the rules of turn taking, often from one routine to the next, and always within the routines themselves. Yet riddling is a distinctive sort of conversation. At the heart of riddling are these pithy and anomalous questions, units of sound remarkable for their departure from conventional question intonation, and for their high phonetic density and organization. From these highly patterned units a succession of turns at speaking spins off, culminating in the definitive affirmation of the riddle solution. Aurally, riddling could be thought of as the quest for intonational stress, for as soon as we hear

A newspaper

we sense that the routine has achieved closure. The intonational pattern reinforces the semantic progress of the riddling, providing the audience and performer with the accessible rhetoric essential to oral communication.

Riddling texture at once appears to serve two purposes. On the one hand, the overriding intent of the riddle proper to deceive is facilitated by the neutralization of elements such as stress and intonation, which would draw the riddlee's attention to a particular segment of the riddle question. To this purpose we can relate the two linguistic anomalies of riddles, the suppression of conventional intonation patterns, and the retention of deletable articles, pronouns, and conjunctions. We have noted that descriptive routines, which are not geared to deception, abandon these practices. On the other hand, riddling texture is sensuous in its adherence to poetic devices. There is every reason to believe that riddling is enjoyed as poetry as well as in other ways. Moreover, the poetic quality of interrogative ludic routines both reflects and maintains their perseverance in oral tradition. They are like the polished stones, rounded off through the incessant action of a brook's water, as their continuous rehearsal on the tongue of the folk endows them with an increasingly graceful and rounded contour. At the same time, this grace of form ensures their perpetuation, rendering them pleasurable and memorable.[4]

It is interesting that these cherished items of oral tradition provide a model for ongoing creativity in the genre. There exists a riddling competence that allows individuals to create from the shards of traditional riddles new items incorporating traditional form and content. And one of the indispensable ingredients of riddling competence is riddle texture. Newborn routines must conform to the dictates of the texture of the genre, however innovative they may be in other ways, if they are to be heard as riddles. Children, those perennial iconoclasts, create the most outlandish conceptual dissonance meant to pass as riddles, yet invariably endow these creations with the proper riddling texture.

The wakeful human is always enveloped within an aural environment pressing in on his consciousness. Within this total sound environment, human speech is of course essential for the negotiation of social intercourse. The ear attends closely to speech, making extremely fine calibrations of the kind entailed in any phonemic system. Nuances of texture in sound are also closely monitored. Constellations of paralinguistic features are diagnostic of the speaker's investment in what he is saying, of his attitude toward addressee, and of a myriad of additional information pertinent to the management of social intercourse. In addition, particular constellations of intonation, stress, pacing, and prosodic organization signal the presence of one specific genre of speech. I have postulated that the genres of verbal performance may be marked by the presence of a highly determined aural texture. We have seen for interrogative ludic routines that a distinctive texture does exist, and that people respond to these textural constraints. For the riddle, and I suspect for other genres as well, texture is the handmaiden of teleology. Through the collaboration of texture and content, riddling achieves its allotted interactive goal and, furthermore, secures some purchase on stability within the oral tradition. I would not assert that the medium is the message, but instead turn Marshall McLuhan's phrase as follows: Medium and message are inseparable.

We are returned to that vibrant universe of sound, the native habitat of all oral literature, with its qualities so well expressed by Walter Ong (1967): acoustic space is inhabited space, alive with energy and potentiality. Within this universe of sound the individual makes increasingly finer distinctions, and every distinction conveys information. The sound environment created by riddling distinguishes this form of communication or enactment from any other. And in the presence of riddling, individuals may anticipate what sort of action is likely to be expected of them, and also what the stakes of that action are. In sum, through textural cues alone, the individual is already oriented to the transaction at hand.

# Structure 4

We now focus our attention on the surface and deep linguistic structures of our material, with three objectives in mind. First, we seek to demonstrate the generative capacity of a few simple syntactic formulas. Inspection of our riddling corpus leads one to suspect that the greater portion of it derives from the operation of a few basic syntactic models, with some leeway built into each model. Second, we will map these surface patterns onto their sources in the underlying semantic component. And third, as a result of steps one and two, we will establish the principle of the interdependence of syntax and semantics, especially visible in the consideration of situated speech genres. For more is at stake in riddling competence than the ability to produce certain syntactic structures. I would argue that riddling presupposes an implicit linguistic analysis, wherein the riddlers navigate between surface and underlying structure, producing surface forms that selectively confine information contained in the semantic substratum to either riddle proposition or riddle solution. The appropriate distribution of information in the surface forms is crucial to the performance of a successful interrogative ludic routine.

## SYNTACTIC STRUCTURE

Turning first to the descriptive routine, which is representative of the entire corpus in this respect, we might inquire: How could we devise a grammar capable of generating the most commonly observed surface forms, and only those forms? The three sorts of descriptive routines, those of classification, instrumentality, and causality, partition the surface forms into three distinctive patterns. Thus each variety entails its own formula, producing a unique form of riddle proposition and solution. Our first category of descriptive routines exhibits several closely related surface forms, all based on a few simple elements, which may occur alone or in combinations. Here are the most productive simple elements (parentheses enclose optional items):

I. What's NP?
   NP goes to a. prepositional phrase
             b. adjective
             c. (article) (adjective) noun (relative clause)
   *Examples*
   a. What's in the dirt . . .
   b. What's red?
   c. What's an animal that has two big horns?

II. What is NP?
   NP goes to a. prepositional phrase
             b. adjective
             c. (article) (adjective) noun (relative clause)
   *Examples*
   a. none
   b. What is white?
   c. What is something . . .

III. It's NP.
   NP goes to a. prepositional phrase
             b. adjective
             c. (article) (adjective) noun (relative clause)
   *Examples*
   a. It's in a hole . . .
   b. It's round . . .
   c. It's a little circle . . .

IV. It is NP.
   NP goes to a. prepositional phrase
             b. adjective
             c. (article) (adjective) noun (relative clause)
   *Examples*
   a. none
   b. none
   c. It is a man that paints stuff . . .

V. What has NP?
NP goes to (article) (adjective) noun (relative clause)
*Example*
What has three wheels . . .

VI. What gots NP?
NP goes to (article) (adjective) noun (relative clause)
*Example*
What gots a lot of colors when it rains?

VII. It has NP.
NP goes to (article) (adjective) noun (relative clause)
*Example*
It has an egg that is in it.

VIII. It gots NP.
NP goes to (article) (adjective) noun (relative clause)
*Example*
It gots the leaves . . .

IX. What VP?
VP goes to V NP
V goes to verb of action
NP goes to a. prepositional phrase
        b. (article) (adjective) noun
*Examples*
a. What lives in the morning . . .
b. What throws water off?

X. It VP.
VP goes to V NP
V goes to verb of action
NP goes to a. prepositional phrase
        b. (article) (adjective) noun
*Examples*
a. . . . it can walk . . .
b. none

These are the fertile simple elements going into the construction of descriptive routines centered on attribution. All the possibilities listed above should occur, though examples for a few of them couldn't be found in the present corpus. Other less productive systems exist, but we will confine our comments to this highly productive set.[1]

Some descriptive routines consist of only a single element:

What's red? (Ib above)

More often, however, simple elements are combined to create compound descriptions of two or more object attributes. Here are some of the typical combinations, the numbers keyed to the list of simple elements presented above.

What's in the dirt, does a hole, and then it's inside the hole?
Ia                      IXb                      IIa

What's square and it gots a point on the top?
Ib                      VIII

It's from a car, it's a Chevrolet, and it's red.
IIIa          IIIc                      IIIb

What's brown and it's round and it gots the leaves on it?
Ib                      IIIb                      VIII

What has two legs, it can walk?
Vb                      X

What's brown and it's round and it's made out of sticks and
Ib                      IIIb                      IIIb

it has an egg in it?
VII

Through the stacking of simple elements, descriptive routines may enumerate as many as three or four attributes of the missing referent. The present analysis is not meant to be a grammar of these routines; a great many other factors would need to be incorporated into the discussion. But it does illustrate the techniques of constructing acceptable routines. Using these simple techniques, the children are able to generate a theoretically infinite corpus of routines.

While my sample of routines of this kind is not sufficient to permit facile generalization, there do appear to be some tendencies in the combination of simple elements. The following chart shows the combinatory anatomy for thirty routines:

Ib: 10 times              IIIb + VIII + IX
IIb: 2 times              IIIc + IIIa
Ib + VIII: 2 times        IIIc + VII
Ib + IIIb + VIII: 2 times V + IIIb
Ib + IIIb + IIIb + VII    V + IX: 2 times
Ib + IIIb                 VI
Ib + IX + IIIa            IX
Ib + IVb + VII
IIc
IIIa + IIIc + IIIb

The simple elements are encountered in these frequencies:

Ia: 1   b: 17   c: 1        VI: 1
IIa: 0  b: 2    c: 1        VII: 2
IIIa: 5 b: 6    c: 3        VIII: 4
IVa: 0  b: 0    c: 1        IX: 6
V: 7                        X: 2

What can be made of these tabulations? Certainly they reflect in part the preferred methods by which the children construct routines of this kind, though they may in part reflect the limitations of our sample.

First, we find that questions predominate over statements. Of roughly fifty-eight simple elements, thirty-five of them begin with question words. Approximately 60 percent of this sample then takes the form of overt interrogation. Second, we find a strong preference for attribution through adjectival description: twenty-three elements in our sample, or just under 30 percent of the total, utilize this mode of attribution. A good many routines, roughly a quarter of the total, involve only a single simple element. Still, there are eight double stacks and six triple stacks in the sample. We even find an occasional piling of four simple elements into a single routine. Finally, we note the extraordinary fact that with only one exception the entire corpus avoids piling like simple elements into a single routine. The children bring diversity into their formulations, drawing on their repertoire of simple elements in such a way as to avoid duplication within any given descriptive routine.

The construction of descriptive routines focusing on attribution could be analogized to playing with building blocks. The blocks are the simple elements, descriptive formulas thoroughly mastered by the children, which are assembled into structures through the operation of a few simple rules: no two identical blocks are to be contiguous or even contained in the same structure; certain kinds of blocks are favored for the foundation of the edifice; blocks will be conjoined in selected patterns. In much the same fashion children assemble descriptive routines from the simple elements. We could call this the architectonics of one variety of children's riddling. We will return to these simple elements when it comes time to take up the underlying semantic of riddling.

The other types of descriptive routines utilize other principles of construction. Those dealing with instrumentality are distinctive in the initial question word they employ and in the way their questions and solutions are formulated. Consider the following representatives:

Why do you need a moustache?   *So you won't be a* bolillo.

How come you have to wear your pants?   *So your underwear won't show.*

In each we can pick out the distinctive traits: the question word *why* or its variant *how come;* the second person singular pronoun, which

sometimes yields to the impersonal *they;* and the presence of a contingency marker such as *need to* or *have to,* which keys the connection between instrument and impact. The solutions, likewise, are marked for contingency, through the morphs *so, so that,* or simply by *to (not) be* as in this one:

How come you need hair?   *To not be bald headed.*

The routines separate instrument and impact, placing the former in the question and the latter in the answer. Yet cognitively the proposition spans these units, in the manner of a discontinuous morpheme.

Thus the logical connection "You need X to do Y" is presented in the following form:

Why do you need X?   *To do Y.*

The case of descriptive routines concerned with causality is similar, though the markings are distinctive. Take the following case:

How come the rabbit eat a lot?   *Cause he wants to get fat.*

Here we have the unitary proposition "The rabbit eats a lot because he wants to get fat" segmented into riddling morphology. In these analyses I have chosen not to provide complete treatments of linguistic processes. The role of negation, the interrogative transformation, relativization, and other standard operations are all taken for granted here in order to keep the discussion away from involuted calculations of a linguistic nature. For our purposes, it is sufficient to observe the overt markers associated with each variety of routine. And we find that our three subcategories pattern quite differently, each displaying its own characteristic syntactic structure. To summarize these findings: descriptive routines of attribution are composed from simple descriptive elements, which are often stacked in sets of as many as four to form complete routines; routines dealing with instrumentality and causality do not exhibit this stacking behavior, but each of them is marked by the presence of characteristic syntactic structures.

I have said of descriptive routines that they reflect the scientific discoveries of the children. In these routines children learn to convey their growing understanding of empirical reality in a language designed for effective communication. The solving of the routine through the correct identification of the described referent is the ultimate and reassuring proof of the communicative power of this social tongue. But let us inspect for a moment the kinds of understandings conveyed in descriptive routines. Those involving straight attribution are of three kinds, essentially:

> *What is*—understandings of diagnostic qualities
> *What has*—understandings of possessed qualities
> *What does*—understandings of habitual behavior

Those involving instrumentality and causality bring with them other kinds of understandings. In the case of the former, the child draws attention to the relation captured in the composite form "You need X to do Y." With the latter, the relationship of causality, "Doing X brings about Y," enters the scene. In every instance, the child consolidates his grasp on experience, and acceptable modes of rendering experience, through a classificatory process based on the logics of attribution, instrumentality, or causality.

A look at true riddles and routines of victimization reveals that they utilize for the most part the construction devices familiar in descriptive routines. One easily matches surface structures of descriptive routines with patterns common to many riddles:

*Attribution*

What is white on the outside and green on the inside and hops? *Frog sandwich.*
IIb                                                      IX

What's big and red and eats rocks?   *A big red rockeater.*
Ib                          IX

What's blue and white and has two cherries on top?   *A police car.*
Ib                          V

What has a tongue and it can't talk?   *Shoe.*
V                          X

*Causality*

Why do the birds fly south?   *Cause it's too far to walk.*
Why did the man take hay to bed?   *To feed the nightmares.*

*Instrumentality*

How do you keep a skunk from smelling? *Hold his nose.*

While the surface form associated with descriptive routines focusing on instrumentality doesn't flourish in other kinds of riddling, those associated with attribution and causality remain fertile models for riddle construction. In my entire riddling corpus, roughly two-thirds of the true riddles utilize these familiar patterns.

Other riddling models appear in true riddles, and these are worthy of consideration. A highly productive formula, explored in some detail later in this book, takes this form:

What did the X say to the Y?

The participants in these fanciful dialogues are not necessarily those we normally consider to be endowed with speech. Instead, they tend to be familiar inanimate objects such as rugs, floors, walls, ceilings. Of interest in these forms is the specificity conveyed in the past tense marker of the verb. We don't find

What would the X say to the Y?

which concedes the contingent nature of these routines. This specificity of tense implies that the dialogue imagined did in fact occur at some given time and place. This deliberate trifling with facticity lends these routines all the more gusto, placing them in a context of make-believe to be taken seriously. The answers to these routines are epigrammatic, generally cliché-ridden bits of reported speech.

> What did the carpet say to the floor?  *"Don't move, I've got you covered."*
>
> What did the big chimney say to the little chimney?  *"You're too young to smoke."*

The trick to these answers is the manner in which they resuscitate the old saw. The familiar expression is placed in a novel context, allowing it to divest itself of its usual meaning. Often this resuscitation is accomplished through the exploitation of alternate meanings contained in the lexical items of clichés, in our examples the reinterpretation of "to cover" and "to smoke."

From the child's viewpoint, these are rather difficult routines. In order to understand and perform them, the child must come to grips with the communicative frame of quotation or reported speech. Languages have a mechanism allowing for the bracketing of segments of discourse as prior speech, so that the contents within the brackets are heard to repeat a segment of speech properly lodged in another discourse situation. The lesson is made clear by the clichés in the answers, which are familiar snippets easily recognized as removed from their native contexts. But the lesson is not a simple one; the child must realize that the pronouns within the brackets are not referring to the same antecedents as those without the brackets (unless, of course, an exchange between speaker and listener is being recapitulated by the same speaker to the same listener). As in so many interrogative ludic routines, we catch the children in their play acquiring and demonstrating a mastery of language skills essential to full participation in their language networks. Mastery of the linguistic resource of reported speech is presupposed in these routines, but this alone is not sufficient. In order to appreciate them properly, the child must also comprehend the de-automatization, to use a term from Mukarovsky of the Prague circle (cf. Garvin 1964), of the cliché within the reported speech segment. This, as we shall see in another chapter, entails important cognitive decoding skills.

Another surface form peculiar to the riddle proper takes the general form:

What kind of X is a Y?

Here the classificatory motive is explicit. Moreover, we are directed toward the sorting out of members of a common taxon. The problem posed is not to order the larger domains of the physical universe, but rather to distinguish closely related tokens within a single category. However, these expectations are reversed in the solution.

What kind of head grows in the garden?    *A head of lettuce.*

The riddle proposition gives us the task of bringing into taxonomic relation two tokens not readily yoked together, in this instance a head and a garden. The solution involves the alternate meaning of a polysemic word. This process too resuscitates a dead metaphor, since we are forced to recognize the metaphoric quality of the expression "a head of lettuce." Thus both of these riddle formulas are vehicles of foregrounding ambiguous possibilities in the language that we normally take for granted. Between these two formulas, and those we discussed in reference to descriptive routines, we have the models for constructing surface forms operant in over 80 percent of my corpus of riddles proper.

Add to these models of surface structures the occasional riddle proposition in propositional form, and we come very close to exhausting the blueprints for formulating riddling structure. It is noteworthy that in riddles proper, relatively few of the riddle questions occur in the form of statements. The figure of nearly 40 percent of descriptive routines in propositional form would read something closer to 5 or 10 percent for riddles proper. The tendencies described for riddles proper would seem to hold for routines of victimization also, though my corpus of the latter is not really large enough to admit of significant generalization. We find, thus, a rather finite group of syntactic models responsible for the generation of a large corpus of interrogative ludic routines.

The inescapable conclusion is, paradoxically, that riddling structure is a major aspect of riddling texture. Along with the other features of texture we discovered in the previous chapter, we must include these predilect syntactic structures as an element in the predictable aural texture of riddling sessions. In addition to the neutral intonation and patterns of stress and sound, we find a limited range of syntactic forms characteristic of the aural composition of riddling. This realization enables us to clarify the puzzling issue of the priority of common syntactic forms to either descriptive routines or riddles proper and routines of victimization. As we have observed, the younger riddlers find the texture of riddling most easily assimilated. Building on their increasingly secure grasp of interrogation in normal language, but reversing this in critical ways, the children first acquire the texture of riddling. They do so by imitating the sound of acceptable riddles modeled for them by older children. It would then appear that the patterns found in descriptive routines are derivative from the conventional patterns of riddles proper. However, the case is skewed by another consideration: riddles proper, like descriptive routines, are derived from the interrogation system in the language. Riddles proper employ the same questioning devices, essential to the flow of information in society, as are employed in descriptive routines. We have then a complex and constant interplay of riddling technique between novice and veteran riddlers. This interplay may well help account for the tendency toward age discrepancy among riddling participants. In any case, the restriction of riddling syntactic structures to a very few archetypes clearly places the surface structure of routines within the scope of riddling texture. As a riddlee readies himself for the posing of a riddle, he knows the kinds of syntactic forms he is likely to encounter. And these forms make a profound contribution to the characteristic fashion in which riddling organizes the sound environment.

## SEMANTIC ARGUMENTS

We find then that only a few syntactic structures characterize by far the greater part of the riddling corpus, and further, that these structures are dispersed in nonrandom fashion among the various kinds of interrogative ludic routines. But it remains to plumb the underlying semantics of the surface structures isolated by our analysis. What are the semantic arguments from which our surface forms derive? Here we address the actual cognitive labor of riddling, the two-way process of shuttling back and forth between an integral semantic unit and its disjointed syntactic representation. It is the process of linearization, the projection of logical relationships onto a temporal sequence, that makes possible the syntactic separation of riddle proposition and solution. At a certain level of riddle competence, as we shall see in a later chapter, the child habitually errs by virtue of infelicitous linearization of a message that could readily have served as appropriate riddle material. The riddler must suppress his awareness of the integral semantic unit underlying his routine in order to produce an appropriately jumbled syntactic translation of it.

The linguistic apparatus we have employed in this chapter so far proceeds from the analysis of syntax. In turning our attention to semantics, we will need to adumbrate another set of terms. One semantic scheme especially suited to our purposes specifies the semantic roles played by noun phrases in sentences. This scheme originates with Wallace Chafe (1970), but here I present Roger Brown's summary of it (Brown 1975):

| role | definition | examples |
|------|-----------|----------|
| agent | Someone or something which instigates an action or process. | *Harriet* sang. |
| patient | Someone or something either in a given state or suffering a change of state. | *The wood* is dry. He cut *the wood*. |
| experiencer | Someone having a given experience or mental disposition. | *Tom* saw the snake. |
| beneficiary | Someone who profits from a state or process, including possession. | This is *Mary's* car. |
| instrument | Something which plays a role in bringing about a process or action. | Tom opened the door with *a key*. |
| location | The place or locus of a state, action, or process. | Tom sat in *the chair*. |
| complement | The verb names an action that brings something into existence. | Mary sang *a song*. |

With this semantic scheme in hand, let's return to the syntactic formulas discussed earlier in the chapter. The first formula, used to generate descriptive routines centering on classification, has three branches:

a. What is NP, where NP goes to prepositional phrase;
b. What is NP, where NP goes to adjective;
c. What is NP, where NP goes to (article)(adjective) N (relative clause)

Chafe handles the first construction by specifying a state verb he calls the "locative," arguing that the *be* of these constructions "is surely not the semantic verb root" but rather a functor designed "to carry the tense and other inflectional units" (Chafe 1970:160). In addition to the locative verb root, these constructions contain a patient and a location. The semantic profile of a unit like

What's in the dirt? *An ant*

might thus be sketched as follows:

| V | N | N |
|------|------|------|
| state | location | patient |
| locative | *dirt* | *ant* |
| *in* | | |

Interrogative ludic routines utilizing the second branch of our first formula incorporate only a few sorts of adjectives:

1. color—What's red?   *A rose.*
2. size—What's big?   *A hen.*
3. shape—What's round . . . ?   *A nest.*
4. potency—What's strong?   *Love.*

These adjectival forms also occur in comparative constructions:

5. color—What's darker than a crow?   *Its feathers.*
6. potency—What's strongest?   *Love.*

In the first set of examples, there is no indication that the qualities referred to should be located along a continuum ranging from high to low saturation. Instead, we encounter qualities that are either entirely present or absent. This set thus evinces the semantic structure:

| V | N |
|---|---|
| state | patient |
| absolutive | *rose* (*nest,* etc.) |
| *red* (*round,* etc.) | |

The second set of examples differs by virtue of reference to a continuum of values for the qualities mentioned. Here we have a different semantic structure:

| V | N |
|---|---|
| state | patient |
| relative | *love* |
| root + relativizer | |
| *strongest* | |

The first set of examples makes a less finely calibrated analysis of experience, reducing a continuum of values to a simple positive/negative dichotomy. It is of interest that the second set, exhibiting a more highly refined analysis of experience, comes from the repertoire of older children. But here we anticipate an argument to be taken up at length below, concerning the acquisition of riddling competence.

Returning to our formulaic structures, we have yet to deal with the case of the noun phrase going to a noun with optional modifiers on either side. The typical form of these routines involves reference to some fairly indefinite object, followed by partial delimitation of that object (often in the form of a relative clause) as in the following examples:

What is one that gives you milk?    *A cow.*

What's an animal that has two horns?    *A longhorn.*

Chafe (1970:143) suggests that these constructions exhibit the following semantic structure:

| V | N |
|---|---|
| state | patient |
| N + predicativizer | count |
| count | potent |
| potent | animate |
| animate | animal |
| *animal* | *longhorn* |

Routines of this kind may thus be characterized as explicitly classificatory. The riddle proposition describes a noun with some degree of semantic specificity, gives the riddlee a further property, and encourages the riddlee to produce the missing referent, coinciding with a noun identical to the one provided in the proposition but possessing one additional level of semantic specification. These routines are exercises in semantic categorization.

Our first riddling formula may be viewed in general terms as an inspection of some of the elementary relations that semantic patients enter into. The first branch locates the patient in some finite spatial niche; the second endows the patient with specific empirical qualities, either calibrated into degrees of saturation or merely attributed to the patient without reference to relative saturation; and the third juxtaposes alternative lists of attributes assignable to patient. The concern in these routines is with states of being, and with the objects we can assign to these states of being. In every instance the child is called upon not only to coordinate the relations obtaining between state and patient, but also to isolate these two semantic elements, consigning one to the riddle proposition and the other to its solution.

We shall see in a later chapter that children manage to achieve this necessary coordination and separation of referents only with considerable difficulty.

A second formula system used to generate descriptive routines centers on the surface characteristic of possession. The standard form is:

What has NP, where NP goes to (article)(adjective) N

Once again, Chafe's discussion proves useful to our investigation. Using the example, "Tom has the tickets," Chafe argues: "No mental experience or disposition on Tom's part is involved in these sentences. Instead, there is a kind of 'benefactive' situation in which Tom can be said (in a broad sense) to be the one who benefits from whatever is communicated by the rest of the sentence" (Chafe 1970:147). Chafe enumerates three kinds of possession encountered in constructions of this kind:

a. be in the transitory possession of
b. be in the nontransitory possession of
c. be the private property of

The great majority of interrogative ludic routines exploiting this form focus on what might be termed the inalienable possessions of objects and creatures. The following example is typical:

What has two eyes, a mouth, and no ears?    *A fish.*

The semantic structure would be:

| V | N |
|---|---|
| benefactive | beneficiary |
| *two eyes,* etc. | *fish* |

The attributes possessed are invariably either anatomical parts or, in the case of inanimate objects, mechanical parts like wheels, pedals, etc. Thus we could observe that the children are focusing in these routines on the essential attributes of the referents incorporated, those attributes inalienably belonging to the referents. This observation confirms our suspicion that descriptive routines engage in a profound analysis of the empirical universe, sorting out those correlations most deeply rooted in our experience.

When we take up the riddle's habit of inversion and reversal, we will find a systematic sporting with the fundamental correlations worked out in the descriptive routine. The specification of inalienable possessions, evidently the task of one large family of descriptive routines, gets its due in riddles like the following:

> You can carry it wherever you go, what is it? *Your name* (or *your shadow*).

Here an older child (an eight-year-old) has skillfully compounded the categories of alienable and inalienable possessions. The riddle proposition appears to refer to a transitory, detachable possession, one that can optionally be carried along; but the solution names one or another object (one's name or shadow) in fact belonging to the category of nontransitory possessions. These riddle transformations of experiential schemata will be treated at length in chapter 5.

One last formula family remains to be discussed, the one incorporating active verbs into the surface statement. The general form is given below:

> What VP where VP goes to V NP, and V is an active verb, and NP goes to either prepositional phrase or (article)(adjective) N.

The underlying semantic structure for a typical instance is given below:

> What throws water off?    *The elephant.*

| V | N | N |
|---|---|---|
| process | patient | agent |
| action | *water* | *elephant* |
| *throw off* | | |

We see the introduction of some new elements here, the active verb (until now all our formula verbs were stative) and its corresponding agent. Chafe (1970:103) notes that "the patient relation is more 'internal' than the agent relation." We find this order of intimacy preserved in the riddling, which segregates verb and patient in the riddle proposition and delivers the agent in the riddle solution. Routines cast in this third formulaic system evidently concern themselves with the habitual actions of objects and creatures, with optional reference to those components of the scene likely to be affected by these activities. In keeping with our earlier impression, we affirm that descriptive routines consistently portray the children as fully engaged in verbal renditions of experience, renditions founded on perspicacious empirical observation and cast in a social tongue conducive to the formulation and eventual confirmation of shared perceptual schemata.

## DERIVATION

Our discussion of syntactic models in riddle construction allowed us to identify a group of formulaic systems responsible for generating a large number of the routines in our collection. Analysis of the underlying semantic structures of these formulas has confronted us with the specific empiricism implicit in the formulation of descriptive routines. We encounter the children adducing phenomenological states and their attendant patients in one kind of formula, possessions and their beneficiaries in a second, and habitual action with associated agents and patients in a third. We have characterized this empiricism as fundamental and profound, centering on the most essential of attributes. We are now in a position to trace the structural transformations conducting the riddler from empirical observation to production of socially shared renditions in the form of interrogative ludic routines.

Each of our formulaic systems accomplishes a transition from underlying semantic core to surface syntactic expression. In general terms, the semantic relations must be correctly segregated into a bifurcate syntactic presentation, the riddle proposition and solution. The entire process involves these steps:

1. specification of semantic roles
2. lexicalization

3. production of lexical gap
4. finalization of postsemantic operations.

Let's see how this works in a specific case.

Final form: What throws water off?  *An elephant.*

Derivation:

a.

| V | N | N |
|---|---|---|
| process | patient | agent |
| action | —count | count |
| | —potent | potent |
| | —animate | animate |
| | | —human |

b.  *throws off*  *water*  *elephant*

c.  WH transformation operates, suppressing agent noun.

d.  Suppressed agent noun reappears as answer to the question.

In attempting to focus on large-scale semantic and syntactic operations, I have deliberately neglected some of the more microscopic processes involved, such as the shuffling of word order, concordance, and the assignment of tense and number. Let us simply leave these final specifications to our fourth category, the finalization of postsemantic operations.

This then, in schematic form, is the cognitive process turning empirical observations into descriptive routines. Incipient riddlers stumble over some of these steps, which appear to be easy enough from the adult's perspective. Even with the semantic content firmly under control, children must master the peculiar splicing of semantic roles entailed in suppressing agent or patient and consigning the same to a separate syntactic unit. Thus we find among the other skills practiced in riddling the purely linguistic dexterity implicit in shuttling back and forth between the integral and fragmented versions of a single semantic structure.

# Content 5

It will be the task of this chapter to examine our corpus of interrogative ludic routines for their characteristic contents and, in the case of riddles proper, to illustrate the conventional forms of deception practiced by riddler on riddlee. We are thus bound to take inventories of items present in riddling questions and answers, classifying these items in a manner likely to bring to the surface the children's perspectives on the social and natural world around them. We will want to ascertain precisely what segment of the children's cosmology enters into riddling and what attitudes are conveyed toward society in these riddling performances. Finally, it will concern us to map the process of deliberate ambiguation whereby children employ riddles to turn the world on its head and shake it once or twice. The overriding theme of this chapter is, then, the relationship of child to cosmology, as revealed in children's riddling practices.

## REFERENTIAL INVENTORY

Any discussion of riddling content necessarily begins with Archer Taylor's observations concerning the limits of European traditions:

> In European riddling . . . the themes of riddles are found almost exclusively in the vicinity of the farmer's house. . . . European riddlers rarely refer to wild animals. It would be hard to find riddles for a stork, a bear, a fox, or a wolf, frequent as these creatures are in folk story. . . . Provisionally, at least, we cay say that modern European traditional riddles deal with the objects in a woman's world or a world as seen from the windows of a house. (Taylor 1951:4–5)

Traditional European riddling, therefore, tends to focus in on the mundane, utilitarian objects of everyday life, and, moreover, tends to adopt a pastoral setting. We can find much evidence of this ambience in children's riddling today, especially in that portion of the corpus which retains a direct linkage to traditional riddles. Unmistakably we find in the corpus riddles that have descended from the same traditional corpus Taylor studies in his *English Riddles from Oral Tradition*. The widely distributed riddle type involving play on the two meanings of the word *leg* still fascinates the children of Austin:

> What has legs but cannot walk?    *A chair.*
>
> How can you leave a room with two legs and come back with six?
> *Bring a chair.*

A substantial portion of the corpus collected in Austin can be fruitfully indexed in Taylor's volume.[1]

However, we would be hard pressed to claim that this children's riddling still confines itself largely to the pastoral farmhouse. Descriptive routines are likely to mention virtually any object regularly encountered in the child's daily perambulation. And parody forms have stretched the referential universe of riddles to include concoctions of fantasy never seen through the window of any house. The riddle proper has been more conservative, since viable block elements are not easily manufactured, yet even here we find a reflection of the changing environment drawn on by riddlers. With these routes of expansion in mind, we still might observe that the humble tokens of quotidian existence remain the primary concern of modern riddling. To this extent, our contemporary tradition has been loyal to its ancestry.

Review of the inventory of common riddling referents among the children clearly points out this conformance to the spirit of traditional European riddling. Solutions to routines are commonly animals familiar in the home and its immediate environs, garden vegetables, household items of a utilitarian sort, body parts, and other related entities. Of new prominence are machines and appliances, items of major importance in the phenomenological experience of the children. The children recreate in these routines the familiar atmosphere of the home environment and adjacent play areas: the home itself, provided with artifacts of recurrent usage; the front and back yards, hospitable to friendly fauna and flora; the street beyond, a place for roller skates, bicycles, cars. Interrogative ludic routines are invested with the tokens of the home, that social environment pervaded with order, hierarchy, predictability. But other realms of the children's experience creep into their routines as well.

A content analysis of the two riddling corpora reveals a tremendous proliferation of items belonging to a rather narrow group of basic categories. While there are interesting differences in content between the corpora, both sets of children conform in general to a single pattern. The classifications I have devised are not always uncontroversial, but I have tried to assign the substantives in the total corpus to the most likely category. Let us consider these categories.

Of first order importance is a category I have labelled *household objects*. We find that children sketch in a remarkably detailed portrait of their homes and the objects within. Our riddling tour takes us around the various niches of the house, from den to kitchen to bedroom. Here is a summary of these substantives:

*kitchen:*

| | |
|---|---|
| refrigerator | flypaper |
| frying pan | candle |
| spoon | match |
| tablecloth | junk (in the sense of trash) |

| | |
|---|---|
| food | apple |
| hamburger | banana |
| fries | carrot |
| cookie | strawberry |
| popcorn | cherry |
| sandwich | *aguacate* (avocado) |
| orange | *plátano* (plantain) |

*den:*

| | |
|---|---|
| pencil | table |
| desk | book |
| chair | |

*parlor:*

| | |
|---|---|
| radio | piano |
| screen | newspaper |
| wall | clock |
| rug | Joker |
| floor | Queen |

*bedroom:*

| | |
|---|---|
| bed | shirt |
| shoe | underwear |
| boots | dress |
| sock | bride's dress |
| pajamas | ball of string |
| coat | ring |
| hat | comb |
| pants | towel |

*general:*

| | |
|---|---|
| house | saw |
| chimney | |

The reader will have noticed that these groupings by dwelling area are quite arbitrary; I simply wanted to indicate the thorough manner in which the children explore their homes in these routines. This category is by far the most numerous and most fully elaborated of the domains presented in children's riddling. It shows that there is still some force in Taylor's description.

Other important categories can be distinguished. A whole set of items comes from the children's habitual *play areas:*

*yard:*

| | |
|---|---|
| tree | egg |
| palm tree | swimming pool |
| grass | walnut |
| fence | rose |
| nest | plant |

*street:*

| | |
|---|---|
| street | Chevrolet |
| road | store |
| highway | twig |
| car | mud |
| police car | sand |
| garbage truck | |

Reading down the list, one senses as with uninflected poetry that this inventory of terms draws a rather vivid portrait of the children's play habitats.

A domain of great interest to the children, which partially overlaps with domains already presented here, is that of *animals*. We find a tremendous array of animals named in these interrogative ludic routines:

*pets:*

| | |
|---|---|
| canary | cat |
| dog | |

*barnyard:*

| | |
|---|---|
| chicken | mare |
| cow | maverick |
| pig | hen |
| horse | |

*play area:*

| | |
|---|---|
| ant | skunk |
| mosquito | rabbit |
| bird | frog |
| swallow | snake |
| mouse | seagull |
| duck | fish |
| crow | |

*zoo and picture book:*

| | |
|---|---|
| monkey | kangaroo |
| elephant | zebra |
| penguin | blue whale |
| guinea pig | great white whale |
| | shark |

These groupings of animals pattern in interesting ways, and we shall return to them below.

The next category in order of numerical importance is a catch-all group of items having in common only their propagation through the *mass media*. Here we can chart in particular the influence of the television and certain forms of popular literature such as the comic book:

*television:*

| | |
|---|---|
| Kojak | Captain Marvel |
| Batman | rocket |
| Robin | Porky Pig |

*literature:*

| | |
|---|---|
| Superman | Moby Dick |
| Ironman | Bigfoot |
| Pooh | |

*school:*

| | |
|---|---|
| Delaware | Lincoln |
| New Jersey | America |
| president | U.S.A. |

Santa Claus

*Body parts* are still instrumental in constructing routines, though the anglo corpus accounts for only five items from a list of nearly twenty.

| | |
|---|---|
| teeth | ears |
| feet | hair |
| face | head |
| eyes | chi chi (nipples) |
| nose | moustache |
| mouth | pimples |
| tongue | belly button |
| legs | leg |
| back of head | |

As is immediately evident, greater attention is addressed to the head and especially the face, which has seven items all to itself.

The children incorporate a number of items belonging to the *natural world* and impinging regularly on their experience:

| | |
|---|---|
| tornado | fire |
| hill | stars |
| snow | sky |
| moon | rainbow |

Finally, there are a few, and only a few, *abstract items* occurring in the corpus:

| | |
|---|---|
| love | Mother Nature |
| age | |

We have, then, the following set of categories:

household objects: fifty-eight items.
yard and street: twenty-four items.
animals: thirty-two items.
popular culture: twenty-four items.
body parts: seventeen items.
natural science: eight items.
abstractions: four items.

I would maintain that this list faithfully traces the children through their daily routine, mapping out the environments they frequent through reference to objects and creatures commonly found in them. The three principal habitats of children, home, street, and school, are represented in our inventory. Yet the picture is distorted in favor of the familiar. Household objects dominate, and other categories focus on the most ordinary of items. We might conclude then that the children explore in their riddling the most intimate segment of their universe. This statement brings to mind Taylor's comments on the scope of traditional European riddles. The surroundings of riddlers have changed, but the focus of riddling remains much the same.

### THE DOMAIN OF ANIMALS

Let's examine one of these domains, the animals, to see how this focus on the more intimate portion of the total universe operates. This domain is, as we have seen, well represented in the riddling.

While thirty-three animal substantives occur, there is of course considerable repetition within single species. We find, for example, eight names for birds including the cover term itself. Of interest here is Claude Lévi-Strauss's theory that the bird world constitutes a "metaphorical human society" (Lévi-Strauss 1966:204). We shall return to this point when we consider the crossing of separate semantic domains in riddles proper. Nonetheless, even allowing for overlap of this kind, we still find an extensive range of animals named in interrogative ludic routines.

We have devised four subcategories: pets, barnyard animals, play area associates, and animals inhabiting zoos and picture books (in the experience of the children). The inventory of pets is scarce, and the few animals named do not recur in either corpus with any frequency. This finding is congruent with Archer Taylor's observation that cats are remarkably scarce in traditional riddling (1951). More attractive to riddlers are the barnyard animals known either from direct contact or from oral tradition within our society. Here we find a remnant of our previous rural and pastoral way of life. These animals have passed from the ordinary experience of most North Americans, yet they retain a position of great respect within our folklore, in tales, proverbs, songs, and riddles, and in our popular culture as well (witness the films of Walt Disney).

A good number of the animals in our sample are play associates of the children. These are creatures that are not really receptive to human overtures, but share the play environments of the children. For this reason, they are familiar though not necessarily friendly. Last, we have a large group of exotic animals that have become highly familiar to the children through regular presentation in children's literature and through visits to the zoo. Thus we can make the case that all the animals featured in riddling are in fact quite familiar to the children. We might invoke here a system of classification used by Edmund Leach (1964:44), classifying animals into categories based on their relationship to human beings:

  1. Those who are very close—"pets"—always strongly inedible.

2. Those who are tame but not very close—"farm animals"
—mostly edible, but only if immature or castrated.
3. Field animals—"game"—a category toward which we
alternate friendship and hostility.
4. Remote wild animals—not subject to human control, inedible.

While this system is not entirely congruent with the one emerging
from consideration of children's riddling, it does correspond to some
degree. Notable for its absence from the routines is Leach's final
category, remote wild animals. Even his category of game animals
is largely unrepresented in our sample. Only those animals inhabiting the secure turf of the home and its environs find their way into
the riddles. Animals such as the deer, bear, wolf, fox, raccoon, and
others of this sort are well enough known to the children, but they
have no presence in riddling, apart from the denatured Pooh of
*Winnie the Pooh*.

Here we have concrete evidence of the riddlers' concentration on
the more familiar and intimate portion of the universe, and their
avoidance of the more isolated and aloof regions. I should note in
passing that the animals neglected in riddling play a central role in
another folkloric genre, that of narrative. In narratives collected from
these same children we find two categories of creatures not represented in riddling: the game and remote wild animals, and certain
part-animal, part-human creatures of fantasy. Animals in tales but
not riddling include the bear, panther, bat, and crocodile. Supernatural figures in the narratives include the witch, devil, ghost, *llorona*
(weeping woman), and Frankenstein. These creatures take human
form but have various animal (nonhuman) characteristics, such as
coming and going at night, feeding on humans, and so forth.[2]

There is no question then but that the children selectively place
certain sorts of animals in riddles or in narrative. Riddling incorporates only the more familiar and commonplace animals, while narratives delve into not only the remote animals not subject to human
control, but also animal-like creatures hovering on the margins of
society and doing harm to its inhabitants. On the face of it, we have

a good case for the conclusion that riddling takes the familiar and renders it strange, while narrative (some narrative, not all) takes the strange and renders it familiar, or more familiar at least, since there is a taming involved even in bringing these strange creatures into human conversation. In other terms, we could say that riddling centers on the societal realm, and more particularly, the heart of this realm: the family, its abode, and nearby locations. Narratives incorporating panthers, witches, and their kin focus on the physical and psychological margins of society, in the form of wild animals roaming the moors and supernatural figures permeating even the securest of environments. Here may lie a partial explanation for the scarcity of cats in traditional riddling: the cat is partly in the inner, societal realm and partly outside it, as the witches' familiar and as a creature associated strongly with other forms of black magic.

This brief excursion into the narratives produced by the same children who have given us our riddling sample serves to highlight the argument of this chapter so far that riddling centers on the familiar. I have suggested, moreover, that riddling renders the familiar strange, thus investing it with new power. It is time to investigate the process of strange-making (cf. Jameson 1972:51) as it occurs in riddling. Two processes are readily discerned, one working in descriptive routines and the other in riddles proper. A third strategy appears to be operating in routines of victimization. Descriptive routines subject the tokens of ordinary existence to an objective, analytical scrutiny. The commonplace is anatomized, as it were. The questions in descriptive routines most often deal with physical attributes of the most fundamental sort: extension, form, members, color, texture—the very roots of empirical knowledge. It is made explicit that roller skates have eight wheels, that trees have branches and leaves. Descriptive routines referring to object attributes (by far the more numerous type) reveal the following modes of description:

1. color—seventeen times
2. composition (texture, material)—sixteen times
3. form—ten times
4. habitual action—eight times

5. habitat—seven times
6. anatomy (members)—seven times.

Here we have a synopsis of the natural science of the children, as they develop a vocabulary of significant observations and share them with one another in the course of riddling. Especially for the younger children, the successful elicitation of a referent through enumeration of its empirical qualities represents an achievement of some magnitude in itself.

To an adult it is hard to find anything strange in this straightforward enunciation of empirical observations, but I would maintain that this skepticism derives from the adult's removal from childhood experiences. To the early riddler, a child of five years, language is still a fairly novel and potent discovery. Linguists working in child language acquisition tell us that the child finishes acquiring the syntactic apparatus of his language right around year five (cf. Brown 1973, McNeill 1970).[3] The child at this stage is competent, but hardly a master of language. Words and phrases still retain a novelty and consequent power that is lost to some extent as the child perfects his language skills during the elementary school years. I would submit that to the early riddler, the real devotee of the descriptive routine, the mere naming of objects in their absence constitutes an act of conjuration, and the matching of objects and their attributes or functions in the disembodied context of riddling appears nothing short of miraculous. Moreover, we cannot overlook the possibility that some routines resembling the descriptive routine may actually anticipate deliberate obfuscation by providing unorthodox descriptions of the objects to be divined.

## LUDIC TRANSFORMATION

In any event, children tire of the descriptive routine by age seven or eight and become increasingly occupied with the riddle proper, defined in this study as an interrogative ludic routine incorporating some form of contrived ambiguity. A great deal of literature treats the problematic of riddle reversal (Petsch 1899, Georges and Dundes

1963, Kongas-Maranda 1971, Todorov 1973, Layton 1976). In the following pages I present a typology of ludic transformation in the interrogative ludic routine drawing in part on insights achieved by these and other scholars, but fashioning a fresh overview of the issue answering to the particular corpus informing our study.

The underlying motive of ludic transformation involves the frustration of linear, strictly referential, or conventional communication through the introduction of ambiguity. Some item in the riddle proposition, ranging from the lower threshold of a single morph to the upper threshold of the entire proposition itself, is endowed with two perfectly legitimate and mutually exclusive interpretations. In many cases, the discourse context points toward precisely that interpretation which does not allow the proper reconciliation of proposition and solution. It becomes the riddlee's business to sift through the ambiguous cues provided and to construct the appropriate semantic frame allowing for successful resolution of the superficially discordant information.

While language is the medium of the riddle, we note that some routines center on the linguistic code itself, whereas others concentrate on the perceptual and conceptual codes articulated in language yet in some sense independent of it. Thus our initial distinction is between deception implicating primarily the linguistic code and deception better located in the cognitive code. This dichotomy is captured by invoking Ferdinand de Saussure's analysis of the linguistic sign into its two components, the signifier or sound-object, and the signified, or concept (1959:67). Ludic transformation in the riddle proper attaches itself to one or the other of these components of the linguistic sign, producing routines that in the first instance plumb the linguistic code itself for ambiguity, and in the second instance plumb our commonsense understandings of ourselves and our environment for ambiguity. We will refer, then, to two loci of ludic transformation, the signifier and the signified.

In addition to these two loci, our analysis identifies two processes of transformation, juxtaposition and comparison. The former process involves the simultaneous or contiguous presentation of contradictory elements in such a way as to facilitate the perception of anomaly. Comparison, on the other hand, involves a transitory association of two similar elements in such a way as to highlight the perception of congruence. Permutation of our two variables, locus and technique, produces the four types of ludic transformation found in our riddling corpus, as displayed in table 2.

TABLE 2.  *Types of Ludic Transformation*

| | | Locus | |
| | | signifier | signified |
| --- | --- | --- | --- |
| *Technique* | juxtaposition | *homophony* | *anomaly* |
| | comparison | *conventional polysemy* | *radical polysemy* |

We examine each of these types of ludic transformation in turn.

### HOMOPHONY

Homophony may be broadly conceived as the capacity of a single phonetic string to produce two or more semantic interpretations, in a manner striking the native speaker as fortuitous. The fundamental logic of natural languages includes the principle of a one-to-one correspondence between phonetic representation and semantic interpretation. That is, we are generally safe in assuming that a given phonetic string implies a particular semantic gloss, even though in some cases the discourse context plays an important role in ruling out semantic duplicity. Only in this way can we insure a reliable coordination of sound and sense, crucial to the referential and broader communicative capacities of language. On the other hand, languages exhibit the principle of parsimony, which restricts the phonological resources to a minimum, the set of phonemes, and stipulates that these be combined and recombined in order to produce the rich lexicon and generative potential we find in natural languages. The principle of parsimony, I suggest, creates a residual category of homophonics, or chance convergences of two or more interpretations to a single phonetic string. These wrinkles in the code, if we may call them such, constitute a threat to the very possibility of language, so they are normally unattended or disambiguated by the discourse context. However, in appropriate circumstances, among them riddling, the wrinkles inherent in the code may become the explicit focus of attention, as we find with homophonic riddles proper.

The favorite ruse of homophonic riddles is the single word encouraging discrepant semantic glosses, thereby juxtaposing two legitimate interpretations of a single morph. The strategy here is to frame the proposition in such a way as to legitimate two possible hearings, while slyly providing discourse cues pointing to the inappropriate option. The following familiar routine can serve as an example:

> What's black and white and (red/read) (all over)?   *A newspaper.*

The kernel of this routine is the ambiguity inherent in the two phonetic strings, /red/ and *all over,* each permitting a pair of interpretations: in the first case, either the color or the past tense of the verb; in the second, either an adjectival or adverbial modifier (there are quite a few modifiers in English that serve either role). Discourse context alerts us to the domain of colors, so we tend to hear the color *red,* a tendency that obscures the proper reading of the riddle, that is, a reading that would lead to divination of the intended referent, *a newspaper.*

In a good many cases, the two semantic glosses occasioned in the riddle entail divergent syntactic analysis as well as lexical duplicity. Consider the following case:

> What has four wheels and flies?   *A garbage truck.*

The ambiguity here begins with the semantic overlap on the string /flayz/. But the deception is abetted by a syntactic process allowing for the deletion of certain inessential morphs in the surface realization. In terms of the underlying arguments, we discern two distinct constructions:

> a.  A garbage truck has four wheels and a garbage truck has flies.
> b.  A garbage truck has four wheels and a garbage truck flies.

These two surface structures derive from rather different phrase markers (fig. 2).

FIG. 2

a.

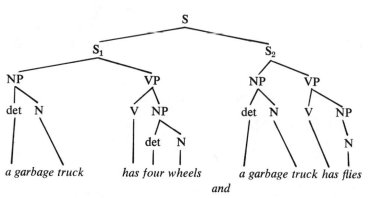

and

b.

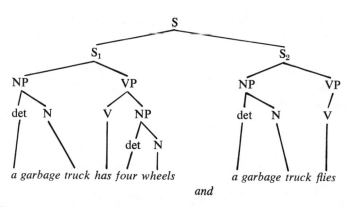

and

In fig. 2a the two conjoined sentences evince the same syntactic structure, while in 2b the two structures are distinct. This difference is also manifest in the underlying semantic structure:

a.

| V | N |
|---|---|
| benefactive | beneficiary |
| *four wheels* | *a garbage truck* |

$+$

| V | N |
|---|---|
| benefactive | beneficiary |
| *flies* | *a garbage truck* |

b.

| V | N |
|---|---|
| benefactive | beneficiary |
| *four wheels* | *a garbage truck* |

+

| V | N |
|---|---|
| process | agent |
| action | *a garbage truck* |
| *flies* | |

Too much information is lost in the conjoining of sentences and resultant deletion of repetitive morphs to allow for a ready disambiguation of interpretations a and b above. In other words, the conjunction *and* is too weak to reflect accurately the underlying arguments. In these deceptions, phonology, syntax, and semantics work hand in glove to produce alternate hearings of the same linguistic fragment. The kernel element, consisting of a linguistic unit with homophonic properties, is embedded within a syntactic structure and semantic argument in such a manner as to enhance the perception of ambiguity. As we have seen, the riddle often provides misleading cues that tip the riddlee to the inappropriate hearing of the ambiguous material. In this fashion riddles juxtapose rival semantic interpretations derivative from the presence of homophony in the linguistic code.

Routines of the kind considered so far constitute the most plentiful class of riddle proper founded on the play of homophony. But kindred forms exist. One of these explores the process of bounding morphs in Spanish and English. The boundaries of morphs are vital to listeners since without them the internal structure and hence the meaning of sentences could not be reliably discerned. Yet these boundaries are compromised in discourse when a single morph is capable of interpretation as a group of morphs. Here we have another instance of semantic duplicity inherent in a given phonetic sequence:

How come you have to go to bed? *Cause the bed won't come to you.*

Here the single lexeme *go to bed* is disassembled and interpreted as a series of independent morphs, giving rise to two legitimate (but irreconcilable) readings:

a. *go to bed* = sleep
b. *go to bed* = move to the bed

Note that the ruse is made possible here by the deletion of the TH marker in the riddle proposition, for the locution, "Why do you have to go to the bed?" lacks the latent semantic duplicity of the actual riddle proposition employed.

The chicano children perform a series of traditional riddles constructed according to the same principle:

Oro no es, plata no es: ¿qué es? (Gold it is not, silver it is not: what is it?)   *Plátano* (*plantain*).

The critical sequence here is *plata no es,* which can be heard in two ways:

a. *plata no es* = silver it is not
b. *plátano es* = it is a plantain

Riddles of this kind can be solved only once the word boundaries are realigned to feature the disguised referent.

A third variety of homophonic interrogative ludic routine exploits the peculiar status of proper names. There is an understanding that proper names are to be exempted from the sort of semantic scrutiny applied to other forms of speech. Thus the proper name is heard as a complete, inviolate unit, which points to a particular (and not a generic) person, place, or thing. But proper names often contain phonetic sequences capable of regular semantic interpretation. Here then is a third route to semantic duplicity of phonetic strings:

What did Della wear (Delaware)? *Her new jersey* (New Jersey).

There are other forms of homophony incorporated into ludic transformations in riddles proper, but perhaps our discussion of these three varieties will be sufficient to convey the general process at work in this category of deception. In every case we begin with a potential ambiguity occasioned by the anomaly of a semantically duplicitous phonetic sequence. The riddle façade features these wrinkles in the code by juxtaposing the two mutually exclusive hearings of the same phonetic material. Resolution of the anomaly derivative from the copresence of two alternate hearings, or from the lack of parity between the conventional hearing and other information provided in the riddle proposition, depends on the riddlee's ability to suppress the more obvious hearing in favor of its less salient alternative. The type of ludic transformation located in the signifier and produced by the technique of juxtaposition can be characterized as a form of sound play, in which the player exploits the fortuitous convergence of two or more semantic glosses on a single phonetic sequence.

### CONVENTIONAL POLYSEMY

We turn our attention to the second form of ludic transformation located in the signifier, but in this instance produced through the technique of comparison, a form I have labelled *conventional polysemy*. Polysemy may be defined as the extension of meaning from one lexeme to another. Polysemy, like homophony, produces multiple semantic interpretations of a single unit of sound, but the underlying process could be described as motivated by perceptual affinity rather than as fortuitous. Here we should perhaps deal with an important definitional problem, namely the tendency of homophony to blend into polysemy in some marginal cases. Polysemy is the motivated co-occurrence of two or more semantic interpretations in a single phonetic string. Motivation, as Geoffrey Leech notes, may stem from two sources: "Two meanings are *historically* related if they can be traced back to the same source, or if the one meaning can be derived from the other; two meanings are *psychologically* related if present-day users of the language feel intuitively that they are related, and therefore tend to assume that they are 'different uses of the same word' " (Leech 1974:228). The following instance is cited to illustrate the difficulty of deciding between homophony and polysemy in certain cases:

| | |
|---|---|
| *ear* (organ of hearing) | Old English *eare* |
| | (compare Latin *auris,* 'ear') |
| *ear* (head of corn) | Old English *ear* |
| | (compare Latin *acus, aceris,* 'husk') |

Here the historical and psychological interpretations are likely to be at odds; thus we tend to assume that the two meanings are historically related, when in fact etymological analysis indicates that they are not. How then do we classify the following riddle, as an instance of homophony or polysemy?

> Something has an ear and cannot hear. *Ear of corn.* (Taylor
> 1951:#285)

Upon reflection, we incline toward the interpretation of polysemy, following the intuitive perception of a semantic relationship between the two lexemes coincident on the phonetic base *ear*. Even awareness of the actual historical picture cannot shake our determination to hear a polysemic relationship in our duplicitous phonetic sequence. The intuitions of native speakers will then serve as the technique for sorting out homophony from polysemy. If the procedure entails some violence to etymological reality, it does have the positive feature of enfranchising the emic perspective, that is, the perceptions of natives in the speech community. Admittedly, marginal cases are difficult to classify, but the majority of the corpus falls easily into one category or the other, thus reinforcing the validity of the categories themselves.

Having provided some clarification on this point, we take up conventional polysemy as it appears in our riddling corpus. Conventional polysemy denotes precisely those instances of polysemy which are codified in the daily usage of a language. They may at one time have been productive of surprise, but in current usage they have become as regular as any other lexeme encountered in the language. This category of ludic transformation thus rests on an historical act of comparison, responsible for the initial extension of meaning from one referent to another, and for this reason I attribute to it the fundamental move of comparison. Yet it also has affinity with the category of homophonic ludic transformation, in that the featured phonetic unit is productive of dual semantic interpretation. One might say that the original items compared in conventional polysemy are juxtaposed in the interrogative ludic routine. We have then a fusion of linguistic and conceptual motives here: current usage favors the juxtaposition of available hearings, but these alternative hearings derive from an historical act of comparison.

The concept of foregrounding, as developed by the Prague circle of linguists, facilitates discussion of ludic transformation based on conventional polysemy. "The more an act is automatized, the less it is concisely executed; the more it is foregrounded, the more completely conscious does it become. Objectively speaking, automatization schematizes an event; foregrounding means the violation of the scheme" (Mukarovsky 1964:19). Riddles in general, but particularly riddles breathing life into dead words, appear to be a tool of deautomatization, as the concept is expounded by these scholars. Ordinary verbal routines rendered second nature or automatic by frequent usage are presented in such a fashion as to force reinterpretation along novel lines. Here again, conforming to our reigning theme, the ordinary is made to appear extraordinary in the riddle forum.

Riddles dedicated to the resurrection of automatized language may work in two ways. A good many of them establish imaginary snippets of speech through use of the formula:

What did the X say to the Y.

The answer to these riddles is some fragment of reported speech. These fragments will be familiar phrases, clichés, but interpreted in a new light. Once again, it will be a pivot word entering into polysemy or homophony that will force reinterpretation of the familiar phrase. The four favorites are given below:

What did the rug say to the floor?  *"I've got you covered."*

What did the wall say to the other wall?  *"Meet you at the corner."*

What did the big chimney say to the little chimney? *"You're too young to smoke."*

What did one firecracker say to another firecracker?  *"My pop is bigger than your pop."*

In each case, a pivot word allows for an unconventional reading of the fragment of reported speech, and the situation projected in the riddle question authorizes this unconventional reading. Thus two possible senses of the word *cover* are exploited in the first example, resulting in contrastive understandings of the same phrase. In addition to the resuscitation of automatic speech routines, these riddles perform another reversal of the ordinary. Creatures and entities not normally endowed with human speech capability are portrayed in imaginary conversational scenarios. We have then a reversal of the cultural code determining appropriate senders and receivers of verbal messages.

Some riddles bring old sayings back to life, or literalize dead metaphors (Sapir 1977), without recourse to a conversational frame:

> Why does time fly? *Cause people are always trying to kill it.*
> Why did the boy throw the clock out the window? *To see time fly.*

In these examples two figurative expressions concerning the passage of time are taken literally, thereby foregrounding the potential ambiguity enclosed in clichés of this kind. The first example is particularly clever, managing a correlation of literalized clichés lodged in the proposition and solution:

> *Time flies* because people are trying *to kill time*
> (proposition)                    (solution)

Prominent among the routines constructed on the device of conventional polysemy are those traditional items taking the form:

> What has an X but cannot Y

where X is some element of the human anatomy, and Y a physiological function normally associated with X. The comparison links the element of anatomy with an element of some inanimate entity on the basis of formal congruity. No functional equivalence is entailed, thus giving rise to the discontinuity sighted in riddles incorporating these comparisons. Below are some familiar examples:

What has an eye but cannot see?    *A potato.*
What has a tongue but cannot talk?    *A shoe.*
What has teeth but cannot eat?    *A saw.*

These routines are constructed according to the logic of privational contradiction, as discussed by Robert Georges and Alan Dundes (1963), meaning that the second part of the riddle proposition denies a logical or natural attribute of the first. The apparent contradiction is resolved once the central figure of speech is taken literally, or de-automatized. Regardless of superficial variation, the routines built on conventional polysemy operate according to a single logic: a frozen figure of speech is thawed and vitalized in a riddle façade precipitating a simultaneous recognition of the literal and figurative interpretations. In this manner old language is invested with new life.

One other form of ludic transformation centered on the signifier and involving juxtaposition of contrary elements deserves our attention. In some routines the children pose questions that in themselves are apparently innocuous, but in effect send the riddlee on a cognitive wild goose chase. The best known instances of this kind are given below:

Why do the birds fly south?    *Because it's too far to walk.*
Why did the chicken cross the road?    *To get to the other side.*

The riddlee's attention is drawn to weightier questions, and these tautological (and hence trivial) responses catch him by surprise. Interrogative ludic routines of this kind victimize the riddlee above and beyond the normal state of affairs in riddling, in that they violate one of the felicity conditions for riddling as discussed in chapter 2:

There is a piece of information (Y) of which the riddler is uniquely possessed (felicity condition #1).

In tautologies of the kind examined above, the riddlee is by definition possessed of the solution, since the solution follows logically from the proposition. Therefore, riddles of this kind turn in on the foundation of riddling itself in order to enmesh riddlee in their deceptions.

Related to these tautological routines are a group of metariddles, literally riddles about riddling. Two examples appear below:

What's black and white and red all over?    *An embarrassed zebra*
or *A skunk with a heat rash.*
Why did the chicken cross the road?    *Because Colonel Sanders*
*was chasing him.*

Each of these is based on a well-known riddle that itself has become too familiar to deceive most riddlees. The first example returns to the more salient interpretation of the proposition, since the original reversal is by now common knowledge. In the second example, the standard reply is suppressed in favor of its modern update.

Ludic transformation operating at the level of the signifier may thus work according to two logics, that of juxtaposition, in which ambiguity latent in the linguistic code is brought into uncompromising focus, and that of comparison, whereby a dead metaphor is resuscitated through the resurrection of its literal meaning. In either case the seed of confusion resides within the linguistic code, in the form of semantic duplicity attaching to lesser or greater segments of the signifier. Riddles focusing on the signifier are essentially about language. They indicate points of tension inherent in natural languages, wrinkles hostile to the reliable semantic interpretation of given phonetic sequences. It is an interesting discovery that riddlers and linguists alike are students of language; and further, that riddles often focus attention precisely on those anomalous margins of linguistic process that are of special theoretical significance to the linguist. In this light, we might characterize riddling as a form of folk linguistics, a penetrating if not comprehensive commentary on the linguistic code by ordinary users.

### RADICAL POLYSEMY

The category of ludic transformation termed radical polysemy introduces some new considerations into the argument. In the first place, we relocate our kernel of deception in the conceptual code, or that component of the linguistic sign referred to as the signified. While language necessarily facilitates these deceptions, we will find that the primary source for them lies in the perception of affinity (in the case of radical polysemy) or anomaly (in the case of our fourth type of ludic transformation) resident in the extralinguistic experiential universe. Moreover, in taking up radical polysemy we depart from those comparisons enfranchised in ordinary usage. We are now concerned with the extension of meaning from one referent to another without the prior sanction of conventional usage. The general case involves the transitory association of two objects on the basis of some common feature. In most interrogative ludic routines exploiting this form of ludic transformation, the commonality exists at the level of appearances. In other respects the compared objects may be entirely discrepant, but these incongruities are momentarily held in abeyance while the common features are brought into focus.

In exploring this third category of ludic transformation, we will be guided by some of the insights provided by Tzvetan Todorov (1973), building on the work of Kongas-Maranda (1971) and Georges and Dundes (1963). In riddles focused on the signified, the riddle proposition and riddle solution articulate a pair of referents bound together through some form of comparison. Todorov identifies a symbolizer and a symbolized. always segregated into riddle question and solution respectively. The following relationships between symbolizer and symbolized commonly occur in riddles:

1. *metaphor:* the symbolizer entire is mapped onto the symbolized.
    a. What are polka dots on your face?  *Pimples.*
    b. A thousand lights in a dish.  *Stars.*

2. *synecdoche:* the symbolized is rendered by reference to its parts or properties.
    a. It gots blue and white and two cherries on top.  *A police car.*

3. *diagram:* one relationship designated by means of another.
    a. The tree has only two leaves.  *A man and his ears.*

Other relationships of the symbolizer and symbolized are possible, but these three account for the comparisons located within our corpus of interrogative ludic routines. We should note in passing that competence in these forms of figurative thinking is basic to the mastery of rhetorical and expressive codes. Riddles thus rehearse children in these subtle rhetorical devices of their native expressive systems.

We have identified two strategies of comparison in our corpus, those marking a conventional extension of meaning from one referent to another (and thus tied to the signifier) and those fashioning unconventional bonds among referents (and thereby located in the signified). The former strategy we have termed conventional polysemy; the latter, radical polysemy. Taking these two sources of comparison together we can describe a grammar of riddle comparisons operating over the course of the entire riddling corpus at our disposal. In a later chapter I will argue that an entire riddling session can be usefully approached as a complete unit in itself, a unit of discourse displaying large-scale regularity and patterning. Here I am suggesting that we consider the entire corpus of riddling collected in Austin as a discourse in its own right, with specific inventories and structures of comparison. The basic motive remains constant, of comparing like to unlike, but this motive manifests itself across a wide spectrum of perceptual experience and conceptual orderings.

Below I present an inventory of comparisons gleaned from our riddling corpus.

Comparisons originating in novel polysemy:
1. cherry/police car lights
2. pimples/polka dots
3. stars/lights
4. sky/dish
5. old lady/candle
6. eyes/holes in screen
7. shell of turtle/mushroom
8. tree/man
9. leaves/ears

Comparisons originating in conventional polysemy:
10. tongue of being/tongue of shoe
11. teeth of being/teeth of saw
12. teeth of being/teeth of comb
13. leg of being/leg of chair
14. head of being/head of lettuce
15. coat of cloth/coat of paint
16. key of door/key of piano
17. trunk of being/trunk of luggage

In unison, these comparisons constitute an attack on our conventional ordering of experience. Tokens from discrepant conceptual categories are housed together, in the following combinations:

human being or part of human anatomy/artifact (#2, 5, 6, 10–13)

human being or part of human anatomy/flora (#8, 9, 14)

artifact/natural world (#3, 4)

artifact/artifact (#15, 16)

animal/artifact (#17)

flora/artifact (#1)

flora/natural world (#7)

The categories used above are delineated as follows:

*human being*
+ animate
+ human

*artifact*
− animate
+ artifact

*flora*
+ animate
− animal
+ flora

*natural world*
− animate
− artifact
+ natural

*animal*
+ animate
+ animal

Following Elli Kongas-Maranda (1971b:215), we could design a taxonomy for the categories isolated in our analysis of riddle comparisons; note that a taxonomy of this kind allows for the calibration of the audacity of comparisons across domains (fig. 3).

FIG. 3

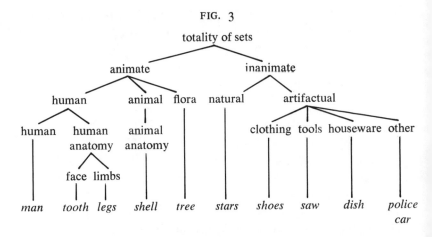

Our juvenile riddlers provide excellent data here regarding their parsing of experience into its appropriate conceptual units. We encounter again the riddle archetype of an underlying system transmuted in the ludic framework of riddling, in this instance the conceptual orders originating in our commerce with the social and natural environment. These orders are, as we have seen, selectively violated in the comparisons enclosed in some of the interrogative ludic routines within our corpus. Most frequent are comparisons of human beings (or parts of the human anatomy) to either cultural artifacts or flora, but a range of other comparisons also occurs. Treating the entire set of comparisons as a whole, the following themes emerge as dominant in children's riddling:

1. Culture vs. nature: All but three or four of the comparisons involve a pair of tokens, one drawn from the cultural domain (i.e., a realm of artifacts and mentefacts imposed on natural raw materials by collective intervention) and the other drawn from the natural domain (i.e., a realm of objects and beings existing independently of human intervention).

2. Animate vs. inanimate: Just over half the inventory compares tokens across this fundamental taxonomic watershed.

3. Mankind vs. other forms of life: A small series within the inventory compares humans or human parts to nonhuman beings.
4. Artifact vs. artifact: Another small series compares different artifacts to one another.

Viewing our riddling corpus as one large unit of discourse, we find these four dominant themes explored through the mechanism of comparing the incomparable. Principal among them is the theme of culture vs. nature, also a pivotal theme in Claude Lévi-Strauss's analysis of primitive mythology (Lévi-Strauss 1968, Leach 1970). Here the children address the basic problematic of the natural and cultural realms of experience. The realm of culture displays patterning and adaptation to human purposes. Nature, in contrast, is characterized by particularity and indifference to human purposes. A second major dichotomy addressed in children's riddling is that between the animate and inanimate portions of existence. Third, the children focus more narrowly on the distinction between mankind and other forms of life. The children's riddling, taken as a single and complete unit of discourse, thus delivers a cosmos as the children perceive it, placing man in the center of the universe, exploring his technological capacity, and contrasting him with other significant entities in the natural world. We have here further demonstration of the capacity, perhaps the unique capacity, of anti- or counterstructure to comment on the everyday orders (Babcock 1978:27). These riddling comparisons, by inverting the ordinary arrangement of tokens, have drawn for us a most intriguing taxonomy of the conventional cognitive order.

## ANOMALY

We come finally to the fourth type of ludic transformation animating our riddling corpus, a type I term anomaly. Anomaly operates in the signified through the process of juxtaposition. The kernel of deception here derives from an empirical and reflective stance toward the experiential universe. Close inspection of the world around us uncovers any number of anomalies not readily assimilated into our commonsense notions of reality. Once again, Todorov (1973) facilitates discussion of this domain. Todorov notes that only a small portion of the figures of speech found in riddles actually involves a linguistic contradiction, i.e., a contradiction in the sense of the words themselves. But he argues that the category of riddles termed oppositional by Georges and Dundes (1963) should be expanded to include contradictions located in the world around us, in what Todorov refers to as the social psychology or cultural context (Todorov 1973:148). He provides the following chart:

| underlying truism— | commonplace | tautology | enthymeme |
| riddle reversal— | improbability | paradox | contradiction |

Riddles violating the sense of their words are based on tautology, and involve the figure of paradox. An example from our corpus:

What travels but never moves?    *A road.*

These routines operate at the level of the signifier, and therefore properly belong to the categories of homophony and conventional polysemy.

Riddles violating commonplaces and enthymemes, on the other hand, are properly treated under the label of anomaly. A commonplace is a state of affairs so regular and predictable that we come to think of it as necessary, a notion the riddle is only too ready to dispel. Take the following examples:

It is taller sitting than standing.    *A dog.*

What goes up and never comes down?    *Your age.*

In each of these routines the solution resolves an incongruity that seems to deny certain facets of reality we take for granted, producing, in Todorov's terms, the effect of improbability.

An enthymeme entails a lesser degree of certainty than the commonplace. Here we enter a territory of probable inference or rough calculation. Reversal of the enthymeme produces contradiction, as illustrated below:

How many balls of string does it take to reach the moon?    *One big one.*

The children perform a good number of routines generating un-natural facts, that is, contrived creatures blending real world attributes into combinations purely fantastic. These creatures of imagination are best treated as a special instance of improbability or contradiction:

a big red rockeater

elephants jumping over palm trees, ensconcing themselves in re-frigerators, abusing credit cards

a frog sandwich

a sparrow or crow with a machine gun

a ten-thousand-pound canary

a zebra with roller skates.

In these violations of commonplaces and enthymemes, the real world provides the materials that are recombined into imaginary entities belonging to a world of fantasy. As in those riddles incorporating comparison, we find in these examples a very instructive crossing of cognitive categories.

Before bringing this chapter to a close, I should note that some of the routines involving real world anomaly present a challenge to the very epistemological axioms that make knowledge possible. A series of routines performed by the Austin children explore difficulties in-herent in the naming and identification of objects. Consider the fol-lowing routines:

How many balls of string does it take to reach the moon?  *One big one.*

What is darker than a crow?  *Its feathers.*

The anomaly here turns on the definitional boundaries of the major referents named, the ball of string and the crow. The basic enigma animating these routines could be formulated along the lines of the classic philosophical puzzle, the one or the many? The part or the whole? How are we to bound and label tokens of our experience? We have then a conceptual parallel to the riddles toying with the boundaries of morphs. In all cognition it is necessary to carve experience into discrete units, but the nature of these units depends on arbitrary social convention as much as on qualities immanent in experience. These routines allude to the essential compromise involved in the act of identification, which inevitably forces us to elevate some perceptual units over others. A large ball of string is composed of smaller balls of string; a crow is in part a composite of feathers. These subsidiary units are made prominent in the two routines cited above, thereby casting light on the disparity between perceptual neutrality and cognitive convention.

Another instructive instance follows:

> I can see it you cannot.   *The back of your head.*

This routine points to the interesting paradox that one of our chief sensory instruments has no reflexive capacity. Our own physiognomy remains in part mysterious to us throughout our lives, since that portion of our anatomy lying in closest proximity to the eyes cannot be directly perceived by the eyes.

The process of reproduction in the natural world is laden with implausibility, and riddles are quick to draw our attention to this fact:

> What has a head like a cat, a body like a cat, and a tail like a cat?
> *A kitten.*
> What do kangaroos have that nobody else has?   *Baby kangaroos.*

The first riddle raises the problem of identity once again, this time not in terms of parts or wholes, but in terms of the A/not A principle of logic. Our sensory apparatus gives us perceptions of single objects that are uniquely themselves. We take for granted the formula that if some object is A it cannot simultaneously be not A. Yet this precept, vital to all human reasoning, is challenged by the likeness of infant to parent in the natural world. A kitten is both a cat and not a cat. The same logical anomaly lies behind the kangaroo riddle. This peculiar identity between parent and offspring is highlighted in the riddles as a natural phenomenon complicating our fundamental assumptions about the world we inhabit.

Let me bring into the discussion one other riddle, this one focusing on yet another aspect of assigning secure identities to the multifarious world around us. Consider this riddle:

What goes up white and comes down yellow?    *An egg.*

Here we come to grips with the capacity of a single item, the egg, to take on rather different phenomenal states. Once again, the identity of the egg is less certain than our everyday logic would recognize. The riddler brings this gap between everyday logic and multifarious reality to the forefront.

This sampling of riddles posed in the form of puzzles derived from naturalistic observation reveals in the genre a strong hint of folk philosophy. We have seen that routines examine the thorny issue of identity from several points of view:

a. The A or not A principle: Some objects can be reasonably described as both A and not A.
b. The part vs. the whole issue: On what basis do we establish boundaries in a continuous universe?
c. The one and the many: Again, a matter of boundaries; how do we determine the basic units of perception?
d. The dilemma of impermanence: At what point does an object undergoing change become another object?
e. The paradox of irreflexivity: A sensory mechanism that is unequipped to sample itself.

These simple puzzles in riddle form assault the fundamental processes of cognition by questioning the procedures we rely on to complete the perceptual cycle of discovery, classification, and reorientation. In previous pages we found riddlers anticipating the concerns of linguists; here we find them treading firmly on the turf of philosophers. Riddles dwelling on real world anomaly scrutinize the epistemology underlying commonsense understandings of the world, suggesting that even the most basic and essential cognitive processes are fraught with uncertainty.

We established early in this chapter that the content of riddling still adheres to the familiar domain of our experience, the modern equivalent of Archer Taylor's world as viewed from the windows of a farm-house (1951). The riddle proper proceeds to render strange this familiar expanse through deliberate exploitation of incongruities encountered daily in the linguistic and conceptual codes but generally suppressed to facilitate the necessary illusion of order and security. Riddles, safely housed in their riddling sessions, implicitly defined as "just play," broach these sources of ambiguity and anomaly, thereby infusing the familiar realm about us with a new vitality. We come toward an understanding in riddling that the world taken for granted is in fact full of mystery. Conceding that our grasp on reality is a tremendous phenomenological compromise, we inevitably return to our conceptual and linguistic orders without which social life is impossible. In the interim, in a field of absolute possibility, riddler and riddlee confront the inherent weakness of cognitive systems in comparison to the wealth of experiential data provided in the sensorium. At this level of abstraction the riddle proper functions as a cultural instrument for defining the limits of culture.

# Negotiation 6

Riddles, much like other forms of conversational folklore, tend to cluster into prolonged discourse sessions composed of numerous instances of the given genre along with other associated material. The performance of a single riddle, if conditions are favorable, will stimulate the performance of additional riddles. Favorable conditions entail the capacity and inclination of participants to preserve the riddling frame. Rarely does one find a solitary riddle lodged in other forms of conversation. More often, one encounters a series of riddles very likely interspersed with other performance genres such as stories and jokes and with other unlabelled conversational gambits thrown in for good measure. Thus we come to speak of riddling sessions, often embedded in larger discourse units.[1]

Drawing on the work of William Labov (1972:160), we may say that a riddle opens a field that is meant to be sustained. A riddle is presented with the expectation that another riddle will be offered in response, and that this second riddle may be modeled on the initial riddle in terms of either form or content or both. It is not difficult to see why riddles tend to cluster into sessions. First, they are short and tidy and thus may be stacked together with relative ease and without the elapsing of a great deal of conversational time. Interrogative ludic routines have clearly demarcated boundaries, facilitating the transaction of unrelated business without disruption of the riddling frame. Second, riddles are interactional forms, bringing at least two (and preferably more) individuals into social intercourse, but they are asymmetrical in terms of the roles they assign to participants. The riddler is the instigator and the sole authority figure for the duration of the riddle. Riddlee is allowed an active part, but one of subservience to the riddler. More than one student of the genre has remarked on this asymmetry, often in reference to the classroom lorded over by the teacher as a model for the riddling format (Roberts and Forman

1972, Sutton-Smith 1976). License is granted to one individual to assume this authoritative role with the understanding that the role will later be available to all participants in the riddling who petition for it. But this equal access rule is operative only if the riddling field is sustained, thus providing ample opportunity for the role of authority figure or riddler to circulate among all interested participants. Finally, riddling embarks on a particular sort of collective contemplation, one that explores nature's transcendence of culture, and the full, sometimes exquisite impact of this exercise only develops through a prolonged process of culmination, i.e., through the aggregation of a series of related episodes.

The time has come to examine riddling in its syntagmatic aspect. Here we are concerned with sequencing at various levels: the order of events generating and bringing to closure a single riddle act; the ordering of riddle acts into riddling sessions; and the riddling etiquette, establishing norms and limits of behavior, by which children successfully negotiate the social transactions entailed in riddling. Concerning the first matter, perhaps enough has been said in previous chapters. We have seen that the riddle act displays a remarkable tenacity of form in riddling traditions around the world. Following Tom Burns (1976), we have identified the riddling skeleton:

   I. riddle act initiation
   II. riddler's statement
   III. riddlee's initial response
   IV. riddler-riddlee interaction in the contemplation period
   V. riddle answer sequence

As we inquire into actual riddling sessions, we will further elaborate this riddling skeleton.

Regarding the second point, the ordering of riddle acts into riddling sessions, we will explore a largely virgin territory. Only a few sources (Goldstein 1963, Evans 1976) have seriously pursued this question. In his article David Evans (1976:170) asserts, quite correctly, that "the total number of riddles told and the order in which they are told constitute part of the context of any single riddle." Within our riddling fields, we can trace the evocative influence of prior material on both form and content, the interplay of creativity and tradition, the selective mixing of genres and riddle types, and the participant strategies that shape and constantly modify the role of each individual in the interaction. In short, we may view the entire riddling session as an integral discourse unit, with patterns of structure and content evolved in the performance.

Riddling etiquette, as we shall see, is an extremely interesting topic. In order to perceive its scope, we might take a look at Jean Piaget's work with the children's game of marbles, which I find closely related to our own present concern. Piaget observed children at play in the game of marbles, and interviewed them regarding their understanding of the rules of the game. He found that at different ages children display markedly different understandings concerning the nature and status of rules. A summary of this work points to three stages of development: "*egocentrism,* where each child does not know the rules or how to apply them but thinks he does; *incipient cooperation,* where mastery of the rules has improved and the children begin to share them in order to compete; and finally, the stage of *genuine coopera-tion,* where children know the rules well and enjoy elaborating on them" (Ginsberg and Opper 1969:102). Of particular interest is the veteran player of marbles, who shows a kind of legalistic fascination with the rules. We will find that riddlers also progress through stages of this sort, and that veteran riddlers likewise display a kind of legalistic fascination with the negotiation of moves in riddling. In fact, we will find a series of portraits: the veteran riddler, with his legalistic attitude; the newcomer to riddling, uncertain of the rules of the game but with ploys of his own invention for gaining a turn; the newly arrived master, with his inventory of traditional riddle material. Riddling, no less than the game of marbles, provides insight into the child's sense of rules and norms governing social intercourse. One im-portant ingredient overlooked by Piaget but irrepressible in our own material is the children's increasing capacity to develop situational strategies allowable within the limits of the rules and conducive to furthering their personal interests in the affair.

In presenting materials for the syntagmatic analysis of riddling, two procedures will be followed. I will present some verbatim transcripts from riddling sessions I recorded in Austin, Texas, thereby allowing the reader to follow the entire verbal transaction. In other cases, I will merely present selections from riddling sessions, when these are sufficient to the argument being made. In all cases, the excerpts are faithfully presented as I transcribed them from my tapes. Moreover, each excerpt is in some sense faithful to the entire corpus of riddling. I have selected representative cases to illustrate fundamental characteristics of riddling encountered throughout the corpus.

Excerpt I

First I present a transcript of a minor riddling field, one occupying an interstice between two spooky stories narrated by an excellent young raconteur. The child I refer to here as Margarita is an accomplished verbal artist. Though younger than her sister, she excels the older sibling in a range of verbal forms. Additional commentary will follow presentation of the excerpt.

Margarita (age 8): M
Linda (age 11): L (The two girls are sisters.)
Investigator: I
Setting: the front porch of their house in East Austin
Date: June 1975

M:   . . . and then the police came and they said it was the devil.
I:   Did that really happen?
M:   I don't know. I know another one.
L:   You know lots of them.
M:   What's a thing, it's a big old round thing and it gots water? What's a big old round thing and it gots water in it?
I:   A water tank, no, a swimming pool?
M:   Right.
L:   Ah what's uh brown, and it has things like that (gestures with the fingers of the right hand to suggest appliance controls), it gots buttons?
I:   Television.
L:   Yeah.
M:   What's, it's in a circle, gots little sticks, and they got something planted?

I:     Garden?

M:    No, it's a big old long thing.

L:     A tree.

M:    It's a tree, she said it. What's yellow, no no no, what's pink, and uh, what's pink and white?

I:     I don't know.

M:    It's a raincoat.

L:     What's a (draws a roundish figure with index finger of right hand)?

I:     I don't know.

L:     An ice cream with a cherry in the top.

M:    What's (draws a complicated figure in the air)?

L:     A design?

M:    A banana split, with cherries.

I:     Do you know any more stories?

M:    Yeah, um let me see, hey you know that little girl, she had a mother but the mother was a witch . . .

Several points of interest are illustrated in this brief excerpt. The field of interrogative ludic routines is initiated by Margarita, the principal storyteller. The riddling frame is dissolved by the investigator, myself, who requests more stories. The field persists for a total of only six routines, all of them descriptive routines, evidently formulated on the spot from related models and deep structures. I have found in collecting various forms of folklore that interrogative ludic routines are highly appreciated as a means of establishing welcome interludes in the midst of other performance genres. We thus find riddling as a field within another field. The riddle appears to bring relief from those performance genres which allow for only an infrequent exchange of roles between performer and audience. A crisp exchange of riddles and the group returns to the larger field. This is precisely the role of riddles in Yoruba storytelling (Abodunde 1977).

We find only descriptive routines in this excerpt because earlier the children had already performed all the traditional riddle material known to them, and there is a rule of riddling etiquette specifying that *a given riddle may not be performed twice in the same session.*

Here is our first encounter with the precepts of riddling etiquette, an unwritten code of riddling decorum enforced by riddling participants through a variety of social control mechanisms.

Our first excerpt is representative of the ambience of performance within the controlling ambience of the home. The home, presided over by the absolute authority of the parents and evoking the children's strongest allegiance, tends to select for courteous, contemplative behavior. With a visitor present, the children are on their best behavior. Some children actually find it difficult to perform folklore around the house, especially if the parents are present. In one collecting excursion, I was ushered into the backyard by a solicitous mother who then instructed her children to perform. The children remained silent, except to insist that they didn't know anything like stories, riddles, rhymes. As I reluctantly took my leave, the little ones followed me around to the front yard and there, beyond the watchful gaze of the parent, the children launched into a series of riddles, rhymes, and stories. The point is that children carefully monitor and control their expressivity in the home environment, especially when strangers are present. This constraint is evident in our first riddling excerpt, in which the children quite deliberately explore a series of descriptive routines. Absent are routines of victimization, which would be out of place in the home environment. The tone of dignity, even tranquillity, pervading the brief interaction I have excerpted above is typical of folklore performance around the home.

The riddling apparatus is minimal in this excerpt. We note only a few distinctive moves: the posing of the riddle, the provision of a clue, and announcement of the solution on riddler's part; attempts at divining the solution and statements of surrender on riddlee's part. Since the exchange is not contentious, the children have no need of the legalistic apparatus we find in more rambunctious sessions. In our next excerpt, we shall investigate some of the legalistic ploys used by riddling participants to advance their specific causes. Riddling on the front porch confines children to their most cooperative personas: there is no squabbling over turns and other matters as we find in street and schoolyard riddling sessions.

One other point is worthy of mention in reference to our first excerpt. Two of the descriptive routines are remarkable for the fusion they occasion of verbal and kinetic elements. In these routines the description of physical attributes becomes an iconography, through the agency of finger drawing. Thus the boundaries of speech and gesture are crossed at will, because the descriptive segment focuses on simple empirical data such as shape, form, anatomy, data capable of schematic visual representation. The two routines illustrate another recurrent phenomenon, the power of suggestion enabling the prior discourse context to precondition subsequent events. Thus Margarita's banana split with cherries may be seen as a topping (not in the confectionary sense) of her sister's ice cream with a cherry on top. The later routine clearly builds on the earlier one as a model, not by repeating it verbatim, for this is proscribed, but by embellishing it with additional descriptive detail.

Excerpt 2

In order to savor the contrast, let's shift settings radically to the schoolyard of an East Austin elementary school. I present excerpts from a prolonged riddling session with rather different characteristics than the sample we have just examined.

Albert (age 9): A
Paula (age 8): P
Tomás (age 7): T
David (age 6): D (Tomás and David are brothers.)
Investigator: I
Setting: East Austin elementary schoolyard

A: I'm nine years old.
P: Estás lyando tú, ¿es verdad que no tiene nine years old? Dile spooky stories.
T: I know one. How come you have to wear your pants? So
5    your underwear won't show.
D: Why do you need to wear your shirt? So they won't see your chi chi.
A: What flies up, it gots some green on it, it gots string?
I: A kite?

10  A:  No, a balloon.
    P:  Wait, what's orange and has a little thing on top?
    T:  A pumpkin.
    P:  Yeah.
    A:  What takes people up in the air?
15  T:  An airplane.
    A:  Yeah.
    D:  What is a slip?
    I:  What is a sleep?
    D:  A slip, you know, when you put up your slip, you know
20      how you go like this? (imitates girlishly the action of hik-
        ing up a slip)
    T:  Why do you need the street? (pause) So the cars can go
        through the highway.
    D:  How come you need a car?
25  I:  I don't know.
    D:  To drive it stupid. Why do you need a bag? (pause) To
        carry candies.
    T:  Why do you need a mask for? (pause) Halloween.
    D:  Hey, how come you need hair? (pause) To not be bald
30      headed.
    T:  Why do you need a moustache? Do you know? (to I)
    I:  No.
    T:  So you won't be a *bolillo*.
    I:  What's a *bolillo*?
35  A:  It's a white.
    I:  And what are you?
    A:  Mejicano, I'm born in Texas, chicano.
    T:  What is this: How come people go inside the bank?
        (pause) To pay the money.
40  D:  How come they need fence the house?
    I:  I don't know.
    D:  You don't know?
    I:  To keep the people out?
    D:  No.
45  I:  Why?

D:  So the dog won't go through to the street.

T:  What's up in the sky and it's white? (pause) The moon.

D:  What's up in the sky and lives up in the sky?

I:  Birds?

50  D:  No, you know.

I:  No.

D:  That you talk to when you go to church.

I:  Oh, God.

D:  Yeah.

55  T:  How come the leaves are falling off the trees?

P:  Because the cold wind.

I:  Because it's winter.

T:  No, because they saw your face and screamed.

A:  What's yellow, what's yellow up there in the sky?

60  T:  The sun.

D:  What's red and it has tires?

I:  A car.

D:  Yeah. How come the trees are growing leaves?

I:  I don't know.

65  D:  Because they saw your pee pee and they screamed. (laughter)

                Look up look down
                Look all around
                Your pants are falling down. (laughter)

70  P:  How come the birds are all out? (pause) Because it's not sunny and it ain't cold.

D:  What is black and you can wear them?

I:  Black and you can wear them.

A:  Pants.

75  I:  Pants.

D:  No, that you can wear on the, you know, shoes.

T:  Socks?

D:  There's something that you go, put them in the hole, and then you go like that (struts) and start walking.

80  T:  Um skates.

D:  No.

T:    You put them on, you tie them.

A:    Shoes.

D:    Yeah.

85  P:    Hey, what's green, what's green and are leaves?

I:    Leaves.

P:    Yeah. (laughs)

T:    What's green and orange? (pause) A pumpkin.

D:    What's orange and has a green thing on top?

90  I:    A pumpkin.

D:    No.

T:    A orange.

D:    It has a light on it.

T:    Candle?

95  I:    Lantern.

T:    I know what, a pumpkin.

I:    What?

D:    Then you make holes in it.

I:    Makes holes in it, a paper bag?

100  D:    No.

P:    A jack-a-lantern.

D:    And there's a string and then you go (makes the motion of pulling a string).

A:    A ball.

105  T:    A jack-a-lantern.

A:    A light bulb.

D:    Unh huh.

A:    A string.

I:    I give up.

110  D:    Lamp.

A:    Well that's what he said.

P:    That's the same thing as a light.

(A great many more routines of this kind follow, along with a few knock-knock jokes, a narrative, and other odds and ends. The session comes to an end with the segment given below.)

D:    Well how come there' cage around here for animals?

|       | I: | I don't know, why? |
|-------|----|----|
| 115   | D: | Why, tell me why. |
|       | I: | So they don't get away. |
|       | D: | It's something because. |
|       | P: | Why do you need a glass for? |
|       | I: | I don't know. |
| 120   | D: | For curtains? |
|       | P: | No, for your cola. What do you need a playground for? |
|       | D: | To play. |
|       | I: | To have fun? |
|       | P: | No, to play. |
| 125   | D: | How come you need a glass for? |
|       | I: | I don't know. |
|       | D: | You know why? You got to tell me the answer. To paint. How come the leaves fall? How come winter comes? |
|       | I: | Because it gets cold, I don't know. |
| 130   | D: | You got to tell me the answer. |
|       | I: | I can't tell you. |
|       | P: | Hey you know why we never go with strangers? |
|       | I: | Why? |
|       | P: | Cause they could kidnap us. |
| 135   | I: | Well I'm going to have to go now. |

I have reproduced this lengthy excerpt in order to convey something of the flavor of a typical session of what I would call contentious riddling. We may examine it from several points of view and contrast it with the other riddling excerpt we have examined already. First, let's correlate the tone of interaction here to the setting of interaction. The children are verbally aggressive in this session, taking liberties with one another and with the adult investigator. The initial sign of aggressive uses of language is the accusation levelled against Albert concerning his assertion that he is nine years old. The next sign is the introduction of obscenity, a feature carefully edited from conversation around the home, but prevalent enough in the schoolyard. Throughout the session we find mention of taboo items such as underwear, chi chi (nipples), pee pee, a girl's slip, etc. Direct verbal attacks are launched: in line 26 a participant is called stupid; in line 58 a participant is alleged to have caused the trees to lose their leaves; again in line 65 a participant is portrayed as some sort of natural spook. The children engage in routines of victimization here, exploiting the riddle form and format for frontal attacks on their coriddlers. But the sounding is ritualistic, and no offense is taken.

Also characteristic of contentious riddling are two exchanges with larger sociopolitical overtones. In one of these (lines 31–37), the children use the riddle form and format to explore the differential ethnic identity of children vis-à-vis investigator. The latter is anglo; the children are chicano. One of the obvious visible markers of *chicanismo* is the presence of the moustache generally cultivated by chicano male adults. The riddle broaching this potentially delicate topic is addressed by Tomás specifically to investigator. Also addressed to the investigator is the final routine bringing up another situationally controversial topic, the possibility of kidnapping (lines 132–35). Both these routines have reference to sensitive issues inherent in the circumstances of this particular riddling session. These topics, both risky and fascinating, are ingeniously broached by the children through the formulation of perfectly legitimate routines. They may in this fashion be dealt with safely within the circumscribed riddling format.

All these features, the aggressive use of language, the presence of obscenity, utilization of routines of victimization, mark this excerpt as language of the street or schoolyard. The interaction has a tone of slightly embittered contest, evident also in the incipient bickering between investigator and the youngest riddler, David. The tone contrasts sharply with the amiability noted in excerpt 1, recorded on a front porch well within the sphere of influence of the home.

In this excerpt, as in the first one, most of the routines are descriptive routines. The absence of riddles proper (actually five occur in the long middle section not included here) derives from the fact that I had already spoken earlier with Paula and Albert and exhausted their corpus of traditional riddles. Neither of the younger children had much to contribute in the way of traditional riddle material. The scene was conducive, however, to the formulation of several routines of victimization. These, like the greater part of the descriptive routine corpus, appear to have been coined on the spot along lines similar to those discussed in reference to the first excerpt.

The sequence of events is also quite abbreviated for the most part, frequently involving only three steps:

1. posing of riddle
2. pause
3. delivery of solution.

The intervening pause, marking riddlee's prerogative, was shortened to the bare minimum since competition for the floor was keen enough to militate against the development of conversational lag. In any case, some of the routines mushroomed into larger sequences, and these we will find instructive concerning the moves provided for riddler and riddlee by the riddling etiquette. We will take a close look at one of these longer sequences.

The lengthy sequence of turns within a single riddle act beginning with line 89 runs through the following inventory of moves:

1. proposition (riddler)
2. unacceptable solution (riddlee)
3. rejection of 2 (riddler)
4. unacceptable solution (riddlee)
5. clue (riddler)
6. unacceptable solution (riddlee)
7. unacceptable solution (riddlee)
8. unacceptable solution (riddlee)
9. request for solution (riddlee)
10. clue (riddler)
11. repetition of clue (riddler)
12. unacceptable solution (riddlee)
13. rejection of 12 (riddler)
14. unacceptable solution (riddlee)
15. clue (riddler)
16. unacceptable solution (riddlee)
17. unacceptable solution (riddlee)
18. unacceptable solution (riddlee)
19. rejection of 18 (riddler)
20. unacceptable solution (riddlee)

21. surrender (riddlee)
22. correct solution (riddler)
23. challenge (riddlee)
24. challenge (riddlee)

For the most part, these moves have been discussed already, but there are a few new elements: the request for solution, the surrender, and the challenge. By the former two, the riddlee attempts to terminate the riddle act, although as the above series indicates, this tactic need not be heeded by the riddler if he is determined to prolong the agony. The challenge is a legalistic device whereby the riddlee questions the appropriateness of riddler's behavior. In our series, the challengers assert that the correct answer had been provided, and riddler had denied it and thereby illegally prolonged the routine. Challenges are essentially like miniature legal briefs, alleging particular infractions of riddling etiquette. They signal the existence of a riddling decorum governing the control of access to the floor, the aptness of clues, and the pertinence of solutions, among other things. The arbitrary authority of the riddler is thus tempered by the riddlee's court of appeal. Here we have uncovered another fundamental principle of riddling etiquette: *riddler may not disavow a correct answer provided by riddlee.*[2]

Other routines delivered in this session bring up additional moves not dealt with so far. The riddler admonishes the riddlee (lines 115, 127, 130) when he senses that the latter's morale is slackening. This move furthers riddler's reign, by encouraging riddlee to pursue the quest for an acceptable answer. Riddler may thereby hold on to his solution all the longer. In one instance above, David refuses to divulge the correct answer in order to prompt further attempts at divination, and the routine remains unsolved as the children move on to other matters (lines 113–18).

A single interrogative ludic routine performed within some definite social context thus potentially gives rise to a variety of social transactions. One set of moves facilitates the posing and solving of routines. Here we find:

1. proposition
2. clue

3. rejection of unacceptable solution
4. affirmation of correct solution
5. delivery of correct solution.

These five are in the domain of the riddler. Note that at least two sorts of clues are found in the sample: additional attributes (lines 52, 76, 102), and formal clues as in line 117, "It's something *because*." The riddlee, on the other hand, has recourse to the following moves:

1. request for clue
2. request for clarification
3. proposed solution.

These moves associated with the mechanics of posing and delivering solutions to interrogative ludic routines alternate in comprehensible patterns, riddler maintaining control over the interaction.

Another set of moves is concerned with monitoring the behavior of riddler. These are devices available to riddlee to correct abuses on the part of riddler. Here we encounter:

1. request for solution
2. surrender
3. challenge.

The first two give the riddlee some access to the pacing of the routine, enabling him either to bring the routine to a close, or to disengage himself from the action. Challenges are lodged only in special circumstances, when the riddler has clearly violated some precept of riddling decorum. The challenge works within the system to promote adherence to riddling etiquette; it is not, in itself, subversive.

Finally, we can infer the existence of a set of moves whereby the riddler consolidates his own position in the exchange. We have two moves for this purpose:

1. encouraging the riddlee
2. refusing to supply requested solution.

Through these moves, riddler holds on to the solution and thereby prolongs his stay as sole authority figure, since *no routine is complete until the solution has been provided or acknowledged by riddler*.[3]

When I speak of the negotiation of riddling I am not using a figure of speech. Riddling entails the adroit manipulation of a set of rules that are pliable in their application to specific circumstances. Each player in the routine has certain rights and responsibilities limiting the scope of his initiative and response. Riddling occurs through the contract of participants. Riddler is allotted for the duration of the routine the authority to direct events and pass final judgment on the aptness of suggested answers. The riddlee acquiesces in the interests of pursuing an enjoyable exchange and because he knows his turn will come. Another pillar of riddling decorum holds that *no individual will repeat as riddler in the face of competition for that post*. Riddling depends for its very existence on universal access of qualified individuals to the position of riddler. Riddler's power is bounded, as we have seen. He is obliged to resolve the routine satisfactorily and to observe other conventions for the duration of his reign. Thus he must judge proffered solutions fairly, relinquish his role within reasonable periods of time, and accede to the will of the majority on matters such as clues and pacing.

It should be apparent that apart from certain pillars of riddling decorum, the rules governing riddling are not cut-and-dried mechanisms of control. The problem is that in concrete situations the claims of riddlers and riddlees may come into conflict. The rules of riddling etiquette are vague and partial, and allow, indeed encourage, the application of diplomacy and strategy in their fitting to specific occasions. The rules are little more than a skeletal contract within which riddler and riddlee negotiate particular moves. Successful manipulation of this system, from the point of view of riddler or riddlee, requires considerable sense of the personalities present, the prevailing mood, and other incidental matters that can make or break any given strategy.

As we have seen, the majority of routines come and go without plunging the children into disputes of a legalistic sort. These mechanisms are available in the event that the normal riddling process breaks down. They resemble, in this sense, what Erving Goffman (1971:95) has called remedial interchanges, that is, sanctioned means of restoring tranquillity after a breach in decorum has occurred and been publicly noted. This level of interaction might be termed meta-transactional, since it entails transactions about transacting, though the term legalistic seems to do just as well.

## ANATOMY OF AN EXCERPT

In our second excerpt, each child plays a unique role, and it will further our analysis to follow each of them through the session, plotting their achievements and their extravagances. David, the youngest, is the most energetic and opportunistic riddler and shows great presence of mind in the ready formulation of acceptable routines. He also revels in the power of being the riddler, lording it over his older associates and squeezing the last drop of authority out of the riddler's license. In one instance he illegally prolongs his turn at riddler, thereby incurring challenges from two of the older children. All but two or three of his routines are descriptive. He does produce the enigmatic

What's up in the sky and lives in the sky?    *God*

which could be assigned to either the category of descriptive routines or riddles proper. He also produces an occasional routine of victimization, based on models supplied by the older children.

David's riddling is opportunistic for a variety of reasons. He has little command of traditional riddling material and is thus perforce thrown back on his own wits. All his routines appear to be spontaneous coinings, generally inspired by material provided in the routines of the older children. Well over half his routines take their topic or form from material found in previous discourse context. The following link is typical:

T: Why do you need the street? (pause) *So the cars can go through the highway.*

D: How come you need a car? etc. (cf. lines 22 ff.).

In this sequence David appropriates both form and content to fashion his own contribution to the riddling. The same is true of the following pair:

T: How come the leaves are falling off the trees? *Because they saw your face and screamed.*

D: How come the trees are growing leaves? *Because they saw your pee pee and they screamed.*

It will be noted immediately that David's routines are not mere copies but clever variations on a theme. In this instance, he copies the tone and structure of the model routine. His proposition is actually an inversion of Tomás's in that he refers to the coming rather than the falling of leaves. In addition, he adds a naughty element, a mildly obscene touch in the solution. David's transformation loses something, since the connection between shock and loss of leaves is more plausible than that between shock and the growing of leaves. Still, he comes up with a routine acceptable to the group, which responds with laughter.

Another diagnostic feature of David's riddling is the absence of block elements. At six years, he stands just shy of the great cognitive watershed. By age seven he will acquire an understanding of the characteristic modes of reversal, both linguistic and cognitive, animating the riddle proper. But for the moment the riddle is still a puzzling question with an arbitrary answer (to use Sutton-Smith's phrase) or a simple matching of object and attribute.

One conspicuous mark of David's energy and guile is his proclivity to retain the post of riddler for two or more consecutive turns. As we have seen, one tenet of riddling decorum is the tendency to alternate turns at posing the riddles among all those present who wish to participate in this manner. Certainly special circumstances allow for occasional violations of this tenet: one individual may have an especially delectable store of routines, or there may be no other pretenders to the throne. But David repeatedly holds on for consecutive turns even in the absence of these mitigating factors. On three occasions he seizes a second turn without pause or gesture of apology. The only other child to take two consecutive turns is Paula, and she does so only once.

In all these ways, David represents a very typical six-year-old riddling participant. There is no question but that he is hooked on the genre; he inserts his own routines at every possible turn. Since he has not developed a grasp on the kinds of reversals to be found in riddles, and since he knows little or no traditional material, his participation necessarily takes the form of newly coined descriptive routines. Though he hasn't mastered some of the cognitive mysteries of the riddle proper, he does well enough at defending himself in the transaction of riddling. Here his energy, enthusiasm, and ingenuity carry him a long way.

Albert, the oldest participant in the session, takes an active role at the outset, but as the riddling progresses becomes less and less involved. Though he recites no routines after the first minutes, he does enter into the guessing of solutions throughout the session. And he rallies to present the challenge to David when the latter illegally prolongs one of his turns as riddler. Albert maintains an attitude of bemused detachment; he allows the younger children to frolic with the riddling.

The most avid participant after David is Tomás, who poses routines constantly throughout the session. As we have seen, he initiates the victimization strain, which is later imitated by David. He also brings ethnic consciousness to the surface in his clever routine about moustaches. Tomás, unlike David, also takes an active interest in solving routines, proposing eight solutions to David's two. He eschews the excesses we have noted in David's behavior, such as monopolizing the post of riddler and drawing out routines beyond the span of the group's patience. Tomás also takes cues from formerly enunciated routines, but the majority of his routines do not spring from the prior discourse context. With his greater innovative capacity, his ability to move from one type to another, his dwelling on themes of special interest (such as ethnic identity), his participation in solving routines, and his conformance to riddling etiquette, Tomás comes across as a mature riddling participant. He shares David's enthusiasm, but exhibits more control over its expenditure.

The other participant, Paula, is slightly marginal to the interaction. She does not take part throughout, but hovers about tossing in an occasional routine or solution. Around the middle of the session, she provides some relief from riddling by telling a story about a sinister figure known as Bloody Bones. She is evidently somewhat discomfited during the session, and even produces a totally flawed routine:

What is green and are leaves?    *Leaves.*

Neither of her proposed solutions is accepted. The fact that she is the only female present in a group of fairly aggressive males may partially explain her marginality, for in other recording sessions I found her a competent riddler and an outstanding teller of spooky stories. She does come through at the end with that curious routine

Hey you know why we never go with strangers?    *Cause they could kidnap us*

which in the performance context appears to be more than a mere ludic routine. In fact, this is a classic example of the adaptation of folklore to the expression of immediate social phenomena too explosive to be dealt with openly.

As a means of summing up these observations regarding the differential participation of each child in the riddling, I present the score card in table 3.

TABLE 3

|  | David | Tomás | Paula | Albert | Investigator |
|---|---|---|---|---|---|
| Number of routines | 12 | 8 | 6 | 4 | 0 |
| Direct contextual stimulus | 7 | 4 | 2 | 1 | — |
| Flawed | 3 | 0 | 1 | 0 | — |
| Number of solutions | 2 | 8 | 2 | 5 | 13 |
| Accepted | 1 | 3 | 0 | 1 | 3 |
| Violations of etiquette | 3 | 0 | 1 | 0 | 0 |
| Challenges made | 0 | 0 | 1 | 1 | 0 |
| Challenges received | 2 | 0 | 0 | 0 | 0 |

The score card portrays the role played by each participant in the riddling and further characterizes typical patterns of participation by children of various ages throughout our riddling corpus. The number of routines performed decreases steadily with the increase of age. This is not a typical feature in itself; if Albert had had a riddling equal to compete with he might have taken a more active role, and we have already discussed Paula's marginal status. Interestingly, the ratio of modeled to original material also decreases steadily with increasing age. The younger children are more likely to rely on previous discourse material for their inspiration, the older children more likely to introduce novel material. Of interest is the fact that the most active poser of riddles is among the least active posers of solutions. The most well-rounded participant poses both riddles and solutions to those posed by others. Violations and challenges are likewise clearly patterned with respect to age. The youngest child commits all but one of the total inventory of violations and receives both challenges made. The two older children are the ones to make the challenges.

The roles portrayed by these numbers are typical in many respects. Over time I became familiar with each of the personas contained in them: the ambitious but untried youngster, who gains performance time through his wits; the riddling master, manifesting a well-oiled expertise; the seasoned older partners, who maintain a certain detachment from the proceedings, intervening from time to time in the interests of order, stability, justice. Not all riddling sessions follow the same pattern as our excerpt 2, but these riddling profiles recur again and again in riddling sessions among children.

One final point: there is a continuity of theme evident in this excerpt, centering on Halloween, which was right around the corner when this recording was made. The pumpkin, jack-o-lantern, mask, bag, and wintry weather weave in and out of the session. But this is to anticipate the theme of the following chapter, which deals with certain constancies of form and content maintained over the entire trajectory of a riddling session. In conclusion, I present a précis of the riddling contract as we have discovered it in this chapter:

1. There are two participant roles, riddler and riddlee.
2. The riddle proposition and solution are provided by riddler.

3. Riddlee has a turn following delivery of the riddle proposition in which he or she may seek to divine the riddle solution.

4. Since more than one referent may fit the bill, riddler is final authority on the correct solution.

5. Riddler may not disavow a correct solution provided by riddlee.

6. No riddle act is complete until the solution is provided or confirmed by riddler.

7. The same routine should not be performed twice in a single riddling session (the arrival of new personnel may trigger a new session).

8. No individual will repeat as riddler for consecutive turns in the face of competition for that post.

None of these stipulations is sacrosanct in the turbulent arena of the peer group, though there is a tendency to conform to them so that riddling may proceed. A set of standard moves allows for the proper discharge of each participant role, and a set of remedial moves may be called into play to deal with perceived violations of the riddling contract. Finally, we have noted that children exhibit divergent attitudes toward the riddling contract, depending on their personalities, ages, and levels of riddling competence.

# Sessions 7

In the previous chapter, we have seen that the occasional riddle tends to open a riddling field, conducive to sustained performance within the genre. One riddle begets another, all other factors being amenable. We also remarked that riddling interacts in predictable fashion with other performance genres, stories for example, providing for a stimulating and enjoyable alternation of cognitive and social interactional frames. One common pattern I noted was the interspersing of spooky stories and short riddling sessions. These two genres of verbal performance are contrastive on several scales: while the former makes the strange familiar, the latter makes the familiar strange; the former allots performance time to a single individual in large units, consigning all others present to comparative silence and inactivity, while the latter draws all participants into highly active roles, either as posers or solvers of riddles. Yoruba storytellers recognize the utility of riddles thrown in among stories as a device to keep audiences on their toes (Abodunde 1977). These two genres, stories and riddles, thus complement one another in the conversational flow, creating a pleasing alternation of effect.

This characteristic patterning of conversational genres indicates that amidst the seemingly capricious flow of words, styles, and topics in conversation, there exist principles of order that are inherently aesthetic in nature. Conversational settings with all their apparent spontaneity and informality are actually far from random affairs. In fact, a group of scholars sometimes known as ethnomethodologists is marshalling evidence to substantiate the proposition that even casual talk is highly patterned and regulated through the operation of unwritten codes (cf. Sudnow 1972). In more recent work, exhaustive study of laughter among conversants shows conformance to patterns tending to synchronize participants' indulgence in the chuckle and guffaw and regulating the interaction of laughing sequences and talk (Jefferson 1976). In this matter of laughing, as in many others, we

133

confront a rigorous patterning, which belies the apparently haphazard progress of talk. Roger Abrahams (1977) suggests that conversants in our society cultivate the illusion of conversational spontaneity in order to preserve the notion of the authentic, unrehearsed self manifest in apparently unstudied speech. Adherence to this illusion may well account for the invisibility of codes actually responsible for the regulation of casual talk.

In any case, there can be little doubt that discourse is a highly patterned human activity and that a good deal of this patterning answers to primarily aesthetic motives. Roman Jakobson (1966) refers to parallelism as the constitutive device of all verbal art, evident in the least conspicuous of locutions as in the highest poetry. Something of this concern for balance and pattern enters into all conversational gambits. In the present chapter, we shall inspect a pair of riddling sessions for the presence of large-scale patterning in form and content. We shall find that these sessions are highly saturated with patterning and that participants attend closely to the emerging structure of riddling sessions even while these are in progress. In consideration of both form and content, we come across the central role played by immediately prior discourse in the shaping of subsequent discourse. Without this self-referentiality of discourse, the patterning of talk into large-scale regularities would be incomplete at best.

In the typical riddling session, purely fortuitous considerations initiate a particular stylistic and semantic thrust. Quite often, sessions open with the performance of the stock of traditional items known to the children. If the participants are seasoned riddlers, the entire session may comprise riddles drawn from this traditional stock. This situation would most likely obtain among adult riddlers. Even so, as David Evans (1976) shows, we might expect to find tangible cognitive routes displayed in the riddling. Among children, the supply of traditional items is frequently exhausted before the riddling thirst is slaked, in which case the children are likely to turn to what I have called descriptive routines, routines evolving from riddling competence but freshly devised on the spot. Younger children may find that their only access to the position of riddler lies in their capacity to formulate descriptive routines. Thus children's riddling typically begins with the performance of one or a few traditional items, but then moves on to the performance of newly made routines partaking of riddle texture. This circumstance endows the riddlers with a free hand to manipulate emerging patterns of form and content. The result is a riddling session taking the form of a symposium, in which a particular topic or formal structure receives collective scrutiny. Form and content provided in the initial traditional material serve as a stimulus for the production of numerous reformulations and transformations.

I have selected two riddling sessions for consideration in this chapter, one displaying primarily formal manipulation, the other primarily semantic. These sessions are highly representative of the patterning found throughout the riddling corpus, but they are in themselves unusual for the intensity of patterning they display. Here we find the children at their most manipulative, paying almost scholastic attention to developing formal and semantic structures. For this reason, these sessions are particularly instructive regarding the patterning of form and content present in lesser degree throughout the entire corpus of riddling sessions. Since our concern here is with global patterns of form and content, I have simply extracted the pertinent interrogative ludic routines from the session, not bothering to include complete transcripts as in the previous chapter, where the concern was with interactional strategies.

## SESSION I: A SYMPOSIUM ON LOCOMOTION

The first session we will consider most nearly approximates a symposium in riddle format. The children present devoted themselves to the exploration of a single semantic domain, that of locomotion, through the promulgation of repeated routines marking out the dimensions of this domain. Not all material performed during this session ties directly into their chosen theme. Other topics weave in and out as the session progresses, but the children insistently return to the original theme. Below I present the eleven routines, performed over the space of about half an hour, dealing with this theme. Other intervening material has been edited out, not because I feel that it is cognitively unrelated but because I wish to concentrate for the moment on the consummate structuring of a single domain. My presentation here retains the original order of occurrence:

1. What has eight wheels and rolls?    *Roller skates.*
2. What has two wheels and pedals?    *A bicycle.*
3. What has four wheels, no pedals, and a steering wheel?    *A car.*
4. What has four legs and can run?    *A mustang.*
5. What has three wheels and pedals?    *A tricycle.*
6. What has four legs and can't walk?    *A chair.*
7. What has two legs, it can walk?    *A monkey.*
8. What has long legs and it's hard to walk?    *A seagull.*
9. What has two seats, four wheels, and they can roll?    *A car.*
10. What has lots of windows and they can fly?    *Airplane.*
11. What are those little clocks and its in your car?    *A dragger.*

We have here a corpus of interrogative ludic routines for the most part of the transparent sort, involving unambiguous questions whose answers are uniquely determined by the interrogator. Items 1 and 6 are traditional and appear to exert considerable influence over the direction pursued in the riddling, orienting the riddlers to the domain of moving things. Item 4 appears to be a spontaneous coining, remarkable in that it revives the dead metaphor implicit in naming an automobile after a kind of horse. The remaining items are descriptive routines, cast indelibly in conformance with riddle texture but encapsulating little or nothing in the way of a block element. This riddling sample, produced by a trio of chicano children ages six through eight, is thus transitional between neophyte and more experienced riddling. The riddlers have mastered the texture of their genre, and are making tentative stabs into appropriate methods of deception.

To claim that this riddling sample constitutes a symposium on modes of locomotion is merely to state the obvious. The interest here lies in the methodical process whereby the children lay bare the organization of that domain. The final, cumulative impact of the session is nothing less than the dissection of their chosen semantic domain into its constituent parts through the operation of logic. I would say that the children adopt in this session a scholastic, or scientific, attitude before the materials they discuss. Implied in the sets of contrasting tokens is a taxonomy of locomotion. The children overtly supply only the tokens or concrete objects in the taxonomy, and the distinctive features or points of significant contrast. The remainder of the taxonomic apparatus is, nonetheless, presupposed in the sorting of tokens into categories. The children provide, then, the following set of tokens: roller skates, bicycle, car, mustang, tricycle, chair, monkey, seagull, airplane, dragger (stock car). In addition, we are given three major points of contrast, wheels, legs, pedals, and several minor points of contrast, number of wheels and legs, effectiveness of legs, and so forth. Yet as the theme of locomotion is explored and developed, one routine begetting another, one senses that underlying this contemplative kind of performance there lurks a rather fully determined folk taxonomy.

Utilizing the data provided by the children, I have attempted to furnish the taxonomy implicit in this riddling sample in order to demonstrate the rigor and perspicacity of thinking revealed in children's riddling. The patterning of content in our sample is sufficiently intense that it merits presentation in taxonomic form. That the children chose to elaborate this taxonomy in the enjoyable format of riddling tells us something about the instructive capacity of nonpedagogic settings. I would suggest that the cognitive rigor and sophistication displayed in these pleasurable vessels is closer to typical than atypical of children's play in verbal genres.

Fig. 4 presents my reconstruction of the folk taxonomy focused on the semantic domain of locomotion implicit in the aggregate of routines dealing with this topic. While the taxonomy is obviously not exhaustive, it is equally obviously highly structured and logically arranged within its chosen realm. There are several tiers to the taxonomy, each level comprising contrasts that are in turn assimilated into continuities at the next higher level. Thus the airplane and automobile stand in contrast to one another at one level, but at a higher

FIG. 4.    *The taxonomy of locomotion*

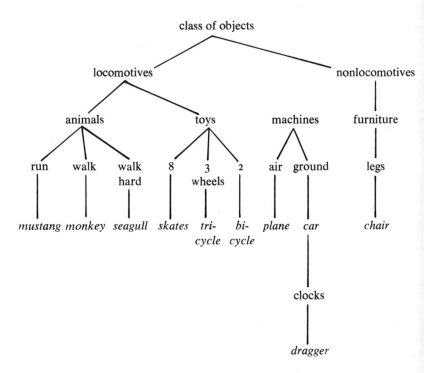

level of generalization it can be seen that they are in fact continuous in opposition to toys and animals. In this manner, the taxonomy sorts out the rather complex structure of relationship among the tokens named in the interrogative ludic routines under consideration, specifying relations and levels of inclusion and exclusion. Things are, as it were, put in their logical places.

This logic inherent in the riddling sample and captured in our taxonomy can be isolated through a distinctive feature analysis of our four segregates, animals, toys, machines, and furniture. With reference to a small number of critical variables, each category displays a positive or negative quality. The constellation of such values is unique to each category:

| animals | toys | machines | furniture |
|---------|------|----------|-----------|
| +legs | −legs | −legs | −legs |
| −wheels | +wheels | +wheels | −wheels |
| −pedals | +pedals | −pedals | −pedals |
| +mobile | +mobile | +mobile | −mobile |

Furniture is clearly the odd man out in this set, distinguished from the other categories simply by the feature −mobile, or by the pair of features −legs, −wheels. It is, of course, the single representative holding down the domain of nonlocomotives, not otherwise treated in our riddling symposium. The category of animals is distinguished from the others on the basis of the three distinctive features +legs, −pedals, +mobile. The two features −legs and +pedals distinguish toys, while machines are notable for lacking both legs and pedals. This distinctive feature analysis can be seen to tally with a system involving modes of locomotion not directly anticipated but nonetheless implicit in the routines performed by the children. Animals, having legs and being mobile while lacking wheels and pedals, are, in the strictest sense, locomotive. Toys, moving on wheels through the device of pedals, achieve motion through the intervention of human energy. Machines, lacking both legs and pedals, achieve motion through the intervention of some nonhuman energy supply. Furniture, of course, does not move at all though it possesses objects sometimes referred to as legs.

We observe then that the distinctions and inclusions brought to attention in the children's riddling correlate with basic, socially endorsed understandings of our society's phenomenological universe. The descriptive routine is in fact a means of checking on the social endorsement of idiosyncratic perceptions. Moreover, the domain selected for elaboration in this riddling is one that lies at the heart of the children's experience of the world. All around them, the children perceive motion. They are themselves moving objects. The nuances and intricacies of motion continue to fascinate us, from the rocking of the cradle to the rocking of the rocking chair. We celebrate our understanding of motion in highly demanding art forms and games. In short, the children here seize on a topic of evident instinctive and cultural salience, and specify within that topic some of the major lines of affinity and contrast.

However, the intention of this folk taxonomy is in the last analysis operational rather than speculative. The folk taxonomy is adapted to practical purposes, while the scientific taxonomy attends rigorously to all the phenomena in its ken. The practical orientation of the folk taxonomy is suggested in the following children's riddle:

> What's the difference between a loaf of bread and an elephant?
> (I don't know).
> Remind me not to send you to the grocery store for bread!

The classification system contained in a folk taxonomy sustains basic cultural competence even at the most mundane level. The folk taxonomy is a working taxonomy, facilitating culturally acceptable action. It seeks for general guidelines rather than exhaustive coverage within a domain. Folk taxonomies contain a flexibility allowing for on the spot improvisation. They capture the pronounced outlines of cultural conventions, without attending zealously to marginal cases inevitably available in the flux of nature, which is more continuous and less discrete than our taxonomies would suggest.

The taxonomy presented here is not, for all that, unscientific. In their grouping of tokens the children have implied a structure transcending what Claude Lévi-Strauss calls "classification at the level of sensible properties" (Lévi-Strauss 1966:15). The taxonomy in fig. 4 rests on the union of form and function. We have seen that legs, wheels, and pedals are not casually but causally related to modes of locomotion. The sensible properties demarcated in the routines correlate to basic functional distinctions, thus establishing the taxonomy on a more secure foundation than mere empirical contradistinction. The formulation of such a taxonomy, emerging as it does in the arena of verbal play, is no mean or trivial task. It is time to give credit to the cerebral child, diligently exploring the predetermined fit of cultural category to natural diversity. Children, in the riddling and other formats, engage in sustained and powerful intellection, a fact sometimes concealed in our tendency to despise the products of childish cognition.

In the analysis thus far, we have confined our vision to the children in their structuring persona, dwelling rather methodically in the course of a riddling session on cognitive structures prevalent in their culture. We have seen a diverse collection of tokens systematically compared and contrasted on the basis of a very few criterial attributes. Children's play across the whole spectrum of verbal and nonverbal genres appears to display this ordering facet, and one might speculate that without the informal, entertaining format provided by the ludic genres, children would acquire only with great difficulty if at all the fundamental cognitive and interactional abilities and flexibilities required of adults in society. Indeed, the practice gained in the arena of children's folklore would appear to be a critical phase of the enculturation process, the process whereby the child acquires mastery over his own culture.

Resting our case here, with the ordering facet of children's play, would be a mistake. There is present in much children's folklore, including riddling, an opposite tendency, another vector of intellection, entailing the dismemberment of cultural orders and their reassembly into culturally anomalous formulations. We have seen in an earlier chapter the operation of linguistic and nonlinguistic reversal in the riddle proper. At that point we speculated that riddling is a cultural mechanism for measuring the transcendence of nature over cultural forms. In our riddling sample we are able to observe this restructuring facet of children's riddling at close hand. Two routines of the eleven, items 4 and 6, depart from transparent questioning procedures and incorporate ambiguity. These routines tend to subvert the very same cognitive orders developed in the other routines performed during the session. As with the proverbial sand castle, the building and dismantling of structure are equally attractive procedures.

Material subversive to our taxonomy appears in the renovation of metaphors now taken for granted, but initially entailing a radical comparison of two items only casually related to one another. The metaphor whereby a chair is attributed legs, or an automobile is associated with a wild horse, introduces a logic that runs counter to the prevailing logic of the taxonomy. This contrary logic suggests possibilities of restructuring the same tokens into quite another taxonomy. The cognitive order so methodically traced in the other routines is momentarily stood on its head by virtue of the unorthodox relationships countenanced in these metaphors.

But let us look closely into this matter. The traditional item in our corpus enclosing a metaphor is the familiar:

What has four legs and can't walk?    *A chair.*

In the context of the other routines, as in the shared cognitive order, legs serve as a distinctive feature setting the category of animals apart from toys and machines. Legs as anatomical features are related to a characteristic mode of conveyance, namely self-conveyance. As we have noted, this feature has both formal and functional cogency in the folk taxonomy underlying our corpus. In this metaphor, however, the legs of an animal are analogized to the legs of a chair on formal grounds only, since the chair's legs are not correlated to mobility. The metaphor thus proposes another logic, one at variance with the controlling logic of the taxonomy. Or to put the matter differently, the metaphor proposes another taxonomy, one in which legged furniture and animals would be subsumed together under a single rubric constituted on the basis of the shared feature +legs. This metaphor is correctly thought of as subversive precisely because it broaches the possibility of alternative slicings of the experiential world. Other, ghostly taxonomies flicker into existence, challenging momentarily the conventional logic by ordering the same tokens into different categories.

The other metaphor resides in the word "mustang," which names both a type of horse and a car model, tokens we find separated from one another in the conventional taxonomy. These tokens are momentarily conjoined in the metaphor, which proposes a grouping of diverse tokens united only in their fleetness, or what we might refer to as locomotive expertise. As in the previous example, this metaphor throws into relief an alternative taxonomy, knitting some of the same tokens into a quite different logical structure. The children are evidently at that watershed point in their development in which they become aware of the dual potency of language to render shared cognitive structures and to rearrange these structures into alternative forms. Each of these processes is adequately reflected in our riddling sample.

It is noteworthy that the conventional taxonomy, with its solid foundation on formal and functional equivalence, prevails over the alternate taxonomies lacking as substantial a footing. The metaphorical connections remain pale and fleeting in comparison to the more stable conventional taxonomy. In fact, we can measure the imaginative force of each metaphor in terms of its departure from the conventional taxonomy. The leap of metaphor drawing chair and animal into mutual association is large indeed, spanning a cognitive distance resolved only at the highest level of the taxonomy. The two referents of the word "mustang," on the other hand, are separated from one another by a less imposing cognitive gap. In the long run, there is probably a trade-off between conventional and unorthodox taxonomy, the latter forcing a reassessment of the former, and we are led to ponder the vulnerability of conventional taxonomy; yet unorthodox linkages are ultimately measured with reference to the conventional. Conventional taxonomies receive constant refinement and confirmation, while their less orthodox counterparts are only fortuitously articulated in the insulated format of verbal play. The ultimate lesson in all this appears to be that language and classification are cognitive tools, absolutely essential in the transaction of social intercourse, but nonetheless lacking any neat one-to-one correspondence to the world outside of culture.

The end product of a lesson of this sort might be a certain studied flexibility of attitude toward the orders of language and culture. Concerning this point, Ian Hamnet observes: "Classification is a prerequisite of the intelligible ordering of experience, but if conceptual categories are reified, they become obstacles rather than means to a proper understanding and control of both physical and social reality. The ability to construct categories and also to transcend them is central to adaptive learning" (Hamnet 1967:385). The riddling sample under consideration exemplifies this dual process of construction and transcendence. The pleasurable format of children's riddling allows children to develop and display expertise in both areas. We have here, then, a concrete illustration of William Bascom's observation that in some settings "riddles serve as a didactic device to sharpen the wits of young children" (Bascom 1954:294).

But the present example affords us some idea as to the nature of wits and how they might be sharpened. We are concerned here with cognitive skills associated with the classification of the tokens of experience; with the capacity to articulate shared cognitive structures; and with the complementary ability to transcend these. In this context, riddling may indeed be viewed as a didactic mechanism, conducive to experimentation with received notions of order and elaboration of novel cognitive orders. Riddling allows children to work through the dual vectors of language, toward order and toward anti-order, in a stimulating and enjoyable social context. At various stages of riddling, children learn to formulate culturally appropriate classifications, to articulate classifications at variance with cultural standards, and finally to assess language and indeed classification as in part arbitrary instruments reflecting only partially the continuous texture of experience.

We can perhaps anticipate yet another great humanistic wave, the discovery of the cerebral child. Claude Lévi-Strauss (1966) introduced us to the cerebral savage, whose primitive speculation represents another, not a cognitively inferior, science. The time may be ripe to turn our humanistic energies to those savages among us and discover at our very portals the cerebral child, concerned in his or her verbal art with complex matters of rationality, logic, sociability, and aesthetics. Certainly in the riddling corpus discussed above, we find prolonged contemplation of a cognitive field, transpiring in a format conducive to artful expression and dependent on some degree of social harmony. Crossing the triviality barrier, we readily perceive the consequential nature of children's verbal play. A folkloristics of enculturation must be developed to investigate fully the place of children's folklore in the persistence and modification of culture.

Finally, returning to the chicano children who produced this riddling corpus, we must inquire into their choice of semantic fields. The field of locomotion is a most interesting one, and the content patterning within this field even more so. For one thing, the setting in which the riddling took place nominated certain tokens for inclusion in the riddling. At the edge of the curb we were in the midst of cars and bicycles. An occasional plane flew by overhead. Through the process of scene incorporation, these tokens of the urban setting found their way into the riddling. Not that the tokens on hand exert any control over riddling content, for the children also draw on familiar tokens stored in their memories of past experience.

The basic antinomy established in our session appears to be that between animals and machines. At the very least, this topic is undeniably present in the riddling. This antinomy is of course crucial in the context of modern, industrial society, in which machines rather than our animal brethren surround us with animistic contrast to ourselves. This development may well be all the more intensified among people like the central Texas chicanos, who have very recent pastoral roots but currently reside primarily in urban environments. James Fernandez (1974) remarks that in urban settings children play at being machines, while in pastoral settings they play at being animals. The folk taxonomy presented in this chapter, straddling as it does both the pastoral and mechanical universe, may well reflect the transitional status of the community between a rural past, preserved in oral tradition, and an urban present. Would it be possible that the children in this riddling session are working through basic anomalies in their cultural apparatus, much as primitives examine apparent contradictions through the logical tool of mythology, to borrow the diction of Lévi-Strauss?

To argue that the riddling under consideration here constitutes a symposium on matters of conscious and perhaps subconscious concern to the children does less violence to our materials than to dismiss them as inconsequential, the common scholarly attitude until very recent times. But the crusade for a proper evaluation of children's materials has led us a bit astray from our topic, the patterning of form and content in riddling sessions. I would suggest that the situation obtaining in our sample is instructive: children's riddling, if sustained over a sufficient expanse of time, tends to cluster about certain topics of special concern to the community. Content is patterned to a sufficient degree to encourage one to characterize the riddling as a symposium. Not many sessions are as elaborately organized as the one we have selected for discussion here, but all of them show some tendency to organize content in this fashion.

## SESSION 2 : PROBABLE AND IMPROBABLE CONVERSANTS

For a change of pace, let us turn our attention to a second selection of routines produced over the course of a single riddling session. This group of interrogative ludic routines owes its existence to improvisation on a given form, though content is also patterned here in interesting ways. Here are the routines we will consider:

1. What did the big chimney say to the little chimney?
2. What did the Aggie say to the other Aggie?
3. What did the three Aggies say to the other four Aggies?
4. What did the rug say to the floor?
5. What did the dead penguin say to the live penguin?
6. What did the rug say to the floor?
7. What did the ten Aggies say to the one Aggie?
8. What did the one Aggie say to the zero Aggie?
9. What did the blue whale say to the duck?
10. What did the whale shark say to the great white?
11. What did the live duck say to the other live duck?
12. What did the baby say to the cradle?
13. What did the blue whale say to the great white?
14. What did the (burping noise) say to the great white?
15. What did the uhhhh say to the great white?
16. What did the burp say to the great white?
17. What did Spiderman say to Ironman?
18. What did the Martian say to the human?
19. What did the man say to the store?

Before I launch into the analysis of these routines, a few words should be said concerning the group of children responsible for them. These are anglo, middle-class children, performing for themselves and adult observers in an Austin studio.[1] There are four children,

two boys and two girls, all age six. All these particulars are consequential in accounting for their riddling production. With the presence of adults and video cameras, the children are understandably a
little hyperactive. Nonetheless, the peer group is preserved and the
riddling here is immediately recognizable as congruent with riddling
to be found in more naturalistic settings. The fact that they are six-
year-olds helps account for the extreme bending of the given models.
Six-year-olds tend to be exploratory by nature, and across a wide
range of performance genres they will be found engaging in virtually
free manipulation of models provided for them by older children.
The two girls are rather shy, and they account for only two items
of the total nineteen: as it happens, the two traditional items in our
list, numbers 1 and 6. The ·boys, a bit more rambunctious, are responsible for the balance of the routines performed. Again, these
personas are familiar in the study of children's folklore. While there
are no hard and fast rules to this effect, I find a consistent tendency
for girls to perform in complete, traditional items, while boys are
much more likely to produce freewheeling improvisations. Finally,
the fact that these are anglo, middle-class children is not without
significance. As we will see in a later chapter, the riddle production
of anglo and chicano children is distinctive, reflecting the different
modes of socialization affecting the two groups.

I have omitted the solutions here because in point of fact the children were rather unconcerned with providing solutions. Many of these
routines were left unsolved; others received only the most casual of
solutions. For example, routine number 5 bears the solution:

"I'm dying, help me, I'm dying."

The children's attention clearly rests primarily on the formulation
of amusing scenarios of talk, through utilization of the traditional
formula:

What did the X say to the Y?

Our corpus contains two traditional models of this formula, each of
them performed, as I have noted, by the girls present. These are:

What did the big chimney say to the little chimney? *"You're too young to smoke."*

What did the rug say to the floor? *"I've got you covered."*

The initial item establishes the pattern; item 6 reinforces it. On the basis of this formula the verbally agitated boys perform a total of seventeen variations. A close look at the method of these improvisations will point up some interesting facts.

First, we note that the traditional models are alike in establishing an imaginary dialogue between two conversants. The identity of the conversants is specified in the question; the riddlee's task is to divine the ensuing dialogue. The two traditional models involve word play, which is not fully comprehended by the boys, and which would be, in any case, very difficult for children of this age to coin spontaneously. For this reason, perhaps, the actual dialogues recede in importance, and the improvisations are concerned with the specification of extraordinary conversants. I would suggest that the children are exploring in these routines, as in our former sample, certain very consequential dimensions of their own experience and their cultural inheritance. In this corpus, we find tampering with the conversational norms of speaker/listener availabilities, and, as I shall argue below, this device serves as a vehicle for plumbing the orders of the received cosmology.

As we have come to expect, the interrogative ludic routine reverses assumptions based on experience in the real world. One of the characteristics of both model routines is their consistent attribution of speech to inappropriate vessels. Rugs, floors, and chimneys are inanimate objects not generally accorded speaker/listener capacity. The most conspicuous feature of these models is their allocation of conversational availability to entities normally excluded from this category. But the choice of interlocutors is far from random. There must be some palpable excuse for alleging dialogue between the chosen odd parties, and the models display two lines of rationalization. In the case of the talking chimneys, we have two like objects. The principle in operation here appears to be that like might very well communicate with like. This premise of human sociability is preserved in the routines. The other model presents two unlike objects, which are, however, in habitual proximity to one another. Rug and floor might enter conversation because they share the same physical environment. This principle, of speech among neighbors, entails another carry-over from normal conversational practice. It is the identity of the speakers and receivers that violates normal expectations; other conversational expectations, notably the motivation for talk, are preserved in these routines.

To summarize, then, the models present to the children the following set of rules:

1. The question specifies two entities allegedly in conversation.
2. Neither of these entities is normally included in the category of speech participants.
3. A motivation for dialogue between the two entities must exist, either in the form of shared identity or habitual proximity.

These are the preconditions, spelled out in the traditional models, governing the children's improvisations on the formula: What did the X say to the Y? We must now attend to the patterning of improvisation and its extremely consequential implications.

The children's improvisations examine somewhat methodically the range of improbable conversants, beginning with entities only marginally unsuited to the task of conversation and arriving in later routines at some rather bizarre conversational settings. The formulation of these improbable speech acts rests solidly on an awareness of the actual sociolinguistic system governing speech availability. Otherwise, how could the routines unflinchingly avoid standard conversational scenarios? The rudimentary procedure of placing odd entities in a state of talk undergoes a series of transformations creating increasingly skewed conversational scenarios. The children hold fast to the principle modeled for them in the traditional routines that nonconversants should be construed as being in conversation. In addition, some of the routines develop a second source of anomaly not contained in the models, namely the lack of ontological equivalence among conversational participants.

There is a general drift in the improvisations moving from the least anomalous of settings to the most anomalous of settings for the fanciful speech acts. This drift is not in every case consistent, but does describe the overall progression of improvisation. The early numbers, following directly upon the traditional model placing two like objects in conversation, similarly envision dialogues among like entities, specifically Aggies. In central Texas, the Aggie or scholastic at Texas A & M University, occupies the unenviable position of numbskull in joking routines of the sort sometimes referred to elsewhere as ethnic jokes. The Aggie is human or humanoid, and thus capable of speech, but perhaps not capable of intelligent speech in the eyes of the children producing these routines. Aggies are conceived of as marginal humans, possessing the outward form of the species but lacking some of its central faculties, such as reason and physical coordination. Among the early improvisations on our list, we find three (items 2, 3, 7) that are anomalous merely for the presence of Aggies in the dialogues. Item 8 is apparently kindred, but the extraordinary intervention of the "zero Aggie" sets this routine apart from the other Aggie routines. Sandwiched in between these routines featuring Aggies are the second traditional model, performed twice, and a routine featuring a live and dead penguin. In this routine, item 5, we depart momentarily from the human sphere and attribute human language capacity to animals occupying lower niches in the phylogenetic scale. The detail of a dead animal further removes the conversational setting from plausibility.

The middle portion of our list involves primarily an exploration of the domain of familiar waterborne creatures. In a sequence of association we move from penguin to duck, blue whale, whale shark, and great white. These latter great fish share the status accorded in earlier chapters to elephants and kangaroos: they are exotic creatures rendered familiar through the office of popular culture. Moreover, they are topical at the time of the riddling because of the popular impact of the recently released movie *Jaws*. Another contributory source would be the campaign to save the whales, which was stirring up a good deal of controversy at the time. In any event, some of these routines preserve very faithfully the pattern established in the models. Items 9, 10, 11, 13 portray these creatures in dialogue with one another. The principle of like conversing with like is maintained, since all these creatures share the significant common features of being aquatic and wild. One item embedded in this sequence, item 12, involves another marginal human, a baby, addressing its cradle. Here we have the attribution of speech to an unlikely candidate, and the motivation is provided in the habitual proximity of baby and cradle. It is clear that both strategies for motivating these improbable dialogues contained in the models are exploited by the children. When Spiderman addresses Ironman, as in item 17, we note the principle of like participants in speech. On the other hand, when the man addresses the store, as in item 19, we are willing to concede that the two participants are in a state of habitual if not constant mutual proximity.

To date we have discussed the gradual extension of conversational participants from marginal human status to animal and even inanimate object status. But we have passed over several routines imposing an even more radical deviation from conversational norms. These items represent an intensification of the basic procedure of attributing speech to inappropriate classes of objects. In item 8, we find a "zero Aggie" engaged in speech. As is well known, nature provides no zeros; the concept of zero is entirely dependent on human conceptualization. A zero Aggie has no phenomenological existence like the other speaker/listeners we have encountered in the routines. The zero Aggie is an analytical, not a material entity. Here the children have transcended the phenomenological universe and reached into the noumena of human rationality to procure their inappropriate speech receptor. In the remaining routines to be considered, the children achieve a comparable transcendence of basic ontological category in their efforts to incorporate increasingly bizarre entities into the fanciful speech acts. Thus in item 14 we find a veritable burp engaged in conversation with the great white; in item 16, the linguistic label for the same entity is similarly engaged; and item 15 places the verbal stall "uhhhh" in a similar conversational format.

These three entities depart radically from the domain of normal conversational participants. The veritable burp, a product of human and animal physiology, is an event or process with a material manifestation evolving through time. The word "burp" is of course the onomatopoeic sound image corresponding to that same event or process. The stall syllable "uhhhh" is a purely linguistic phenomenon, without a referent in the real world, but conventionally signifying stupidity or the lesser condition of being at a loss for words. With these routines we have indeed superseded the received cosmology.

We encounter in this corpus, then, a wide range of disparity in conversational scenarios. At the most conventional pole of the continuum we find the human of item 18 and the man of item 19. Moving progressively further away from these allowable conversants, we run through a collection of improbable conversants including humanoids, animals, dead animals, material objects, physical processes, and purely analytical constructs lacking any objective existence outside of man's cognition. What the children have done, utilizing the ludic formula contained in our traditional models, is to parse the cosmology into its logically distinct segments. The inner circle is the human being, with its remarkable gift of speech. Attributing this uniquely human characteristic to other than human entities in the children's experience, the routines carry us into successively more distant reaches of the experiential universe, eventually landing us in a domain with an entirely different ontological status from our starting point.

Componential analysis of the alleged participants in these anomalous speech acts will afford some insight into the analytical process underlying these routines. We begin with the inner circle and work our way outward through the entire set of fanciful speakers and listeners. The grids to follow attribute a constellation of positive values, involving several parameters, to the inner circle of human beings. Each move away from this inner circle exhibits the demise of one or more of these positive values. The parameters used are the following:

a. *material*—entities possessing physical form and substance apart from human cognition.
b. *objective*—entities perceived as maintaining a stable

identity; contrasts with *process,* a material progression
lacking a stable identity.

c. *animate*—that which has life.

d. *human*—specifically Homo sapiens.

e. *age of reason*—humans capable of mature human cognition.

These parameters are implicit in the children's improvisations and
constitute in themselves a rudimentary metaphysics, a child's guide
to ontology. Every one of these features is crucial in determining the
structure of our cosmology and the place of our own species within it.

On the basis of the parameters listed above, the conversants provided by the children in their improvisations fall into the following
categories:

1. *human being* (exemplified by *human,* item 18, and *man,*
   item 19)
   + material
   + objective
   + animate
   + human
   + age of reason

2. *humanoid* (exemplified by *Aggies,* items 2, 3, 7, 8, and
   *baby,* item 12)
   + material
   + objective
   + animate
   + human
   − age of reason

3. *animal* (exemplified by *penguins, whales, ducks,* etc.,
   items 5, 9–11)
   + material
   + objective
   + animate
   − human
   − age of reason

3a. *dead animal* (exemplified by item 5, *dead penguin*)
+ material
+ objective
− animate (though formerly + animate)
− human
− age of reason

4. *objects* (exemplified by *cradle,* item 12, and *store,* item 19)
+ material
+ objective
− animate
− human
− age of reason

5. *processes* (exemplified by the burps of items 14 and 16)
+ material
− objective
− animate
− human
− age of reason

6. *cognitive constructs* (two kinds, see below)
− material
− objective
− animate
− human
− age of reason

Type A: *fanciful beings* (exemplified by *Martian,* item 18, *Spiderman* and *Ironman,* item 17). Here the construct is conceived of as if it possessed material, objective, and animate status.

Type B: *analytical concepts* (exemplified by *zero Aggie,* item 8, and *uhhhh,* item 15). Here the constructs are conceived of as existing entirely within human cognitive systems.

The children's quest for increasingly unconventional conversants leads them into the articulation of these diverse strata of their experiential universe. We begin with the inner circle of the rational human being, then enumerate certain ontological cousins, that is, creatures and objects sharing a comparable mode of existence, and finally wind up with items manifesting an entirely different ontological status from that of rational human beings. Dressed up in analytic language, this sort of mental exercise might earn the label of philosophy. Once again, as in the first corpus examined in this chapter, we encounter the cerebral child, contemplating the orders of his cognitive universe through the instruments of verbal play. Again, the conventional orders become explicit as they are violated. The attribution of talk to entities excluded from the sociolinguistic category of speech participants is the ludic transformation imposed in these routines. But in exploring the ranges of unacceptable speakers and listeners, the children reveal a sophisticated awareness of the states of being as experienced and defined in their culture.

One strategy for skewing these conversational settings not provided in the traditional models but nonetheless seized on by the children is the juxtaposition of ontologically distinct conversants in a single dialogue. As we have seen, the models present interlocutors with some cause for talking, either physical proximity or shared identity. Most of the routines stick to this formula. But the more radical routines engage speakers proceeding from one corner of the cosmology with listeners proceeding from quite another. The Martian and human pairing of item 18 is not really too bizarre, since the speakers exhibit at least the commonality of being denizens of their respective planets in the same solar system. But the juxtaposition of cognitive constructs and processes with waterborne animals is somewhat more jarring. Here the children assault with redoubled vigor the conventional scenarios of talk. In creating routines like items 14–16, the children demonstrate complete intellectual flexibility, complete freedom from the constraints of conventional classification.

It is curious that these extreme forms of manipulation appeal more to children than to adults. Adult witticism is more likely to select a more modest and more telling reversal of norm. Manipulation of classificatory schemes is not properly indulged in for its own sake. To account for the disparity in children's and adults' wit we must return to one of the master concepts informing our research: children's verbal play reflects their level of acquisition of cognitive, linguistic, and social competencies. Children in the age range of five to eight years are actively engaged in ordering their experience into the tidy categories we adults take for granted (and then rediscover in our philosophical treatises). The perception of order and the realization that this order is not sacrosanct are exciting cognitive breakthroughs. In addition, we must realize that children in this age bracket enjoy free access to antiorder, which they will lose as they move into adult roles demanding the suppression of alternate visions. As newcomers to the cognitive orders around them, they are uniquely capable of tampering with them. Later these same orders will become second nature and lose the psychological saliency they possess during these preadolescent years. A rationale of this sort might account for the greater appeal of riddling in our society as in many others to children than to adults. Riddling, after all, entails a rather unscrupulous manipulation of ambiguity and reversal, and this cognitive exercise appears to come most readily to some children, artists, poets, and jokesters, all of whom enjoy a significant cognitive disassociation from the mundane cognitive orders essential to the fulfillment of conventional adult roles in society.

The two riddling excerpts examined in this chapter substantiate the allegation that children's riddling can be highly patterned in terms of form and content. In both instances, the children perform a series of routines tending to cluster about an emerging theme. By the same token, formal models articulated early in the session exert a telling influence on the formulation of subsequent routines. These observations suggest that riddling sessions may be profitably viewed as integral, organic units in their own right. We have found that there is indeed a method to the children's mad improvisation on set formulas and themes. The interrogative ludic routine becomes in the hands of the children a tool for investigating the cognitive orders their cultures encourage them to identify in their experience. These routines are lenses affording vistas into the structure of experience. In this manner they perform a vital function, assisting the children in their quest for understanding of themselves and of the world around them. There can be little question that in the employment of these routines children acquire and polish cognitive and social skills essential to later stages of their lives. But at the same time it should be recognized that these routines confer understanding that is equally essential to the child as child. Manipulation of cognitive orders and social environments enables the children to gain a handle on the bewildering diversity of the world as they experience it. Without this learning mechanism, we might wonder whether enculturation could proceed to any significant degree at all.

I will conclude this chapter by affirming that children's riddling sessions do indeed tend to exhibit the methodical, contemplative ethos of a symposium. Often one must look beneath the diversity of content and search out the underlying organization tying the whole series together. We have examined two riddling units, one of which dedicated itself to exploring the cognitive field of locomotion and certain anomalies related to it, and the other of which carried out an ontological analysis of the cosmology. The thinking underlying both sessions is acutely logical. While it is true that the children's attention is not focused on the analysis itself, but rather on the fruits of the underlying analysis, it remains the case that the sequence of routines formulated depends on a logical analysis of the kind I have attempted to illustrate through taxonomy and componential analysis in this chapter. The same sorts of insight, when deliberately culled from collective experience, are known as philosophy. Admittedly, the intentions of riddler and philosopher are not entirely congruent, but there is a significant overlap in terms of intellectual underpinnings.

Finally, we should stress that these symposia of folk philosophy are conducted in the pleasing and exhilarating guise of animated social intercourse. These are madcap philosophers, playfully jousting with words and in the process uncovering the elementary orders of their experience. The social ambience of riddling and the built-in repartee between riddler and riddlee ensure that these excursions into order and antiorder receive immediate social confirmation or rejection. In this way, a certain uniformity of cognition is stimulated, and the children work out collectively a structuring of experience with maximal social validity. The regular feature of age differential among riddlers provides a conduit for the entrance of adolescent and adult understandings into the riddling. In short, we are in the presence of a powerful device of enculturation, wherein understandings proceeding from experience and structured by social convention are articulated and eventually assimilated by cultural novices.

# Class and Ethnic Variables 8

We are possessed of a bifurcate riddling corpus, with interrogative ludic routines proceeding from two communities, the East Austin chicano community and the university-centered anglo community in the same town. These two communities are contrastive on several points, generally subsumed under the rubrics of class and ethnic affiliation. Yet children in both communities clearly subscribe to the same basic riddling activity. Chicano and anglo children in Austin participate avidly in riddling, sharing a similar understanding of the texture, structure, content, and etiquette associated with this form of verbal play. In all rudimentary aspects, the riddling of the two groups is comparable. Upon closer inspection, however, it will be seen that within this mutual adherence to a common set of riddling procedures, there remains room for idiosyncratic patterning of form, content, and affect. It would be fair to say that both chicanos and anglos riddle, but each group adapts the genre to its own particular circumstances.

Riddling, unmistakably present in both communities but assuming a unique disposition in each, thereby becomes a powerful diagnostic tool for setting forth the constellation of values, attitudes, and underlying beliefs characteristic of each of our sample communities. The fundamental premise of this chapter's argument can be stated baldly as the assumption that the forms of folklore reflect in significant fashion the cultural constitutions of the communities in which they emerge and are perpetuated. The roots of this premise lie deep within the soil of contemporary intellectual currents. To cite two hallowed figures, both Sigmund Freud and Karl Marx posit a more than casual relationship between expressive forms and underlying psychic and economic realities. More recent, and more pertinent, is Franz Boas's contention that folklore constitutes a mirror of culture. In the following passage, the basic concept of the reflexivity, or self-commentary, of some cultural forms (in this instance myth and folktale) is formulated: "Material of this kind does not represent a systematic description of the ethnology of the people, but it has the merit of bringing out those points which are of interest to the people themselves. *They present in a way an autobiography of the tribe* [italics mine]" (Boas 1940). Subsequent formulations have modified and amplified this kernel idea. Thus Ruth Benedict (1935) shows, with respect to Zuni folktales, that the mirror image is not always a true one, but may be inverted. But scholars documenting the elusive tenets of world view have continued to turn to expressive forms (Colby 1966, Stross 1973). And recently, the notion of certain expressive forms as diagnostic of cultural systems and their cognitive structures has gained a special prominence (Spradley 1972, Babcock 1978). Representative of current thinking is Clifford Geertz's characterization of the Balinese cockfight as "a Balinese reading of Balinese experience; a story they tell themselves about themselves" (Geertz 1972:926).

## CHICANOS AND ANGLOS

In the following pages, I shall be utilizing interrogative ludic routines as a diagnostic indicator of cultural values and orientations differentially manifest in the chicano and anglo communities of central Texas. The two Austin communities tapped for their riddling are ethnically discrete and homogeneous. The chicano *barrio* of East Austin is in some ways a world apart, and many of its residents have minimal contact with their anglo surroundings. By the same token, most of the anglos consulted for this project have little contact with the chicano neighborhoods. To a remarkable extent, exempting marginal elements in both groups that circulate freely across the ethnic boundary, the two communities coexist in an attitude of friendly (for the most part) detachment from one another. As a result, we can describe the communities as differentially constituted, allowing for the presence of somewhat distinctive oral traditions and world views.

Nonetheless, certain homogenizing influences do exist. Among these, the public school system, with its uniform curriculum and conventionally trained personnel, figures prominently as a point of intersection for the two communities. The possible impact of the school system is reduced by its failure to win the affection or identification of its chicano wards. From my observation, many chicano youth display an attitude of indifference to school curricula and personnel, which could be better labelled hostility in some cases. The schools in East Austin remain alien institutions, treated as anglo implants into the prevailing chicano environment. Perhaps with the expansion of bilingual and bicultural educational programs this unfortunate state of affairs could be remedied.

Another homogenizing influence is that of popular culture in all its various manifestations. Chicanos and anglos alike have access to such public media as television, radio, newspapers, and comic books, though our evidence suggests that the impact of these sources is far greater in the anglo community than in the chicano community. The two communities come into contact in some work and recreation locales, though even here the tendency to form fast friendships across community boundaries is minimal indeed. In sum, we are presented with two North American populations maintaining only the most casual forms of association with one another despite habitation of the same central Texas city. This casual, superficial interaction of the two communities tallies with our proposition that their children share a common genre of verbal play but exploit this common genre in quite distinctive fashions.

We have observed some of the commonalities between our two communities. What are some of the more salient differences? First, we note the contrasting heritage of ethnic and national origin. Chicanos are a people with strong roots in the Mexican experience. Ethnically then, they are typically *mestizo,* an ethnic mixing of European (primarily Spanish) and Indian blood. While much of the Mexican experience evinces a subtle Indian admixture, many of the more conspicuous elements in the Mexican heritage derive from the Spanish culture imposed on the colony by the mother country. Sorting out these two threads and noting the occasional contribution of Afro-American ingredients can be fascinating and frustrating, so thorough is their blending. Among the chicanos, much of the traditional food is Indian (*tamal, chile, enchilada,* for example, are words from indigenous tongues), while the language and many of the forms of expressive culture are evidently Spanish in origin. The discussion occasioned by the Mexican *corrido,* a native balladry, is typical. While the prosodics and thematics of the genre recall the earlier Spanish *romance,* brought over by the conquistadores, there are those who detect a peculiarly indigenous tone to the *corrido* (Serrano Martinez 1950, Paredes 1976). The Brazilian sociologist Darcy Ribeiro (1964) describes the Mexicans as a new people, emerging from the blending of old and new world populations, and the chicanos of central Texas adequately reflect these Mexican mestizo roots.

The anglo community, on the other hand, is representative of the mobile, broadly middle-class population sector to be found in all parts of the United States. This anglo community is not rooted in the historical development of the Southwest, but instead reflects the comparatively recent and continuous movement into central Texas fostered by the presence of state government, a large university, and an increasingly visible light industry site in the Austin area. We are dealing then, on the one hand, with a regional ethnic group, highly marked in terms of language, tradition, and socioeconomic status, with firm roots in the Mexican and southwestern United States; and, on the other hand, a mobile and diversified North American population, exhibiting a more or less describable national consciousness. Central Texas has been one of the historical meeting grounds of these two groups, and as Américo Paredes (1958) surmises, the encounter has not always been friendly.

The cultivation of the Spanish tongue and the development of Spanish-English creoles are two of the more tangible manifestations of the chicano bicultural destiny. Chicanos in East Austin rely on the Spanish language and its regional dialects for the great majority of in-group communication. A Spanish-language radio station is favored by nearly two-thirds of the residents of East Austin (1970 Census). While facility in Spanish is most evident among the older generations, the young ones today are learning this language also, frequently as their mother tongue. Out of the fifty children interviewed and observed in some depth for this project, thirty-six were either competent or fluent in Spanish. Only five of the total appeared to have little or no Spanish (McDowell 1975:86).

We might linger over language affiliation for a moment, since this feature is diagnostic of other less visible cultural processes affecting communities in culture contact. I have stated that the chicanos have recent and constantly reinforced roots in the Mexican heritage. But it is equally true that the destiny of these people has placed them squarely within the North American experience. This dual affiliation has left its trace in language usage among chicanos. While one may very likely encounter correct Mexican Spanish in East Austin, there are at least equal odds that one will hear a more local dialect with palpable English admixture. The general linguistic situation in the Southwestern chicano community has been described as follows:

> The Spanish spoken by the "old folks" . . . which contains many archaic forms; the language of the middle generation, which keeps some of the archaic forms but adds a large vocabulary of Anglicisms developed to meet the needs of trade or business; the speech of the "youngest group," which increases the confusion by the use of slang expressions current among their schoolmates; and lastly, the jargon of the city gangs, identical with the third grouping above except that expressions of a shady, sinister, or double meaning have been added. (McWilliams 1968:292)

Among some East Austin children the two linguistic resources have become so entwined that one might speak of the fusion of Spanish and English into a creole. From the snippets of this kind of speech (which is generally reserved for use in the peer group) I have been able to monitor, it appears that the controlling syntax is Spanish, but its composition in terms of lexicon draws in approximately equal measure from both English and Spanish. Consider the following segment (English translations are in parentheses; solid underlining indicates English loan words; dotted underlining indicates hispanicized English root):

No es lies   (it's not lies)
just dije que, este, que el abuelito (I just said that, well, that
   grandpa)
I mean el tío (I mean uncle)
se fue pa la casa (went to the house)

y ya feel algo que le tochaba (and then felt something touching him)

In this speech segment, the English loan words retain their native phonology, though the word *feel* appears uninflected. While code-switching might account for speech of this kind, it is clear that the grammar of code-switching would be quite complex indeed. Thus we have to allow for the switching of immediate constituents at all levels or nodes of the phrase marker. As flexible as our grammar of code-switching must be, it cannot allow any conceivable splicing of English and Spanish elements, for exposure to this dialect immediately convinces one that switching is a far from random affair. It will not serve our purposes to pursue chicano code-switching any further at this point, but current research in the field may be consulted to flesh out the brief sketch provided here (Gingras 1974, McDowell 1975, Elias Olivares 1976). Some discussion of specific interrogative ludic routines incorporating code-switching appears below.

We find in the domain of everyday speech that the combination of Mexican and United States elements has produced a novelty, a speech community possessed of each of the original codes plus a code concocted from their intersection. These patterns, which are traced with relative ease in reference to language, are also present in other, less accessible, cultural domains. In the area of expressive culture, for example, we find among chicanos cultivation of forms and traditions brought from Mexico, and also traditions encountered and assimilated in the course of their odyssey in the United States. Consider the repertoire of contemporary chicano *conjuntos,* or musical ensembles, conversant with traditional Mexican genres like the *corrido* and the *ranchera,* but also adept in Afro-American blues and soul and predominantly anglo rock and roll. Children's folklore contains many a display of this bicultural competence. The following juxtaposition of parody rhymes based on the Popeye ditty tells it all:

I'm Popeye the sailor man          Popeye nació en Torreón
                                   (Popeye was born in Torreon)

| | |
|---|---|
| I live in a garbage can | Encima de una sillón |
| | (on top of a toilet seat) |
| I eat all the worms | Mató su tía |
| | (he killed his Aunt) |
| And spit out the germs | Con una tortilla |
| | (with a tortilla) |
| I'm Popeye the sailor man. | Popeye nació en Torreón. |
| | (Popeye was born in Torreon.) |

The chicano child, having access to both traditions, delights in performing routines premised on the availability of English and Spanish. The following knock-knock joke will illustrate this point:

Knock knock
(Who's there?)
Kelly.
(Kelly who?)
Que le importa. (Spanish for "What's it to you")

Here the customary reinterpretation of the initial phonetic string (in this case *Kelly*) pivots on the integration of this string into a longer, Spanish locution. We will find that in riddling, also, the chicano children manifest their community's straddling of Mexican heritage and United States experience.

Much more could be said about the cultural distinctiveness of the central Texas chicano, but let me merely underline the basic point that we are presented with a highly distinctive, regional ethnic group that contrasts on many indices with our mobile, middle-class anglo sample. In addition to these cultural factors, the two communities contrast in terms of socioeconomic status. As an historical legacy of culture contact in the Southwest, the ancestors of the present-day chicano came to occupy a position of economic subordination to the incoming yankees. The initial pattern of yankee apprenticeship to a Mexican community that had developed the means of coping with the generally uncooperative ecology of the area gradually gave way to yankee ascendancy as northern population and technology streamed into this section of the country. Several sources trace the passing of economic control from Mexican to anglo (Pitt 1968, Williams 1968, Meinig 1969). D. W. Meinig's depiction of the events affecting central Texas is representative:

> Cattle and cotton were the mainstays of much of Central Texas, but it was only here that the plantation and the hacienda, the two great patriarchal landed institutions richly idealized by the contending cultures, really met. But it was an unbalanced encounter of forces, and the military triumph of the one drove out the leadership of the other, so that both institutions were now ruled by the anglo, the one worked by the negro slave, the other still worked by the *mestizo* vaquero. (Meinig 1969:54–55)

Subsequent migration of Mexican and chicano families into these formerly Mexican-controlled areas served to reinforce the new anglo dispensation. Meinig continues:

> There was immigration from south of the Rio Grande also, which gradually over these years reinforced the Hispanic character of all South Texas. The movement was sporadic but it was never wholly checked by the recurrent brigandry in the Nueces country and persistent social antagonism between anglo and hispano. With the building of the railroads and the fencing of the open ranges the whole region was gradually domesticated into a uniform pattern in town, farm, and ranch of anglo rule over an hispano population. (Meinig 1969:65)

The contemporary central Texas chicanos have inherited from these historical processes their present social and economic status. By any standard of measurement, the chicanos of East Austin occupy a disadvantageous social and economic position in the city of Austin. The census data reflect some of the prominent features of the East Austin community. Taking tract 10 as representative of the total East Austin community, we have a population less than 1 percent black and only roughly 10 percent anglo. The remaining 90 percent is chicano. The average household is large, on the order of 4.12 persons. Just under four-fifths of the population is native of native parentage, that is, third-generation American. Still, some 15 percent of the population in East Austin is native born of foreign parentage, and a small but significant element (5 percent) is itself foreign born. Over two-thirds of this population claims Spanish as its native tongue.

The educational level of this community is at variance with the general situation in Austin. The median number of years of school completed is 7.1, as compared with 12.5 for the city overall. Only 10.9 percent of this community's residents have completed high school, compared with 62 percent for the city overall. These figures provide the strongest possible indictment of the public school system, which has failed to respond effectively to the special educational needs of the central Texas chicano. One need only recall that less than ten years ago it was against the law, punishable by corporal methods, to speak Spanish on the grounds of any Texas public school.

The occupational level of members of the East Austin community is also at variance with figures for the city overall. Chicanos in East Austin tend to occupy the less prestigious and less lucrative jobs in high numbers, while relatively few are found in the higher niches of the employment scale. With a total employed from tract 10 of 1655, the following occupational distribution is reported:

| | |
|---|---|
| professional, technical | 25 |
| managers, administrators | 88 |
| sales persons | 112 |
| clerical | 162 |
| craftsmen | 283 |
| operatives | 327 |
| laborers | 301 |
| service | 351 |

The figures reveal that well under 10 percent of the employed persons in this community occupy high-prestige positions, while approximately two-thirds are engaged in menial or subordinate positions. When these figures are translated into income levels, then their real significance becomes apparent. The median family income in tract 10 is $5,083 per year. A typical anglo tract in the city, where many of the children interviewed for this project reside, features a comparable figure of $14,025. Other indices are also of interest. In East Austin, over 11 percent of the families earn less than half of the poverty level income as determined by HEW. Consider these figures:

| percent of families with income less than | East Austin | Anglo Tract | City |
|---|---|---|---|
| one-half poverty level | 11.4 | 1.3 | 3.8 |
| three-fourths poverty level | 23.2 | 2.6 | 7.0 |
| poverty level | 35.5 | 3.3 | 11.0 |

On the other hand, only 7.8 percent of the families in East Austin have incomes three or more times the poverty level, while the corresponding figure for our comparative anglo tract is 71 percent.

The statistics on education, employment, and income levels lend support to Rodolfo Acuña's characterization of the chicanos as an internal colony, segregated by race and language, and exploited as a source of cheap or menial labor (Acuna 1972:iii). We have an unmistakable portrait of a working-class community, occupying the lower rungs of the employment scale, deprived of access to substantial income, and alienated from the educational system of the community. The contrast between the two communities represented in our sample could not be more clearly drawn. All indices point to a prosperous middle-class anglo community and an economically marginal working-class chicano community. Our two controlling variables, class and ethnic identity, thus differentiate the two communities in the most definitive manner.

As we move into a consideration of behavioral traits further distinguishing the two communities, it will not always be possible to ascribe perceived differences to specifically one or the other of our controlling variables, class and ethnic identity. But we will find in a range of activities, including socialization within the family and, of course, riddling, systematic differences clearly pointing to the existence of two distinctive currents, the anglo middle-class mainstream and the regional, chicano, primarily working-class tributary within our pluralistic North American society.

We now have some sense of the broad sociological factors distinguishing our two sample communities. Let's return to the matter of child socialization, taking as our guide the useful analysis provided by M. D. Shipman (1972) of contemporary trends affecting family life. We will find it convenient to bring in contrasting evidence on the chicano family of south Texas gleaned from the work of William Madsen (1964) and Arthur Rubel (1966). There are problems with the latter two studies, stemming from their tendency to present stereotypical portraits (see Paredes 1977 for a scholarly redress), but their inclusion in the discussion at this point allows us to pinpoint some of the differences in childhood experience within the anglo and chicano families in our population sample.

### DECREASING FAMILY SIZE

Shipman (1972:19) notes that the average family size among professional and clerical workers in England has shrunk considerably from levels common a century ago. Already by 1949 the figure for these groups was approximately 2.0, a figure roughly comparable to middle-class communities in modern North America. The average family in East Austin in 1970 had 4.12 persons, or over twice the membership of contemporary anglo families. The chicano children responsible for our riddling corpus come from large families, while many of the anglo children consulted are single children or have only one sibling.

Socialization in the chicano setting thus evinces some facets not prevalent in the anglo setting, including the division of parents' attention among a larger constituency, the release of children at a comparatively early age to the care of an older sibling, and a rich sibling peer-group life. Anglo children of the middle class tend to receive the parents' undivided attention longer, and the peer group is likely to consist not of siblings but of the children of neighbors and family friends. The differential size of anglo and chicano families thus entails contrasts on these significant points: the degree and duration of parental attention; time of entry into the peer group; and the composition of that peer group.

### PARENTAL ROLES

Shipman (1972:20) notes that "falling death rates, better health and smaller families have transformed the lives of women." The contemporary woman spends an average of only four years in pregnancy or nursing a child under a year old (Shipman 1970:20). As a consequence, women are released from the pattern of periodic childbirth and associated tasks and tend to find jobs and enter into other sorts of activities away from the home. Many of the children in our anglo sample have experienced relatively little contact with their mothers after the age of two or three. In the chicano family, we find women generally performing a more traditional role. Some chicano mothers work after the children are grown, but the greater proportion of mothers in East Austin perform the role of homemaker. One interesting corollary of the mother's presence in the home is the fact that the institution of baby-sitting is unknown in East Austin. Young children are with their mothers or in the sibling play group. Even in cases where the mother works or engages in other away from home activities, the children are consigned to a near relative, such as an aunt, for the duration.

Another issue conveniently addressed here is the parental attitude displayed in family interactions. Shipman (1972) refers to the interaction of members in the contemporary family as intense. Parents, both mother and father, are affectively engaged in the socialization of their children. The phenomenon of children calling their parents by first names has become foregrounded of late, as a notable sign of the departure from earlier patterns of social intercourse within the family. In reading Madsen, however, one gathers a rather different impression of the south Texas chicano family. He portrays the chicano father as one "aloof, absolute, and forceful in the administration of justice" (Madsen 1964:51). Arthur Rubel (1966:61) affords us a similar view: the chicano father is "gruff and firm, yet neither capricious nor tyrannous." Neither source attributes much in the way of overt affective involvement to the father, with the exception of the early years, when the father may "drop his dignity to cradle a child, care for his needs, or even crawl on hands and knees to play with him" (Madsen 1964:51).

The position of women in the family also conforms to a rather different pattern than the one adduced by Shipman as characteristic of the modern family: "The wife is expected to give comfort and pleasure to her husband. She must acknowledge his authority and superiority and think of his needs before her own. She is supposed to accept abuse without complaint" (Madsen 1964:48). Naturally this is an idealized role, and Madsen gives plenty of evidence of problems deriving from some women's refusal to conform. Yet Rubel is again confirmatory: "A wife and mother is, ideally, submissive, unworldly, and chaste. She is interested primarily in the welfare of her husband and children" (1966:67). Certainly we must allow for some deviation from this ideal even in south Texas, and even more in the urban environment of central Texas, but nonetheless we find in East Austin considerable evidence indicating the persistence of the patterns described by Madsen and Rubel. Needless to say, these parental roles stand in vivid contrast with Shipman's description of the liberated mother and involved father typical of the contemporary British and North American family, particularly among the middle and upper classes.

### NUCLEAR AND EXTENDED FAMILIES

Shipman (1972:41–42) quite properly notes the intimacy of the small modern family. The anglo middle-class family has divested itself of many of the traditional ties of kinship binding nuclear units into larger kinship networks. The anglo middle-class home is likely to be uni- or bigenerational; only rarely will a grandparent be found on the premises. Social engagements outside the home are likely to involve acquaintances rather than kin, though periodic contact with selected kin may be maintained. Playmates of the children are rarely cousins, since siblings in the parent's generation most likely reside in different cities or states.

By way of contrast, consider Madsen's description of the south Texas chicano family:

The nucleus of the Mexican-American family consists of parents and their off-spring but the bond between parents and children extends over three generations. . . . Uncles and Aunts are well-known and frequently visited. First cousins are almost as close as one's own brothers and sisters. . . . Mexican-Americans think it is wonderful to have many relatives and keep in touch with them. . . . The range of kinship is extended beyond genetic links by the institution known as *compadrazgo*. (Madsen 1964:46)

East Austin conforms to the pattern developed in Madsen's statement. Chicano children spend a good deal of time playing with cousins, who often live next door or elsewhere in the neighborhood. Throughout the childhood years and even into adolescence and adulthood, the individual's primary associates are likely to be siblings, cousins, and fictive kin known as *compadres*. In addition, chicano children experience constant contact with grandparents and aunts and uncles, many of whom are likely to reside in the child's own neighborhood.

PROFESSIONALIZATION OF SOCIALIZATION

Shipman (1972:23) speaks of a barrage of "fluctuating professional advice" inundating the modern family with a message centered on the "bright, sanitary, well-nourished and healthy family of two children." Messages of this kind are spread through a host of public service agencies, through advertisements in the mass media, and through professionals working in the areas of health and education. As Shipman suggests, these professional sources have moved in to pick up the slack as the extended and nuclear family becomes less and less dedicated to the socialization of its young. In other words, the professionalization of socialization is a function of some of the other processes modifying the family and its scope of operations over the last century or so.

While no family in residence in North America can be entirely beyond the reach of these professional sources, there is reason to believe that chicano and anglo families are affected in different measure. Recalling that socialization remains largely in the hands of parents and siblings in the chicano family, we might expect professionalization to exert a minimal impact. The anglo middle-class child, on the other hand, moves from baby-sitter to day-care center to nursery school in an unbroken chain of involvement in professionally directed institutions. The children in our anglo sample evince this characteristic involvement in extrafamilial institutions, and thus could be thought of as substantially affected by the trend toward professionalization of socialization.

## THE PACKAGED WORLD

Shipman (1972:25) observes somewhat ominously that "even though we cannot gauge the effects of our action on children, we have nevertheless organized for them an early life in which little is left to chance." Partly as a consequence of some factors already discussed, the modern family tends toward the total programming of its children's lives. The anglo child in our sample spends the great majority of his time in activities structured according to adult prerogatives. Even his play time during and after school hours is often dedicated to organized activities under adult supervision. The exhilarating experience of unbridled play is increasingly at a premium in these children's lives.

In contrast, the chicano children enjoy comparatively larger segments of unsupervised play, as the sibling peer group is generally left to its own devices outside of school hours. These children wander about the neighborhood, meet and scramble in the parks, and linger quietly in yards and on sidewalks without direct guidance from their parents or other adults. For this reason, chicano children are readily encountered and observed, while anglo middle-class children are less accessible to the meandering folklorist. The former group is likely to be abroad on its own in the after-school hours, but one frequently runs into an adult hovering about the latter group even when it is at play.

## PENETRATION OF SCHOOLING

In earlier pages, I have noted that chicano children in East Austin perceive the public school as an alien institution encouraging little in the way of affective identification. School personnel are predominantly anglo; the curricula reflect a notably anglo bias. Moreover, the chicano child's parents are not likely to have fared well in schools, which were even less amenable to cultural differences a generation back. We have seen the impact of this alienation in the level of education attained by *barrio* residents. A further clue is provided in Bernstein's work, which indicates that public school systems are premised on language and thinking skills associated with the middle class, particularly the elaborated code (Bernstein 1970, 1971).[1]

The disaffection of the chicano child from the public school has no real parallel in the middle-class anglo community. Certainly some youngsters in this community are equally alienated from school, but the general pattern exhibits a great deal of positive involvement in school activities and goals. The parents, who are virtually without exception high school graduates, and often college graduates, foster a positive attitude toward school by rewarding their children for accomplishments and punishing them for failures in school-related activities. Parents and children alike are caught up in curricular and extracurricular activities. The school as an institution has penetrated far more deeply into socialization among middle-class anglos than it has among working-class chicanos.

The list of key variables drawing a contrastive profile between the socialization of children in our two sample communities is now complete:

1. family size
2. parental roles within the family
3. nuclear vs. extended family
4. professionalization of socialization
5. the packaged world
6. penetration of schooling.

We have seen that on each of these points the experience of chicano and anglo child diverges. Whether these deviations attach to ethnic or to class affiliation is uncertain, but there is little doubt that these distinct experiential frameworks create a rather different early life for the children in our two communities. In the remaining pages of this chapter, we first examine some of the characteristic differences manifest in the riddling of chicano working-class and anglo middle-class children, and then interpret these in the light of the contrasting patterns of socialization we have encountered in the two communities.

## DIFFERENTIAL RIDDLING PRODUCTION

As I have noted, sufficient commonality exists in the riddling production of anglo and chicano youth to allow us to speak confidently of a single generic performance tradition present in both communities. On basic matters of texture, structure, composition of the riddle act, and even negotiation, the children of both communities are in substantial agreement. The analytical apparatus developed in earlier chapters of this book suffices in accounting for the riddling of either group. The differences we will be pursuing in this chapter are real enough, but they concern relatively minor matters either marginal to the main guidelines governing riddling or sufficiently minute so as not to throw into doubt the identity of the genre being exploited. Despite the finite nature of variation in riddling practices from one community to the other, we will find that this variation comments forcefully on the differential personality and experience of each.

Beginning with the most conspicuous divergence, the riddling of the chicanos exhibits these children's bilingual heritage. The anglo corpus is without exception an English-language corpus, perhaps with cognate riddles in other language communities, but consistently performed in the English tongue. The chicano corpus, in contrast, includes interrogative ludic routines in the English language, in Spanish, and in a code entailing transition between these two languages. Within the chicano sample are some of the traditional riddles distributed throughout much of the Spanish-speaking world. For example, the following versified riddle is attested in several Latin American countries (Garrido de Boggs 1955):

> Una vieja larga y seca
> Que le escurre la manteca.    *La vela.*
> An old woman long and dry
> Fat is dripping from her.    *The candle.*

The wide dissemination of this riddle indicates an origin in Spain and subsequent implantation in many sections of the Spanish New World. Over the generations the riddle has apparently continued to bemuse and delight, and we find it today on the lips of chicano children in East Austin.

The chapter on content presents an interesting riddling device occurring in several of the Spanish routines, wherein the solution appears in disguised form in the riddle proposition. In that chapter we dwelled on an instance:

Oro no es, plata no es, ¿qué es?   *Plátano.*

Other similarly constituted forms occur in the Spanish corpus:

Yo aquí, tú allá, ¿qué es?   *Toalla.*
I here, you there, what is it?   *Towel.*

Agua pasa por mi casa
Cate de mi corazón.   *Aguacate.*
Water is running through my house
Watch out for my heart.   *Avocado.*

In these riddles the phonetic string corresponding to the solution is hidden in a larger morphological construction. As we have seen, this is but one instance of inherent ambiguity in language brought to the foreground in the riddle format. The underlying anomaly is the capacity of a single phonetic string to lead off into conflicting semantic interpretations.

Other routines in the corpus are simply Spanish equivalents of routines the same children produce in English as well. We have cases of descriptive routines lodged in Spanish rather than English:

¿Qué es blanco y blanco?   *Un vestido de novio.*
What is white and white?   *A wedding dress.*

¿Qué tiene una cosa aquí y que no tiene piernas y que va asina?
*Una culebra.*
What has a thing here and doesn't have legs and goes like this?
*A snake.*

The Spanish corpus thus consists of some traditional Hispanic riddles, as well as Spanish cognates of routines also cultivated in English by the chicano children. It is worthy of attention that the Spanish corpus is small in comparison with the English corpus of the chicano children. These children, many of them fluent or competent in Spanish, choose to perform the great majority of riddles and other interrogative routines in English. The ethnic identity of the field collector might have some bearing on this tendency, but I have observed settings and heard recordings not likely to have been influenced in this manner, and the same tendency to pose routines in English persists.

Bilingual children segment their usage of the two codes in response to a complicated inventory of social and personal considerations. For the chicano children of East Austin, English appeared to be the favored code for the posing of interrogative ludic routines, a fact standing out all the more clearly in view of the children's employment of Spanish for the narrating of traditional stories featuring devils, witches, and the like. One might hypothesize that verbal play associated with school to a considerable degree was more readily lodged in English, while the performance of cherished ethnic traditions tended to preserve the Spanish tongue.

Routines incorporating code-switching between Spanish and English appear frequently in the chicano corpus. The bilingual child takes pleasure in juxtaposing and otherwise toying with the linguistic resources at his disposal. We have already treated code-switching from the linguistic point of view, but in reference to its function in the creation of interrogative ludic routines the signal element of artistic manipulation enters in. In the words of two authorities, "Code-switching is also a communicative skill, which speakers use as a verbal strategy in much the same way that skillful writers switch styles in a short story" (Gumperz and Hernandez 1972:98). Let us consider some of the instances of code-switching provided by our riddling sample.

> What's an animal *que* (that) gots two big horns?   *A longhorn.*
> *Tú* (you), how come the elephants eat a lot?   *They want to get fat.*

In each of these cases, only a single Spanish word appears in an English sentence, essentially functioning as an ethnic identity marker. But consider the following:

> 1st child:  Why did the chicken cross the road, *¿por qué* (why)?
> 2nd child:  *Porque* (because) it's too far to walk.
> 3rd child:  Porque está *too far* pa andá. (Because it's too far to walk)

In this exchange, the two codes are creatively alternated, and the children derive a self-evident pleasure from restating the solution in a form incorporating a larger degree of code-switching. In another instance, the riddler switches to Spanish in a vain effort to clarify a muddled routine:

> Why did the king of animals jump over the moon?    *Cause the house can't . . . porque la casa no puede brincar.*

In this instance, youthful exuberance has led the child to misstate the common routine:

> Why did the cow jump over the house?    *Cause the house can't jump.*

Having found herself in this predicament, the riddler seeks salvation in a switch to Spanish, but the routine remains flawed. These are some of the forms and uses of code-switching as they occur in the chicano riddling corpus; others could be adduced but perhaps we should move along to other considerations.

We have looked into one difference between chicano and anglo riddling that is definitely attributable to cultural diversity. It is the differential ethnic identity and national origin of the chicanos that provides them with their bilingual capacity. Other segments of our population have emigrated from countries speaking languages other than English, but conditions have not always been favorable for them to retain their native tongues. Thus the anglo sample conforms to mainstream expectations and exploits only English in the performance of interrogative ludic routines. But the time has come to take up more subtle variations in riddling between the two groups, variations that will not be directly traceable to language of national origin per se, but that appear to stem instead from the belief systems and cultural practices separating class and ethnic groups in our society.

In the remaining portion of this chapter I will seek to establish a few pivotal ideas regarding the differences between the riddling of anglo and chicano children, and to connect these ideas to the patterns of socialization we have discussed for our two sample communities. The points to be developed are:

1. The differential degree of penetration of North American popular culture into our two riddling groups: we will discuss evidence indicating a greater presence of popular culture figures in the riddling of the anglo children.
2. The discrepant roles played by oral tradition in the two communities: we will adduce evidence leading to the conclusion that chicano children are more substantially involved in face-to-face, oral communication than their anglo peers.
3. The impact of one media-conveyed cultural enrichment program on the riddling of the chicano children.

These three points represent the insight gained by viewing the children's riddling in relationship to the quality of early life in the family and community. The type of social environment experienced by the child is of course the crucial datum, and on this score we have sufficient evidence to draw a contrastive picture of our two sample communities.

For the anglo child, the personages and artifacts propagated through the various channels of popular culture, and television in particular, constitute a major component of the imaginative cosmology. Their riddling abounds with references to fanciful, fictive, and real world celebrities. We find multiple references to perennial favorites such as Moby Dick, the elephant, the Lone Ranger, and the Texas A & M Aggie; likewise represented are figures like the whale, Bigfoot, and Ironman, whose reign in popular culture may be more limited, or even momentary. Anglo children incorporate television heroes, comic book regulars, and even the protagonists of children's literature into their interrogative ludic routines. Their total production reflects a deep involvement in the world of popular culture. Chicano children, in marked contrast, appear to be only peripherally involved in this constantly shifting universe. Outside of Batman and Robin and Porky the Pig, their routines are oblivious to the denizens of television shows, comic books, and children's books.

The comparable inventories for chicano and anglo are presented below:

*anglo*

| | |
|---|---|
| Captain Marvel | Winnie the Pooh |
| Lone Ranger | Moby Dick |
| Kojak | Spiderman |
| Bigfoot | Ironman |

These are figures almost certainly proceeding from popular culture outlets to the children. A good many other figures, such as the shark (recall the movie *Jaws,* popular around the time our field work was carried out) and the various whales (recall the campaign to save the whales), would be likely candidates, though their provenance would be beyond definitive proof.

*chicano*

Batman
Robin
Porky Pig

In a riddling corpus of comparable size, the chicanos incorporate less than half the number of popular culture figures than those appearing in the anglo riddling. This discrepancy increases when marginal candidates such as the whale and shark, the Aggie and the armadillo, are included in the list.

We have then primary evidence to the effect that anglo children are more plugged into the popular media, chicano children more aloof from them. Additional secondary evidence points in the same direction. Anglo children, when quizzed as to where they had acquired a particular interrogative ludic routine, tended to cite such sources as riddle books, the Pink Panther, a television personality given to reciting jokes and riddles, and other comparable input. Furthermore, when disputes developed regarding the propriety of any detail in the riddling, the anglo children tended to recognize these popular culture sources as the ultimate authority on the matter. A seven-year-old boy, when questioned on a detail in a solution he had offered, replies: "That's part of the joke. I don't know. Ask Mr. Riddle Book, he's the one that has all the jokes." Or another child expounds: "I just read 'The big red rockeater' and 'Why do birds fly south?' in a riddle book." Over and over, the anglo children ascribed their riddling to popular culture sources:

—I got it from my *Highlights*. I get *Highlights*.[2]
—My sister has a riddle book and a joke book.
—I have a riddle book. I have two riddle books.
—I'm trying to think back in that riddle book.
—It's in my riddle book.
—I get them from those dixie cups.
—That's in a riddle book, on the last page.

Sometimes the recollections of riddle books are surprisingly vivid: "See the picture, there's this egg carton, it's from a knock-knock joke book, and there's some chick- . . . you know a baby chicken sticking out of its egg. . . ." The use of these sources as ultimate authority can be gauged in the following exchange between child and investigator:

C:   O.K. What did the cow say to the soil?
I:   I give up.
C:   Is my fooder in there?
I:   Fooder? What does that mean?
C:   I don't know. It was on the riddle cup.

Among anglo riddlers, these sources responsible for the mass dissemination of lore directed toward children occupy a position of prominence. Anglo children tend to draw much of their material from them and to rely on these sources for validation of disputed allegations.

One finds nothing comparable among chicano riddlers. Only once in all the time I did field work in East Austin did I encounter a riddle book. Chicano children do not refer their material to these popular culture outlets, nor do they turn to them in order to resolve substantive disputes over riddling. As we shall see below, chicano riddlers tend to call forth another factor, the oral tradition, as the source and ultimate authority for their riddling practices.

We find, then, two kinds of data indicating a differential engagement in the world of popular culture in chicano and anglo riddling. The primary evidence is the ubiquity of the figures of popular culture in anglo riddling; these figures enjoy only a marginal presence in chicano riddling. The secondary evidence is the testimony of the children themselves; anglo children almost invariably refer to riddle books, television comedies, or riddle cups as their sources. The entire riddling corpus of the anglo children appears to be shaped and molded by these popular culture outlets. There can be little doubt that these children are vitally connected to the cultural lifeline of mass media production. Our first point, regarding the differential penetration of North American popular culture in the two riddling groups, is thus established.

The second point, concerning the different role played by oral tradition in the two communities, is a partial corollary of the first point. Now we focus on the chicano corpus and find that instead of responding primarily to the input of popular culture, chicano riddling exhibits a reliance on oral tradition for both the materials and final authority of riddling. Chicano children, when questioned, generally refer a given interrogative ludic routine to a friend or relative. Over and over in the transcripts we find statements to the effect that a parent, sibling, cousin, or friend communicated the routine to the riddler. In cases under dispute this human source is trotted forth. As we have already noted, chicano riddling does not appear to owe much to the proliferation of popular culture sources dealing in this medium.

Perhaps as a consequence of this fact, the content of chicano riddling displays certain interesting contrasts with anglo riddling. Let me seize on one particularly intriguing contrast. Chicano riddlers exploit body parts as comparisons and solutions in riddling to a far greater extent than their anglo counterparts. The comparative lists are given below:

| chicanos | anglos |
|----------|--------|
| mouth | teeth |
| ears | feet |
| leg | face |
| nose | legs |

| | |
|---|---|
| belly button | eyes |
| teeth | |
| hair | |
| head | |
| chi chi (nipples) | |
| moustache | |
| feet | |
| back of head | |
| pimples | |
| tongue | |

As the list indicates, chicano riddlers invoke fourteen different body parts, while their anglo counterparts invoke only five. How shall we account for this disparity?

A glance through Archer Taylor's *English Riddles from Oral Tradition* draws immediate attention to the prevalence of body parts as means of comparison as well as solutions to traditional riddles. The various parts of the body definitely constitute a major, if not the major, conceptual tool utilized in traditional English riddles. Therefore, the preservation of these same body parts in modern riddling must be seen as a conservative tendency, and their neglect as innovative. In short, I would argue that the greater role of body parts in chicano riddling comprises evidence of a closer adherence to traditional riddling content. Anglo riddlers, with their reliance on popular culture sources, are moving away from some of the traditional bases of English riddling. Chicano riddlers, less influenced by these media sources, retain a manner of riddling more homogenous to traditional models.

Further internal confirmation of this point can be found in the differential presence of radical polysemy in the riddles performed by the two groups of children. Radical polysemy, as we discussed it in chapter 5, involves novel comparisons of objects not conventionally associated with one another. It is, I would submit, the most difficult form of ludic transformation to improvise, since the child must locate the kernel affinity in his experience of the world and then design an appropriate verbal vehicle for it. In short, comparisons of this kind are most easily plucked from oral tradition. The riddling of the chicano children is especially rich in radical polysemy, and that of the anglo children notably spare. Once again, we note that traditional riddling exhibits radical polysemy as one of the primary devices of confusion. In fact, in chapter 10 we will examine the presence of radical polysemy, or metaphor as many sources refer to it, as a possible indicator of conservative riddling traditions. Nearly 90 percent of our instances of radical polysemy occur in the chicano corpus, further indicating the importance of oral tradition in the formation of chicano riddling in Austin.

On these two scores, the testimony of chicano children and the prevalence of traditional content, we may conclude that chicano riddling betrays a greater investment in oral tradition. Chicanos avowedly receive much or most of their material from oral transmission, turn to oral tradition as the ultimate authority in riddling disputes, and practice a riddling that conforms more closely to traditional models in terms of riddle content. Differences in riddling between our two communities have thus led us to paint two rather discrepant portraits, one of a community formed in large part through adherence to primarily oral communication involving direct contact between speaker and listener, and another formed in large part through adherence to a common culture derived from mass media sources. Roger Abrahams describes a similar dichotomy: "One of the major cultural differences between the white middle class and ghettoized Afro-Americans is that the latter have preserved an oral-aural world view while the former have invested their creative energies and imaginations heavily in books, in the typographic-chirographic world" (Abrahams 1963:39). Consideration of the riddling of chicano working-class children and anglo middle-class children leads us to a similar understanding of these two communities. The issue is not literacy, but rather investment in primarily oral, immediate modes of communication or in primarily written or electronic and remote modes of communication. The consequences of orientation in one or the other of these directions are anything but trivial, probably filtering through into every dimension of life and influencing directly world view and interpersonal relations. But we cannot afford to take the time at this juncture to follow these interesting differences to their logical conclusions.[3]

Before we rest our case, we must make one last observation. To claim that chicano children are entirely free of influence from the public media would be inaccurate. Though their riddling indicates a cosmology remarkably devoid of popular culture's telling stamp, these same children have nonetheless attended closely to one particular production, the bilingual cultural enrichment program titled "Carrascolendas." This delightful program is filmed in Austin, Texas, at the KRLN studios, and one of its avowed purposes is to present traditional Mexican folklore to the urban chicano juvenile. Included among the materials presented are a good number of traditional rhymes, songs, and riddles. Most of the children included in our chicano sample were aware of the existence of the show; many of them were regular viewers and admitted to having learned material encountered on the show. A few children in our sample had even performed on the show, since "Carrascolendas" at that time made use of local talent in taping some of its skits.

But decisive attribution of sources is complicated here by the fact that much of the material presented on the show exists concurrently in East Austin oral tradition. For example, the traditional riddle

> Una vieja larga y seca
> Que le escurre la manteca

was learned in separate instances from the television show and from an adult relative. Two concluding observations are in order here. First, we have the remarkable fact of selective tapping of the popular media, and particularly of a cultural enrichment program aimed directly at the sector of chicano youth. The reports I received on this program were all very positive, and evidently the children found it both enjoyable and instructive. "Carrascolendas" had made an impact where the commercial programming had made little or none.

Second, the material presented in the show so favorably received was largely congruent with material simultaneously present in the community's oral tradition. Thus the children's exposure to this one television program in no way distorts our findings with regard to the traditionality of their riddling. If anything, exposure to "Carrascolendas" would operate to enhance the traditionality of riddling, since the materials aired on that show were deliberately selected from Mexican oral traditions.

There is a message here for those who would advocate the presentation of folklore via the public media. The manifest success of "Carrascolendas" with its target community is encouraging, but it must be recognized that the folklore displayed on the show possessed a certain cultural vitality and validity.

# Acquisition 9

The foregoing chapters have addressed themselves to the typology of interrogative ludic routines, to the texture, form, and content of this genre, to the negotiation of riddling in actual performance contexts, and to subcultural differences evident in our two riddling samples. Our prior investigation of these manifold dimensions of riddling among children provides a suitable foundation for the examination of the child's gradual indoctrination into the at first mysterious ways of riddling. For it is a manifest fact that children must acquire, often through painstaking and sometimes painful experience, a competence in this genre of verbal performance. The task of this chapter will be to chart the progress of riddling initiates from their fourth year, when riddles appear to be merely puzzling questions with arbitrary answers, to their eighth year, when riddles are performed properly and savored for their linguistic and conceptual intricacies.

We are dealing here with the acquisition of an essentially artistic competence. Children of four or five years come equipped with a mastery of the basic linguistic categories and processes of their native tongue, though subtleties of lexicalization and in other areas remain to be worked out (Chomsky 1969, Brown 1975). By the same token, the five-year-old is no newcomer to artistic performance. Basic aesthetic capacities and responses probably begin to develop in infancy (Jones 1972, Sutton-Smith 1976). By the age of five children already manifest a secure grasp on the performance persona, although the actual performances they produce are often less than entertaining to anyone but themselves. The ensuing years, especially the period five to nine years, are crucial in the development of performance repertoires with general entertainment value. By age nine the performance persona is armed with a set of effective routines, ranging across several genres of verbal folklore. And much to our own purpose here, prominent among this armory of performance skills we find the interrogative ludic routine. The problem awaiting this chapter, then, is to trace the emergence of a consummate artistic skill from an inceptive linguistic and aesthetic competence.

The aesthetic capacities entailed in the acquisition of artistic skills would include the control over formal mechanisms, a familiarity with the cognitive systems of society, and the ability to turn this control and familiarity to account in the crucible of social intercourse. Control over formal mechanisms in riddling involves a feeling for the texture, structure, and content of interrogative ludic routines. Awareness of cultural systems of classification is of course a necessary ingredient, allowing children to construct descriptive routines, which are simply verbal enactments of these orders, and riddles proper, dedicated to momentary sabotage of them. Finally, the code of pragmatics, that is, the strategy enabling the implementation of knowledge, involves a balancing of legal and moral concerns, whereby the child negotiates verbal performance in riddling as in other folkloric genres. These are the aesthetic capacities distinguishing the efforts of beginning and master riddlers. We shall seek to describe the gradual acquisition of these capacities in the riddling arena.

In order to discuss the process of acquisition, we will have recourse to the notion of a developmental sequence. There are two basic concepts involved: first, that the child acquires artistic skills through a series of stages whose order is fixed; and second, that this process has a temporal disposition—it is carried out through time. The first concept is built on the premise that each successive stage depends on the previous stage for its realization. We are dealing with an organic process, one that develops through logical steps from its initial form to some terminal form. The second concept alerts us to the fact that acquisition is not spontaneous but gradual. As Jean Piaget observes, "any development—psychological as well as biological—supposes duration" (1972:1). Duration provides time for practice, for thorough assimilation, and for integration of new skills into preexisting intellectual frameworks.

The developmental sequence as defined here avoids a few more controversial claims. For one thing, no absolute ages can be determined. Each child progresses at his or her own pace, in conformance to a variety of factors including innate capacity, social and material environment, and parental and peer-group encouragement. Approximate ages and the order of acquisition can be specified, with the proviso that there will be a great deal of variation in the former, and very little in the latter. At the same time, this concept need not imply that once a stage has been mastered it will be abandoned or neglected. A child might well return to the use of resources he has thoroughly mastered. The developmental sequence, as I use the term, refers to development of skills through a series of ordered stages, and little else.

## ACQUISITION STUDIES

At the outset, we will cite the limited work already done in the area of the development of artistic competence. We begin with Jean Piaget, whose work displays a pronounced developmental bias, though it is not oriented explicitly toward artistic performance. Piaget envisions a series of stages in intellectual development conducting the child from birth to adolescence. Despite the apparent overlap of his theory and our present concern, it will be seen on inspection that Piaget strikes off in a rather different direction from our own. Piaget is concerned with spontaneous development, i.e., the development of a reasoning capacity tied to the genetic character of the species. He explicitly bars from consideration "the psychosocial aspect, that is, everything the child receives from without and learns in general by family, school, educative transmission" (1972:2). The aspect of development he excludes is precisely the one that concerns us here. Nonetheless, the ideas of Piaget are pertinent to our discussion, since spontaneous and psychosocial development would appear to be mutually dependent. We will find the definite presence of a bridge between Piaget's spontaneous development and the corresponding developmental process indicated in our own riddling materials.

In a recent formulation, Piaget refers to four stages of development:

First we have a stage, before about 18 months, which precedes speech and which we will call that of the sensorimotor intelligence. Secondly, we have a stage which begins with speech and lasts for about 7 or 8 years. We will call this the period of representation. . . . Then, between about 7 and 12, we will distinguish a third period which we will call that of concrete operations. And finally, after 12 years there is the stage of propositional or formal operations. (Piaget 1972:10)

The children responsible for our riddling corpus fall into the two middle stages, representation and concrete operations. The former is in the ascendancy with the acquisition of language; its basic ingredient is the growing manifestation, in speech and apart from speech, of the capacity to symbolize. Thus during this stage play becomes symbolical (Piaget 1972:16). The latter stage, of concrete operations, witnesses the emergence of logic in the child's reasoning. Piaget observes: "This will thus be a logic of classifications, relations, and numbers, and not yet a logic of propositions" (1972:210). Along the same lines, he adds: "It is a logic in the sense that the operations are coordinated, grouped in whole systems which have their laws in terms of totalities" (1972:21).

We will be able to trace with little difficulty levels in the riddling competence of children evidently reflecting the transition from one stage to another in Piaget's sequence of intellectual development. The cognitive processes underlying the acquisition of stages two and three in Piaget's system are first encountered, then explored, and finally mastered in the arena of children's riddling. Our riddling materials allow us to make a case for the interdependence of spontaneous and psychosocial development. Without the expansion of cognitive ability it is doubtful that children could progress in riddling from descriptive routines to riddles proper. Yet it is tempting to suppose (though proof here is probably unattainable) that intellectual development could not proceed without exercise and practice in the ludic genres cultivated by children.

Discussing the stages of intellectual development in detail, Piaget recognizes a level of preparation and a level of completion attaching to each stage (1972:52). We are able to view the child engaging elements of a stage not yet attained, and in due time achieving an equilibrious completion of successive stages. Breaking the acquisition period into substages defined by preparation and completion allows Piaget to refine his focus considerably. The total inventory of stages and substages pertinent to our inquiry now becomes:

*Stage of Representations*
1. from 2 to 3.5 or 4 years: appearance of the symbolical function and beginning of the interiorization of the schemes of action in representations.
2. from 4 to 5.5 years: representative organizations founded either on static configurations or on an assimilation to the action itself.
3. from 5.5 to 7 or 8 years: articulated representative regulations; increasing articulations of classifications, relations of order, etc.

*Stage of Concrete Operations*
1. roughly 7 to 9 years: simple operations, awareness of reversibility and complete systems.
2. 9 to 11 years: completions of whole systems, especially in the fields of space and of time.

*Stage of Formal Operations*
1. 11 to 13 years: preparation of combinative operations, in which any element may be connected with any other.
2. 13 or 14 years: equilibrium.

With these more finely calibrated stages, we are able to trace the intellectual development of the child in sufficient detail to lay bare certain apparent correlations between riddling and stages of spontaneous or psychological development. But we will return to this theme later on in this chapter.

Two researchers have launched a theory more closely tied into our own concerns. Mary Sanches and Barbara Kirshenblatt-Gimblett propose that children's verbal play mirrors their acquisition of language competence. The verbal play of children must be viewed in relation to their language model, which "contains fewer lexical and morphological forms on which to map newly heard phonological sequences" (Sanches and Kirshenblatt-Gimblett 1976:31). To this circumscribed language model the authors attribute some of the prevalent features of children's verbal play, notably the high incidence of nonsense, the central role of sound play, the fascination with seemingly elementary homonymic relationships. As the child's language model develops, his verbal play centers on different problems. The progression is from sound play to sense play, finally culminating in play with sociolinguistic rules. "We would like to visualize the foci of children's speech play —that is, whether the individual form is mainly dominated by phonological, grammatical, semantic, or sociolinguistic structure—as reflecting an exercise in whatever part of the structure the child is currently mastering" (Sanches and Kirshenblatt-Gimblett 1976:43). The theory articulated here is provocative. While it has been criticized for placing undue emphasis on the progression from sound play into sense play (cf. Brady 1974), it usefully draws attention to the relationship between language learning and language play. While the theory proposed by Sanches and Kirshenblatt-Gimblett is obviously pertinent, the work of the previous chapters clearly transcends the purely linguistic perspective. In the context of this study, the language skill is merely one element in a comprehensive structure of conceptual, expressive, and social competencies.

Martha Wolfenstein (1954) has elaborated a developmental scheme concentrating on those aspects of development peripheral to language acquisition. Her theory stems from the psychoanalytic treatment of the growth and individuation of personality. She assumes that joking behavior functions primarily as a release from the pressures and anxieties of everyday life. Working within the Freudian frame, she argues that joking provides a format for the acceptable social expression of desires and hostilities that are normally repressed. She asserts the intriguing proposition that "there is a double aspect to the joke: the sexual or hostile theme, and the joke façade which gets it past inner and outer censorship" (1954:159). The joke façade develops apace as the child matures. Children around the age of four are said to invest little energy in the elaboration of a joke façade: the controversial material springs forth virtually undisguised. By age five Wolfenstein notes the onset of a narrative frame as a means of displacement from the self. By age six the joking riddle with its set form, economy of wit, and impersonality, takes over. At age seven tales reflecting the conflict with authority become prevalent. Joking riddles remain important until age eleven or so, when anecdotal jokes allowing for improvisation replace them as a prime focus of interest. These developments have a design: "There is an increasing indirectness of expression; the child must find ways to gratify his impulses while disclaiming responsibility for them" (1954:161).

This much of Wolfenstein's theory is of use in our own inquiry, though I would describe the joke façade in a more positive vein, as a means of featuring a particular conceptual or linguistic incongruity. But when she wades into her celebrated Freudian interpretations of specific child performances, we must decline to follow her. Her interpretations are ingenious enough, but they necessitate mapping of Freudian notions onto child locutions scarcely capable of bearing such weight. Given the Freudian system, these interpretations stand; but if Freud's understanding of human psychodynamics is once challenged, Wolfenstein's interpretations have no means of independent support. The following example is typical:

> *The child:* Why did the moron put the television on the stove?—Because he wanted to see Hopalong Cassidy ride the range.
>
> *Wolfenstein:* It would seem that this riddle in its latent meaning deals with the child's observation of his parents, his frustration at not seeing everything, his jealous fury against the father, and his vindictive wish that his sexual heat should consume him utterly. (Wolfenstein 1954: 101)

Without the a priori acceptance of the Freudian scheme, one might propose a rather different treatment of the same child performance. We can still speak of the joke façade, comprehending here the entire apparatus of the moron, the television, the stove, the cowboy and his horse, and the kitchen range. These are elements roped together in order to feature the linguistic anomaly of two semantic interpretations attaching to the single morph *range.* Thus far we are in consonance with Freud's theory of humor as elaborated in his delightful volume, *Jokes and Their Relation to the Unconscious,* still the most stimulating work in this area. But it remains to account for the evident delight taken by children and others in the foregrounding of linguistic and conceptual anomaly. Freud's excursions into primeval forces of aggression and hostility as motivating factors are well enough known. In this study, I have found it more appropriate to speak in terms of cultural systems inherently less powerful than our experience in the real world, and the need to rationalize and examine this disparity.

Brian Sutton-Smith (1976) articulates a system of riddle types, each using a specific cognitive operation and corresponding to a particular level of development. Sutton-Smith envisions his system as "a piagetian view of riddle structure as an exercise in classificatory ambiguities" (1976:12). The proposed types are the following:

1. preriddle: "a puzzling question with an arbitrary answer."
2. implicit reclassifications: treat homonyms as synonyms.
3. riddle parodies: "what seems like a riddle turns out to be an obvious question."
4. noncritical relationships: "standing patterns of behavior are changed."
5. explicit reclassifications: homonym masquerades as synonym, and direct reference is made to this fact.
6. noncriterial classifications: "These are not the attributes which would normally be central in a description of this particular class."
7. multiple classifications: conundrums.

These riddle types are acquired roughly in the order presented above, at least among the children Sutton-Smith consulted.

This list of types incorporates both linguistic processes (for example, homonyms and synonyms) and conceptual processes not directly dependent on language ("standard patterns of behavior are changed"). Upon inspection, it will be seen that we have addressed ourselves in different words to each of the types enumerated by Sutton-Smith, with the exceptions of the preriddle and multiple classifications. The latter are not highly developed in our corpus, being somewhat intractable to younger riddlers. The preriddle, as Sutton-Smith defines it, corresponds to the category of misfired routines as I will develop it below.

These then are the prominent sources[1] contributing to the formulation of a theoretical framework capable of handling the process of riddling acquisition as revealed in our riddling corpus. From Piaget's work, we are alerted to the interdependence of the child's reasoning powers and his expressive behavior. Our model of riddling competence conserves two important ties with Piaget's stages of intellectual development: on the one hand, the piagetian stages must be seen as logically prior to the child's acquisition of riddling, a sort of cognitive substratum; on the other, the kinds of riddling cultivated at each stage of riddling development presumably feed into the preparation for the succeeding stage of intellectual development. We will find ample evidence of the dovetailing of psychological and psychosocial development in our riddling corpus. Sanches and Kirshenblatt-Gimblett focus attention on another conceptual system in some sense prior to the production of interrogative ludic routines: the child's language model. Indeed, in the work of some modern linguists the language model is coterminous with the reasoning faculty itself (Chomsky 1968). Another system external to riddling but implicit in its acquisition emerges from consideration of Wolfenstein and Sutton-Smith: the cognitive orders shared by members of society. Wolfenstein notes that children acquire a growing awareness of materials to be censored or handled delicately in performance. And Sutton-Smith indicates that riddling involves some sense of "standing patterns of behavior" and attributes conventionally associated with a particular class of objects. These commentaries could be gathered together under the heading of a general grounding in the classificatory systems of culture.

The foundation we build on thus consists of intellectual faculties and a child's model of language and culture, none of which remains stable itself over time. We will find that certain breakthroughs in riddling technique must await articulation in one of these logically prior domains. But our published sources provide us with additional information not directly related to these intellectual, linguistic, and conceptual substrata. Wolfenstein, for example, introduces into the discussion the useful concept of façade, redefined for our own purposes as a suitable communicative vehicle for the conveyance of cognitive intent in riddling. She observes the gradual elaboration of façade in children's joking; we will have occasion to note a similar process in what might be called the riddling façade. What is required here is a conventionally marked verbal structure conducive to the display of linguistic or conceptual ambiguity. Interrogative ludic routines are marked by patterns of texture, content, and structure immediately diagnosed by members of the culture as riddling devices.

## RIDDLING OUTPUT

We have begun to articulate a model of riddling that analyzes this activity into two aspects, the linguistic or conceptual insight, and the conventional vehicle used to promote or feature this insight. These two aspects achieve final productivity in the performance of mature riddlers, but they develop at different paces toward that apotheosis. The vehicle is ready first: children are producing routines with the proper structure, texture, and content long before the intricacies of homonyms and paradox become available to them. The descriptive routine, as we have developed the concept, is essentially a riddling vehicle without the proper passenger, the linguistic or conceptual insight found in riddles proper. The descriptive routine comes first in children's riddling repertoires. The capacity to produce and understand block elements (a term congruent with our own "linguistic or conceptual insight") comes later, as we shall see, presupposing a preliminary linguistic or conceptual perceptivity, which is itself contingent upon a step forward in the process of intellectual development. In this manner, we can coordinate the different levels of our theory to account for the acquisition of riddling competence.

In order to elaborate a comprehensive model, we rely on two sources of data. First and foremost, the riddling of the children provides us with incontrovertible evidence of a child's riddling capacity. Flawed or misfired attempts are particularly valuable, allowing us to ascertain the precise limits to the child's riddling competence. In addition to misfired or somehow infelicitous routines, we exploit one other source of information, the children's commentary regarding items heard or performed. Through direct questioning or fortuitous comment, the children have provided some evidence concerning their comprehension of riddling material. On the basis of inspection of the children's riddling production and their own commentary regarding the same, we will piece together a developmental scheme charting the acquisition of riddling competence.

We cannot begin where the children begin, with the problematics of formulating acceptable riddle vehicles. At five years, the lower limit to our sample of riddlers, children already exhibit a familiarity with the patterns of texture, structure, and content characteristic of the interrogative ludic routine. Riddling texture includes the distinctive riddle question or proposition, with its muted intonation and quasi-poetic patterning of sound. Riddling structure, as we have described it, involves a narrow range of syntactic forms bridging question and answer, stemming from basic epistemological concerns operating at the level of deep semantic analysis. And riddling content, as we have seen, entails a concentration of referents within the sphere of quotidian existence. In these three dimensions, beginning riddlers display a ready hand, indicating that they have previously assimilated the contours of riddling vehicles. Indeed, access to performance in riddling sessions would presuppose a familiarity with the distinctive perceptual signal diagnostic of the genre. Otherwise the fledgling's locutions would not even register as instances of riddling.

Evidence from our transcripts shows that children are conversant with riddling vehicles well before they learn to deal with the problematics of the semantic fit of question and answer. We find numerous routines formulated in accordance with the conventional patterns of texture, structure, and content, but lacking any appreciable fit of question to answer. We also find routines appropriately formulated and encoding a transparent semantic fit of question and answer. These latter routines we have termed descriptive routines. In either case, the children are producing interrogative ludic routines employing the appropriate vehicles, but the cargo distinctive to the genre is absent. The mechanisms of ludic transformation, productive of the kinds of linguistic and conceptual duplicity found in mature riddling, evidently constitute a major stumbling block en route to riddling competence.

Consider the following instance, one of the more flamboyant of misfired routines in the transcripts:

What's big big big like the fig in the dog? (No solution provided.)

Here the aural texture conforms to standard riddling practice: the line can be scanned as isochronic tetrameter; a tendency toward sound play is evident in the clustering of /ig/ and /g/; in performance the intonation remained neutral, refusing to mark any element in the string as a focus of attention. In structural terms, we find one of the common patterns discussed in chapter 4. The content is appropriate to riddling, dwelling on the familiar domains of food and animals, and singling out the attribute of physical size. In all these particulars, the young riddler has formulated a felicitous interrogative ludic routine. Yet this routine is highly anomalous from the semantic point of view, so much so that it does not readily admit of solution, even to the riddler herself. Here we might make reference to an observation of Sanches and Kirshenblatt-Gimblett to the effect that "phonology, as compared to semantics and syntax, is far more highly developed in the child's language" (1976:39). The phonological components of riddling are acquired earlier than the semantic components, corresponding to the same order of acquisition in the child's developing language model. This disparity may well derive from patterns in the development of intellection, but here we are anticipating an argument we will develop more fully below.

Surveying the overall riddling production of children between the ages five and eight years, we encounter some very consequential patterns. First, as age increases the preponderance of riddles proper over descriptive routines becomes more notable. At age five children perform roughly equal numbers of each kind of interrogative ludic routine. By age eight riddles proper dominate to the tune of two to one. This trend is shown in table 4.

TABLE 4. *Type of Interrogative Routine by Age**

| Age | Descriptive Routines | Riddles Proper |
|-----|----------------------|----------------|
| 5 | 10 | 10 |
| 6 | 22 | 26 |
| 7 | 23 | 31 |
| 8 | 14 | 28 |

* Based on entire sample, with flawed and repeated routines eliminated

The younger children utilize the descriptive routine as a means of securing performance time in riddling sessions in the absence of a firm grasp on the mechanisms productive of riddles proper. As we have seen, the descriptive routine and the inscrutable preriddle are the only options open to the child who has not yet mastered the art of ludic transformation. But increasingly with each year, the children vent their riddling impulses in riddles proper, and by the eighth year the descriptive routine has slipped to a rather marginal position in the child's total repertoire. The older children continue to perform descriptive routines; as we have seen, these routines invoke a collaborative ethos, which the children find rewarding even though it differs substantially from the conventional agonistic arena of riddles proper. The descriptive routines performed by older children tend to cultivate more esoteric tokens, such as starfish, a swimming pool, a wedding dress, an alligator, and even Abraham Lincoln. Moreover, the rendition of attributes becomes crisper, more economical. But there is no question that by age eight the children prefer riddles proper to descriptive routines, however finely made these latter may be. By the eighth year, of course, children are fully competent in the mechanisms of ludic transformation, and therefore able to produce a diverse lot of proper riddles.

Another revealing numerical indicator is the ratio of error to total riddle production. Moving from the youngest to the oldest bracket, we find a significant decrease in the ratio of misfired routines (table 5). The children become increasingly adept at performing felicitous riddles.

TABLE 5. *Rate of Error in Riddle Production by Age**

| Age | Percentage of Error |
| --- | --- |
| 5 | 90 |
| 6 | 46 |
| 7 | 13 |
| 8 | 7 |

* Based on total sample of riddles proper

As these figures indicate, the percentage of flawed routines in the overall riddling production is cut in half between years five to six and seven to eight, while the decrease of error is even more pronounced between years six and seven. At the outset, children rarely manage a viable riddle; by age eight they rarely botch one. Here we have further proof that the period five to eight years is indeed the critical period in the acquisition of riddling competence.

Before moving on to other indicators, we might pause over the infelicitous routines produced at each age level and explore in them the series of hurdles challenging riddlers at each stage in their development. At age five children are led astray by the unorthodox character of riddle questions, which, unlike standard questions, oblige the questioner to provide an answer. Young riddlers often find themselves compromised by a riddle proposition, correctly formulated, to which no plausible solution attaches. A five-year-old boy poses the riddle:

> What did the chair say to the projector?

The audience recognizes the conventional riddling vehicle and awaits the solution. The child who posed the routine had not foreseen this development, and remains speechless. In riddling, interrogatives are transformed into interrogative ludic routines, and the responsibilities of addressor and addressee are reversed (see chapter 2). The five-year-old child will also respond to this dilemma by producing spontaneous solutions marginally related to the riddle question, but uncharacteristic of the economical solutions provided in mature riddling models. The following example is illustrative:

> What did the pig say when he dived in the mud?  *He said, the man said, "You better get out of that mud. That's where I'm planting my crops today, and I'm gonna spank your bottom."*

Some children become quite adept at this maneuver, and manage to fuse the two genres of riddles and narratives greatly to their advantage. Still, from the perspective of riddling competence, these productions are clearly flawed.

In some of the misfired routines of five-year-olds, we note an incipient regard for the coordination of question to answer, though there is little enough success to show for it. The following three instances are representative:

> Why did the farmer pull his coat off when he went in the water? *Those were his best clothes.*
>
> What did the elephant say when he fell in the diving pool with no water? (No solution provided.)
>
> You know what a jokeman said to a joker fireman?    *Bang bang, there's a fire in your hand.*

In each of these misfired routines we can perceive some attention being paid to the problematic of semantic fit. In the first one, the child correctly pairs solution and answer, but the element of paradox or ambiguity is missing. In the latter two, the child has attempted to create an incongruous situation. The middle routine paints an incongruous picture, but the child has not learned to space this incongruity properly across question and answer: the entire notion is enclosed in the riddle proposition. In the final example, the child correctly locates the anomaly in the riddle solution, but the anomaly itself is unmotivated, imprecise. Though each of these routines is infelicitous, we cannot fail to note the fumbling attempts to recreate a riddle effect not yet understood.

The five-year-old child thus produces routines decidedly well formulated as riddling vehicles, but lacking the ludic transformation indicative of cognitive ambivalence. He errs in failing to comprehend the transformation of interrogative systems into interrogative ludic systems, with the attendant reversal of participant roles, and in falling short of the mark in attempting to reproduce the conceptual anomaly he senses in mature riddling. The sixth year brings about new developments. At this point children produce an abundance of near misses, that is, routines that almost, but not quite, capture that elusive cognitive ambivalence. Six-year-old riddlers are riddling enthusiasts. They rambunctiously explore the entire riddling field and their enthusiasm leads them into both success and equivocation. Some of their flawed efforts appear to be spontaneous coinings that fall short of the mark, hinting at a viable ludic transformation but never quite attaining it. Consider the following examples:

> What did the big hill say to the little hill?    *"You're too fancy to be walking around."*

What did the man say when he held up the bank?    *"Pop pop, you're dead, I put popcorn in your mouth."*

What did the baby say to the cradle?    *"It's time for me to fall."*

What comes after the tire?    *The mud.*

The first item above hints at the anomaly of a mobile hill; this is precisely the stuff of riddles, but the arrangement of details does not successfully feature this anomaly. The format, "what did the big X say to the little X," familiar from traditional material, doesn't appear to have been of much help here, and the adjective "fancy" fails to connect to the overall scheme of the routine. Nonetheless, even in this infelicitous effort, we detect a more insistent regard for paradox and ambiguity. The second item actually stumbles upon a polysemic word, "pop," but the format once again operates against the promotion of this ambiguity in the performed routine. Here, as in the previous instance, we get a notion that the riddle sought to incorporate a ludic transformation and missed merely by a faulty arrangement of components. Similar analysis of the final two items given above confirms our growing suspicion that the six-year-old riddler seeks cognitive ambivalence but can't quite hold on to it in performing interrogative ludic routines.

Six-year-olds err in another direction. Not uncommon in their riddling performance are skewed traditional items. They perform traditional material that is imperfectly digested and skew the arrangements requisite to bringing off a successful riddle. Compare these two following routines with their traditional counterparts:

Why does the little boy put ice in his father's bed?    *He's used to it.*

vs.

Why does the little boy put ice in his father's bed?    *He wants an iced pop.*

Why do ducks fly backwards?    *They crack up.*

vs.

What happens when ducks fly upside down?    *They quack up.*

In the first case, the child correctly performed the riddle proposition, but was unable to provide the traditional solution. His own spontaneous offering is flat, to say the least, lacking the element of linguistic duplicity present in the traditional item. In the second case, the child doesn't quite have it right, and his deviation from the traditional routine once again destroys the ambiguity present in the same. Errors of this kind are facilitated by the failure to comprehend material assimilated from oral transmission. Once again, it is that elusive and fortuitous ambiguity that remains intractable to the child's efforts.

Consideration of the errors of six-year-olds points to an essential element in riddling competence: the ability to select pertinent details and arrange them in such a way as to feature the riddle's conceptual twist. In the absence of a firm grasp on the cognitive or linguistic ambiguity to be promoted in the routine, the riddle format easily collapses and the riddler's proposition appears pointless, his proffered solution random. Six-year-olds often fall shy of the mark, but their riddling efforts indicate they are gaining a sense of what goes into successful ludic transformation.

Seven-year-olds rarely go astray, but even their occasional errors are instructive. Let's look at two examples:

> How come mans shave a lot? *Cause grass always grows on them.*
>
> How come plums grow on trees all the time? *Cause it's a plum tree.*

The intention in the first item given above is evidently to compare a man's facial hair to the lawn's grass, and thereby to associate the act of shaving with the act of cutting the grass. The comparison is fertile enough, but the vehicle is clumsily formed. Another format might have featured the comparison with more lucidity, for example:

> Why are a lawn and a man's face alike? *They both need periodic trimming.*

But the child chose to encode her comparison in covert fashion, and one is left with the feeling that her routine needs some reworking. In the second instance an attempt is made to set the riddlee on a wild goose chase, but the riddle question is too direct and the solution consequently comes as no surprise. Again, a refinement of technique is called for.

> Why were so many plums gathered in one place?    *Cause it was a plum tree.*

The reader will no doubt feel that this improvement is in need of the same, but in any case it points to the necessary concealment of ultimate purpose. Roger Abrahams (1974) says of the riddle that it involves epistemological foreplay, which is then consummated in the delivery of the solution. The flawed routines of advanced riddlers fail by virtue of improper deployment of information in the riddle question and solution. Even with a conceptual or linguistic twist in mind, the riddler must slyly deploy his tokens in such a way as to maximize the riddlee's suspense and ultimate satisfaction.

The flawed production of riddlers helps us chart the course of the acquisition of riddling competence. At five years riddlers are uneasy with the obligation to provide an answer to their own questions. They manage only the most attenuated approximations to the semantic fit characteristic of the genre. With the sixth year, children zero in on the wellsprings of desirable ambiguity, sometimes hitting the mark, but missing with equal frequency. By year seven the source of difficulty has shifted, and children err in performing riddles only by virtue of an unfortunate deployment of information. The cognitive twists are forthcoming now, and the child is released to concentrate on effective riddling formats. Errors among eight-year-olds are scarce, and simply point to the same factors adduced in analysis of the flawed production of their younger peers.

We must turn our attention now to the positive side of this coin, the successful riddle production of children ranging in age from five to eight years. Focusing in on the devices of ludic transformation exploited in acceptable routines, we note some interesting trends, which must be considered tentative in view of the limitations of our sample. The deployment of ludic transformation by age is given in table 6.

Inspection of table 6 brings out a few significant observations. First, we see that the six-year-old has access to ludic transformation primarily through the technique of juxtaposition. Riddles constructed on comparisons are hard to come by for the six-year-old, and those incorporating radical or unconventional comparison are apparently quite intractable to the six-year-old riddler.

TABLE 6. *Type of Ludic Transformation by Age*

(Numbers given are numbers of routines)

|  | Age | | | |
| --- | --- | --- | --- | --- |
|  | 5 | 6 | 7 | 8 |
| Homophony | — | 8 | 15 | 8 |
| Conventional Polysemy | — | 2 | 8 | 7 |
| Radical Polysemy | — | — | 6 | 5 |
| Anomaly | — | 5 | 13 | 14 |

Moreover, we notice that riddlers shift their efforts from routines locating ludic transformation in the signifier to those placing ludic transformation in the signified over the period six to eight years of age. Roughly two-thirds of the output of acceptable riddles proper by six-year-olds exhibits ludic transformation lodged in the signifier; the comparable figure for seven-year-olds is 55 percent, and for eight-year-olds, 45 percent. As the chart indicates, a dramatic drop in homophonic routines occurs between the seventh and eighth years in our sample, while the production of routines employing other forms of ludic transformation increases or maintains a constant level during this critical period of development. Our data suggest that children acquire their first notion of reversal in riddling around age six, in the form of manipulation of wrinkles in the linguistic code. In subsequent development, they increasingly move toward deceptions that are conceptually based, though routines founded on language play continue to form a significant minority of riddle production. Whitt and Prentice (1975) record a similar result in their studies.

Inspecting the kinds of conceptual duplicity practiced in these routines brings to light another interesting development. Younger children give roughly equal scope to routines making reference to creatures of fantasy and to routines dwelling on real world anomaly. But in the eighth year, children focus most of their attention on real world anomaly, and creatures of fantasy become much less prominent in the riddling.

The moment has arrived to integrate some of the insights discussed so far into a preliminary profile of the riddler's progress.

Stage 1. Repertoire consists of descriptive routines and preriddles; participation is marginal; attempted riddles proper mostly flawed; riddle vehicle is familiar, but ludic transformation quite mysterious (age 5).

Stage 2. Repertoire consists of descriptive routines and some riddles proper; participation is substantial, enthusiastic; rate of error is high, still nearly 50 percent; ludic transformation involving primarily homophony and anomaly (age 6).

Stage 3. Repertoire consists primarily of riddles proper; participation is substantial; rate of error greatly reduced; ludic transformation secure; strong preference for language-based reversal; equal presence of fantasy and real world paradox; refinement in riddle formats (age 7).

Stage 4. Repertoire consists primarily of riddles proper; descriptive routines are crisper, more exotic; participation is authoritative; rate of error quite low; secure grasp on ludic transformation; mild preference for language-based reversal; real world paradox of special concern; continuing refinement of riddle formats (age 8).

## RIDDLING SKILLS

While the acquisition process is clearly gradual and continuous from the riddler's perspective, we can adopt an analytical perspective of the same events and discern certain broad inconformities from one stage to the next. From the first to the second stage we observe a gradual strengthening of the children's grasp on riddle ambiguity, allowing them to participate more fully in riddling sessions. Five-year-olds are really shooting in the dark, as their high rate of error would suggest; with the sixth year, some awareness of ludic reversal enters in, though flawed routines are still legion. The earliest successful routines tend to incorporate linguistic reversal. These are generally traditional items often encountered in riddling sessions. In some cases they are very likely mouthed without comprehension, though proof of this is hard to come by. But the following comments by a six-year-old who had just performed the well-known "newspaper" riddle indicate that there may well be a lag between performance and comprehension:[2]

Investigator: What's black on a newspaper?
Child: The print.
I:     And what's white?
C:     The background.
I:     And what's red?
C:     The comics. Uh like . . . on top of it? The picture?
I:     Can you think of anything else red means?
C:     The color red?
I:     Or—some other meaning.
C:     The name Red.
I:     And what else? Do you know of any other meaning of red?
C:     I can't think of any.

That the six-year-old is on the brink of comprehension is shown by the following exchange, which also reveals the difficulty of plumbing this issue through direct interviews:

Investigator: How is a newspaper red?
Child: I don't understand that either.
I:     You don't get it? Well what are the different—
C:     Oh, *read!* Read like you read a newspaper.

In any case, six-year-old riddlers mount a ferocious attack on genre and in the end their unbridled experimentation leads them closer and closer to a feeling for ludic transformation in the riddle form.

   The shift in riddling posture from stage 2 to 3 is equally dramatic. In the seventh year children achieve mastery of the ludic sophistication that had previously eluded them, becoming especially adept in routines based on homonymic and polysemic pairings. Now that linguistic and conceptual equivocation have become available to them, the children make fewer errors, and those they make relate to a continuous refinement in the artful deployment of information, so as to best promote the linguistic or conceptual twist of the riddle. Seven-year-old riddlers are fully comfortable in the genre, though further attainments still await them.

With the final stage of riddling competence, the discontinuity is less than the radical shifts we have noted thus far. The riddlers continue to refine their technique, and to expand their repertoire toward the production of increasingly more demanding routines, such as the conundrum and those focusing on real world paradox. The children now reap the fruit of four years travail in the genre, producing a wide range of riddle types and only occasionally misfiring. One might expect further refinements in later years, but my transcripts indicate that sometime in the ninth or tenth year the children's dedication to riddling slackens, and their performance energies find expression in other genres. With the eighth year, the riddler's progress appears to be virtually complete.

Our model for the acquisition of riddling competence specifies a series of skills learned in a particular sequence and culminating in the capacity to produce various kinds of routines that are not only unflawed, but moreover especially telling exempla of the genre. Let us examine this sequence. The first skill, marking the very dawn of riddling competence, is the ability to construct authentic riddling vehicles, incorporating all the textural, structural, and content features distinctive of the riddle. Acquisition of this primary skill is requisite for admission to the club. The ability to construct proper riddling vehicles in turn presupposes a grasp on the interrogative system, and a feeling for the prosodic and strategic modifications of that system in interrogative ludic routines. During the fifth year the final touches in this riddling foundation are completed.

The next skill, occupying the child for a year or more, is the demanding one of turning the cognitive orders on their head to produce ambiguity and confusion in riddles. The descriptive routine, which sounds like a riddle but incorporates no cognitive block, simply rehearses the cognitive orders. There is evidence that this rehearsal of

cognitive orders is productive and rewarding in its own right, especially for the younger children for whom economical renditions of
these orders may still retain a certain novelty and sense of achievement. Descriptive routines come early in a child's riddling experience,
and are most engaging to the younger children. Also available to the
child not yet conversant with the methods of ludic transformation is
the preriddle, which, as Sutton-Smith (1976) notes, reflects the un-
initiated child's perception of the way riddles work. But here we have
a random or nearly random juxtaposition of categories within the
classificatory system, rather than an insightful foregrounding of ambiguity and multivocality lodged within these cultural systems. The
child not yet capable of ludic transformation in the riddling arena
thus pursues one of these two routes, either shying away from obliq-
uity to produce descriptive routines, or producing inscrutable items
that must remain inscrutable, since they are not founded on some
underlying conformity. Either route is innocent of the kind of analytic intelligence implicit in the recognition and harnessing of linguistic
or conceptual ambiguity.

We have followed the children through their quest for ludic transformation. We have noted that their flawed routines approach ever
closer to adequacy, and that fewer of them occur as we move from
the lower to the higher age brackets. The five-year-old has only the
slightest notion of how to produce ludic transformations typical of
riddling, but the six-year-old already shows great progress in this direction. With the seventh year, the process is complete, and certain
kinds of ludic transformation are readily performed by the children.
At this point, the child possesses the ability to transcend cognitive
orders, but primarily through the good offices of homophones and
polysemes, that is, particular vocabulary items encapsulating these
ambiguities. It remains for the eighth year to establish in the children's
repertoires a substantial inventory of interrogative ludic routines independent of linguistic incongruity. In the eighth year we find the children focusing more of their energy on the observation and presentation in riddle form of real world paradox and anomaly.

One other skill goes into the production of good riddles. The vehicle and the cognitive twist are not enough in themselves; addi-

tionally, the child must acquire a feeling for the selection and arrangement of information. Details provided in the riddle proposition must obscure the unorthodox connection to be revealed only in the solution, yet they must allow for a retrospective construction of meaning. Facility with riddle design is present in the riddling of children beginning in their seventh year. Part of their success in this domain stems from their growing capacity to reproduce set items, the traditional routines culled from oral and written sources. Traditional routines exhibit that polished efficacy gained in the course of extensive handling by the folk. As a result, they serve as excellent models of the proper deployment of information, essential to the well-turned riddle. We have seen that the six-year-old still has considerable trouble with traditional items, frequently misplacing critical information to the detriment or devastation of riddle denouement. In the seventh year children handle traditional material with less difficulty, though not until year eight are they fully comfortable with the traditional repertoire.

These observations accord well with data provided by other researchers. Martha Wolfenstein (1954:138) locates the rise of fixed form, joking riddles, in the sixth year, and Sanches and Kirshenblatt-Gimblett (1976) find that children's performance repertoires include a peak saturation of set pieces in their eighth year. The ability to perform traditional material is intimately linked to the development of skills in the areas of ludic transformation and riddle design. The development of these skills facilitates performance of traditional items, while performance of these items presumably enhances the child's awareness of riddle design and ludic transformation. These processes are mutually dependent and mutually reinforcing.

Our model of riddling competence would thus include three principal skills, marking the progress from riddling innocent to riddling master. These are:

1. The ability to construct viable riddling vehicles: presupposes familiarity with interrogative system, and with characteristic patterns of texture, structure, and content.
2. The ability to encode in interrogative ludic routines some

form of ludic transformation, wherein the cognitive orders are explored for ambiguity, anomaly, paradox, or incongruity: presupposes a firm grounding in the cognitive orders, in the principles of classification, and in the device of reversal.

3. The ability to design effective riddle formats: presupposes the capacity stated in number 2 as well as sufficient detachment to encompass riddlee's perspective on the routine being performed.

Let us now return to the theoretical statements discussed at the beginning of this chapter, and thereby integrate this model of riddling competence into a broader understanding of the child's intellectual progress.[3]

## RIDDLING COMPETENCE

In the work of Sanches and Kirshenblatt-Gimblett (1976) we find support for the notion that riddlers first acquire a competence in producing riddling vehicles, and then move on to the subsequent task of incorporating ludic transformation. These authors point out that phonological expertise precedes semantic and syntactic expertise in the child's developing language model. While they assign a greater importance to phonological structure in children's verbal art in general, they especially emphasize its central role in the verbal art produced by younger children, ages five and six. The verbal art of the older set takes up other issues, responding to the current preoccupations deriving from their expanding language model. The authors conclude: "Our analysis of the collection of forms at our disposal corroborates our hypothesis that the child's concern shifts from phonological to grammatical to semantic and finally to the sociolinguistic level of language" (Sanches and Kirshenblatt-Gimblett 1976:51). The child's verbal art moves from a preoccupation with phonological structure to a concern with syntactic and semantic structure as the underlying language model accomplishes the same transition. The shift from sound to sense, from the ability to produce vehicles to the

ability to incorporate ludic transformation, provides a riddling analogue to the theory Sanches and Kirshenblatt-Gimblett have developed in reference to verbal art in general. Their insights allow us to
assimilate the ordered acquisition of skills 1 and 2 in our model of
riddling competence to a broader intellectual process, the child's acquisition of language. In both realms, the child's developing language
model and our own analytic model of riddling competence, there is
a chronologically determined movement from sound to sense.

Martha Wolfenstein's discussion of the joke façade and its development through time is also pertinent to our findings. She notes over
time "an increasing indirectness of expression" (1954:161) as the
child successively lodges controversial material in undisguised form,
narrative form, joking riddles, and finally anecdotal joking forms.
The joking riddle, with its economy and impersonality, constitutes
an appropriately indirect medium for the presentation of controversial
material, according to Wolfenstein the hostile and sexual themes seeking to avert both inner and outer censorship. In our own riddling
model, this controversial material becomes insight into conceptual
and linguistic inconsistencies. Note that it remains controversial, since
in theory at least this material constitutes a threat to the cognitive
status quo. Just as the Freudian views the themes of verbal art as
sufficiently powerful to require special encoding in aesthetic vessels,
so our own model views the insights contained in children's riddling
as sufficiently subversive of the ruling orders as to require treatment
in special, insulated, artistic settings. There exists the possibility of
social and individual trauma in the exercise of these speculative faculties, in tampering with the cognitive orders of society. At this juncture
I would cite Morse Peckham's theory of art, which argues that cultural systems may be manipulated in this fashion only in the pro-
tected arena of the aesthetic (Peckham 1965).

In any case, the child's continuing refinement of the joke façade
could be interestingly related to our own third skill, the ability to design effective riddling formats. In both cases, the controversial material is a given, and the problem becomes one of finding a suitable
format for its presentation. Wolfenstein chooses to emphasize the
need to avoid censorship, either from psychic mechanisms or social

ones. I would prefer to concentrate on acceptability in light of the community's canons governing artistic performance, though I would concede that the two points of view are not in any sense contradictory here. The child riddler, having mastered the technique of constructing riddling vehicles and loading them with ludic transformations of the cognitive orders, must further perfect a method of organizing the information conveyed on either side of the riddlee's first option, that is, in the riddle proposition and solution. Wolfenstein notes the surprising arrival of joking riddles in the child's sixth year, and it is just at this point we find children taking up set pieces garnered from tradition and internalizing successful strategies of format design, a task of performance refinement that will occupy them throughout the remainder of their riddling careers.

As for the sequence of riddle types proposed by Sutton-Smith, definitive comparison is not possible because of the limited size of our riddling corpus. In the general drift of riddling development, our two samples appear to agree rather well. Sutton-Smith notes that riddlers begin with the preriddle, and that riddling expertise is complete with the advent of conundrums. In our profile of the stages of acquisition we posited an analogous riddler's progress. But the correspondence of Sutton-Smith's developmental scheme to our own runs even deeper. Sutton-Smith wraps up his argument with these words:

> Three major periods are typified in this material. There is the preoperational period when a child thinks of objects or sentences in an unidimensional way: when he is asked how many words there are in the sentence, "The man has twenty chocolates," he says there are twenty words (Berlin 1972). By grade three, however, he knows that a sentence can contain two dimensions (possession of twenty chocolates can be communicated by only five words), just as objects can have two dimensions (number and extension) and words can have two meanings (hot dogs and hot dogs). By the fifth grade, his interest in ambiguities, at least as reflected in jokes, focuses dominantly on behavioral expectancies. (Sutton-Smith 1976:119)

Sutton-Smith observes that the younger riddlers begin with pure ambiguity (the preriddle) and move into resolvable ambiguity later on (riddles of implicit reclassification). Finally, their attention is drawn to part-whole relationships and expected behavioral patterns (Sutton-Smith 1976:118).

There are then two kinds of congruity between our own model and that of Sutton-Smith's. First, each model relates progress in children's riddling to Piaget's framework of intellectual development. Second, each model devises a drift in children's riddling toward the artful enshrinement of ambiguity, accompanied by a move from linguistic-based reversal (homonymic riddles) to concept-based reversal (part-whole relationships and reversal of standing patterns of behavior).

One important source of data not yet mentioned in this chapter, the work of developmental psychologists, is usefully added to the discussion at this point. Their observations, though founded on a research methodology quite foreign to my own, nonetheless coincide on two major points with the profile of riddle acquisition elaborated here. First, they identify a critical period in the child's exploitation of the genre between the ages of six and eight years; and second, they provide preliminary evidence for a linkage between these events in the psychosocial arena and concurrent advances in child intellection as described by Piaget, the final topic to be addressed in this chapter.

With respect to the former coincidence, we might cite the work of Thomas Shultz as exemplary. Shultz subjected children in the critical age range to a set of riddle questions and solutions, measuring their response through both direct questioning (funniness rating) and observation (mirth response). The stimulus set presented to the child consisted of a riddle question, the original solution, a resolution-removed solution, and an incongruity-removed solution, as illustrated in the following example taken from his article:

How far can a dog run into a forest? (Question)
Only halfway. After that, he will be running out. (Original answer)
Only halfway. (Resolution-removed answer)
As far as he wants. (Incongruity-removed answer)

His conclusions are summarized as follows:

The transition from a stage of pure incongruity to a stage of resolvable incongruity occurs between the ages of 6 and 8. . . . Children of age 8 and older preferred original forms over resolution-removed forms, while 6-year olds did not. . . . 6-year olds had particular difficulty in detecting the hidden meanings of the ambiguities which are considered necessary for a successful resolution of the incongruity. (Shultz 1974:104)

These results, as I have said, accord well with my own finding that the ability to produce and savor ludic transformation appears in the children's riddling around the seventh year of life. Additional "empirical investigation" (the term developmental psychologists reserve for laboratory experimentation) confirms the finding summarized by Shultz above.

That methods founded on such divergent principles as empirical investigation in laboratory settings (the developmental psychologists), clinical observation (Wolfenstein and Sutton-Smith), and participant observation as employed in my own field work, should produce consonant results is at first somewhat disconcerting, but eventually heartening, lending to our common findings a degree of likelihood not easily obtained in the social sciences. Still, as a folklorist acutely cognizant of the delicacy of human interactional frames, I cannot help but feel uneasy with the methods utilized by the developmental psychologists. Granted, placing a child in a laboratory facilitates control over unwanted variables and quantification of the significant ones. Yet riddling is indigenous to the intricate fabric of social interaction, and transportation to the laboratory must entail some loss of validity. An indication that something is amiss emerges in the failure of mirth ratings and funniness reports to match in experiments of this kind (Whitt and Prentice 1977, McGhee 1976). These measures of affect would appear to be quite problematic, inasmuch as the child finds himself alone in a room with an unfamiliar adult, encouraged to respond to verbal material wrested from its normal habitat. As P. McGhee comments on the disparity of indicators in his experiment, "the experimental situation utilized in these studies simply may not have been conducive to the free expression of such affect" (1976: 426). Despite these misgivings, I am constrained to admit that the carry-over of normal response patterns into the experimental setting is evidently sufficient to produce, in the instance of riddling development, results comparable to those observable in more natural surroundings.

Our final task in this chapter is to tie our findings into the most comprehensive theoretical framework at our disposal, Jean Piaget's scheme of the development of child intellection. The relationship between Piaget's work and our own is both difficult and intriguing. As we have noted, Piaget is concerned with what he terms spontaneous, or psychological development, which he perceives as logically and temporally prior to developments in the psychosocial arena (1972: 20). We have mentioned the possibility of bridging the gap between these two sorts of development with analysis based on our own riddling materials. In our formulation, progress in the psychological domain underlies progress in the psychosocial domain. By the same token, experience in the latter domain may well precipitate developments in the former. Piaget speaks of periods of preparation predating the acquisition of each of his major stages of intellectual development (1972:52). Surely the arena of children's verbal play would constitute an important preparatory forum. Moreover, once a given cognitive skill has been acquired, it must still be integrated over a period of time into the intellectual armament of the child. Here again the arena of children's verbal play would seem to offer one ideal forum for practice and refinement of newly acquired cognitive skills.

Piaget centers in on the development of classificatory skills over the period five to seven years of age. The child from five to seven is capable of identifying true classes and engages in articulations of classifications (1972:58). However, not until the eighth year does the child grasp the important taxonomic principle of inclusion. In the period five to seven years Piaget notes

> a logic which is not based on verbal statements but only on the objects themselves, as manipulable objects. This will be a logic of classifications because objects can be collected all together or in classifications; or else it will be a logic of relations because objects can be combined according to their different relations; or else it will be a logic of numbers because

objects can be materially counted by manipulating them (Piaget 1972: 21).

The notion here is that children's reasoning during this period is determined by physical rather than symbolic manipulation of the environment. We find a suggestive counterpart of this orientation toward classifying, counting, and relating objects in the descriptive routines performed by children of this same age bracket, which similarly count, classify, and relate as they adduce the empirical attributes of the referents to be divined. The rehearsal of cognitive orders in the descriptive routine appears to be a verbal manifestation of the logic of classification that Piaget describes in this period of intellectual activity. We recall that it is during the period five to seven years when children's repertoires are most replete with descriptive routines.

Piaget attributes the limitations of children's reasoning powers up until the age of seven or so to a few basic traits. *Syncretism* involves "the tendency to group together into a confused whole several unrelated things or events"; *juxtaposition* results from "the failure to see the real connections among several things or events" (cf. Ginsberg and Opper 1969:114). While these traits are discussed primarily with reference to the perception and arrangement of physical objects, they have an obvious verbal parallel in the preriddle, a verbal form likewise characterized by an unsystematic jumbling of elements. Thus both options available to the riddler who is still innocent of ludic transformation correlate neatly with the logic and limitations Piaget finds in the reasoning of children of this age. Furthermore, interrogative ludic routines, with their concentration on cognitive orders and alternatives to these orders, would be a laboratory well adapted to both the extension of classificatory skills and the transcendence of the confusions derived from syncretism and juxtaposition.

The great shift in child intellection comes around age seven, according to Piaget, when the preoperational child moves into the sphere of concrete operations. As Piaget has it: "About the age of 7, a fundamental turning point is noted in a child's development. He becomes capable of a certain logic; he becomes capable of coordinating operations in the sense of reversibility, in the sense of the total system" (Piaget 1972:20). The preoperational child is still firmly rooted in his perceptions, and abstracts from the empirical level only with great difficulty (Ginsberg and Opper 1969:151). With the advent of the operational stage around seven years of age, the child becomes capable of forming a mentalistic, or figurative, image of experience, which allows him to abstract considerably from experience. It would appear that the children's growing awareness of taxonomic principles, of total systems, and of reversibility in systems should enable them to grasp the moves of ludic transformation that do in fact begin to appear in his riddling with high levels of accuracy during the seventh year. The emergence of riddles proper as the main element in the riddling repertoires of children in their seventh year thus constitutes a further riddling correlate of spontaneous, psychological development.

As I mentioned above, developmental psychology has also wrestled with the likely interplay of psychological and psychosocial development, and we are beginning to receive direct and explicit evidence to the effect that progress in one domain correlates with progress in the other. Kenneth Whitt and Norman Prentice (1977) find that first graders who have mastered the conservation of liquid (one of Piaget's basic criteria of concrete operations) exhibit "heightened enjoyment and comprehension of homonymic riddles," leading them to conclude as follows:

> The findings suggest that Piaget's tasks tap a transition to increasingly more complex cognitive operations that transcend the confines of specific schemas. Thus the capacity of the concrete operational child for decentering from any single element and making reversible transformations to compare these elements may enable the child to enjoy and comprehend logical incongruities in a variety of domains. (Whitt and Prentice 1977)

To cite one final study, P. McGhee designed an ingenious experimental program involving humorous anecdotes based on the piagetian principles of conservation of mass and weight and class inclusion. Here are two examples from his article:

*conservation of mass and weight*
Mr. Jones went into a restaurant and ordered a whole pizza for dinner.
When the waiter asked if he wanted it cut into 6 or 8 pieces, Mr. Jones
said: "Oh you better make it six; I could never eat eight!"
*class inclusion*
"Please stay out of the house today," Susie's mother said. "I have too
much work to do." "OK," said Susie as she walked to the stairs. "Where
do you think you're going?" her mother asked. "Well," said Susie, "if I
can't stay in the house, I'll just play in my room instead."

McGhee measures responses through smile-laugh ratings and funniness reports (which also fail to correlate for him), arriving at the
following conclusion:

> Children varying in the degree of (or length of time since) acquisition
> of conservation and class inclusion concepts were presented jokes in
> which the humor depicted derived from the violation of these two con-
> cepts. The results indicated that humor appreciation was 'greatest soon
> after the concepts were acquired, with reduced appreciation shown both
> by subjects who did not possess the concepts and by subjects who had
> mastered them several years previously. (McGhee 1976:420)

These results lend some specificity to the claim that progress in the
realm of child sociability is intertwined with progress in the child's
spontaneous psychological development. Particular forms of verbal
play (with their attendant cognitive moves) evidently presuppose a
substratum of broad intellectual capacities. Moreover, these forms
of play lose their hold on the child once the pertinent elements in
this substratum have been thoroughly incorporated into the child's
intellectual arsenal.

Below, in schematic form, I draw together the correlations noted
in our discussion of riddling competence.

age: five years
stage: preoperational
language model: phonological component dominant
riddling output: descriptive routines, preriddles
reversal: none
vehicle: diffuse forms, with appropriate textures

age: six years
stage: late preoperational
language model: phonological component still somewhat dominant
riddling output: descriptive routines, flawed and correct riddles proper
reversal: primarily homophonic, some anomaly (few comparisons)
vehicle: approaches traditional prototypes

age: seven years
stage: concrete operational
language model: parity of phonological and semantic components
riddling output: riddles proper, some descriptive routines
reversal: all kinds, including marked increase in polysemic forms
vehicle: traditional forms

age: eight years
stage: concrete operational
language model: increasingly focused on semantic component
riddling output: riddles proper
reversal: all kinds, decrease in homophonic forms
vehicle: traditional forms

# Enculturation 10

We conceive of the human infant as a cultureless being, a pulsating locus of life with genetic endowment conducive to the acquisition of culture, awaiting incorporation into the surrounding cultural nexus. In every domain of activity we can trace the gradual process whereby the infant's genetic potential is transformed into specific forms of cultural competence: as, for instance, the process transforming the infant's babbling, which touches upon the entire range of phonetic effects found in all natural languages, into the particular phonemic inventory of what is to become his native tongue. In another domain, we have observed in the previous chapter the leisurely process of riddle acquisition. In these domains of activity as in others, the learning of cultural competencies occurs through the dynamic interaction of the individual and his society. The individual observes and experiments, while others within his community contribute a steady stream of positive and negative feedback, as well as models of appropriate behavior. The cumulative product of these learning experiences is the culturally competent adult, who, in Ward Goodenough's formulation, is capable of operating in a manner acceptable to the members of his society (1964:36). Yet surely this determination is an arbitrary one, since we observe around us an incessant dialectic between individual and society, which does not magically cease when a person comes of age, marries, or even grows elderly.

There are two terms conventionally used to discuss the process of cultural acquisition to which I have just alluded: socialization and enculturation. The former has a more confined scope of reference, involving in particular the mechanics of the social dialectic between the individual and his society. Socialization is concerned with the techniques whereby first the family, later the peer group, and finally official and unofficial social authorities influence, contain, or control (depending on your ideological proclivity) the behavior of the individual. In the acquisition of riddling competence, the socialization process resides in the negotiation of riddling, the emergent adjustment of individual forays and strategies to socially sanctioned riddling etiquette. In learning to negotiate riddling, the child learns to formulate proper riddling vehicles, and eventually to produce the telling incongruity native to the genre, in order to participate actively as a valued riddler.

Enculturation invokes a rather different perspective on the same transformational process of infant potentiality into subsequent forms of cultural competence. Here we focus our attention on the categories of knowledge underpinning the competencies acquired through the socialization process. To quote Goodenough again: "Culture, being what people have to learn as distinct from their biological heritage, must consist of the end product of learning: knowledge" (Goodenough 1964:36). Enculturation, then, is defined as the process of induction, wherein the individual acquires competency in his own culture, or the kinds of knowledge requisite to fulfillment of recognized social roles. The central mechanisms in this process are described in terms of socialization. But certainly other mechanisms are at work as well. Our discussion of Jean Piaget's work in the development of intellection suggests that spontaneous, or genetically conditioned, development is to some degree independent of socialization. Internal cognitive processes, such as reflection, contemplation, rehearsal, and anticipation, are important mechanisms of enculturation capable of operating outside of the social arena.

Even prior to William Bascom's influential essay (1954), folklorists recognized an important didactic component to many of the materials they studied. But formulations of the didactic vector of folklore have generally confined themselves to those genres explicitly given over to instruction of the young, such as parables and proverbs, or ancillary instances where the didactic motive is salient, though not exclusive, as in the case of the fairy tale. I would like to propose here a much wider concept of the instructive potential of folklore, in line with our foregoing discussion of socialization and enculturation. In the realm of socialization, our treatment of children's riddling indicates that children gain practice with a considerable range of social skills in the riddling format. A central element in children's riddling is, as we have seen, the negotiation of personal strategy. In the competitive arena of peer-group interaction, children develop a series of skills enabling them to enter into the riddling. These are skills, I would suggest, that not only contribute to success and satisfaction in childhood, but also remain critical to the negotiation of social situations throughout the life of the individual. But apart from this signal role in socialization, children's riddling, and, by extension, the other forms of children's folklore, contribute mightily to the process of enculturation. The oral tradition, in the form of riddles, rhymes, and narratives, instructs, informs, and seasons the child in the entire spectrum of knowledge comprising culture. Let's take up the contribution of children's riddling to socialization and enculturation in more detail.

## SOCIALIZATION

Children's riddling is of course an inherently social activity. The partition of the riddle act into two roles, that of riddler and riddlee, insures the sociable character of riddling. Moreover, the generally competitive ethos of riddling (though descriptive routines are an exception here) lends a particular flavor to riddling sociability, specifically that of the contest. Not unlike the game of marbles, riddling is a game of skill with a loosely determined set of rules allowing for a good deal of situational interpretation. In this respect, we might note in passing, both games are models or analogues of an important class of real world experiences.

Zeroing in on the sociable character of riddling, we might make the fundamental observation that riddling entails the successful management of the conversational roles of riddler, riddlee, and audience. In learning to participate appropriately in riddling sessions, children acquire experience in the elaboration of collective interactional frames. In order to bring off a riddle act each child must conform to the scope of activity provided for the assumed role, and shape and time his moves in accordance with conventional riddling practice. Moreover, the interactional frame of riddling presupposes little or nothing in the way of common esoteric knowledge among riddlers. All that participants must hold in common is a common tongue and a common understanding of what it means to riddle. Thus riddling allows the child to expand his communicative network beyond the immediate circles of kin and close friends. New relationships are facilitated by the availability of riddling as a technique of communication between nonintimates. This function of riddling is especially visible in certain adult manifestations, such as the infamous turtles' club (Bauman 1970).

Riddling consolidates the child's developing familiarity with socially constructed events. The child must attend to the behavior of others and condition his own contribution to the emerging social edifice. Fundamental conversational etiquette, such as the sharing of turns, the avoidance of simultaneous talk, and the concerted attention to the tone and content of discourse, is indispensable to appropriate participation in riddling sessions. The collaborative ethos is implicitly present in all riddling, but particularly conspicuous in the descriptive routine. Here the children painstakingly engineer a correspondence between attributes and objects, and divination of the correct referent is taken as confirmation of a shared social vocabulary. In the riddle proper, this collaborative ethic still operates, though now the explicit ethos is competitive. But the riddle act, with its prescribed sequence of moves allocated among different individuals, could hardly come about without the cooperation of participants. In short, one of the socialization processes evident in riddling is the construction of cooperative interactional frames of the kind suitable for utilization by strangers and new acquaintances as well as family and friends.

In our discussion thus far we have stressed the social dimension of riddling, the cooperative ethos requisite to the construction of conversational edifice. Of equal significance is the scope allotted in riddling to the furtherance of individual goals and strategies. An obligatory adherence to basic interactional conventions interacts with each individual's personal stake in the encounter. Here I allude to the well-known dialectic between community values and the individual's private motives. Riddling sessions afford field training in the legitimate assertion of self within socially determined constraints. We have noted that occupation of the role of riddler confers on the occupant a temporary authority to which the other participants must submit. At the same time, divination of the correct answer to a riddle distinguishes the diviner as a riddling hero. These are strong incentives, permitting individual participants to shine in the eyes of their peers. But in order to secure the riddling limelight, the child must wield an arsenal of interactional skills enabling him to gain access to the floor at the appropriate juncture, and to hold the floor until his turn has run its course.

We return, then, to the negotiation of riddling, the struggle among individuals to control the development of riddling sessions through adroit manipulation of a mutually recognized system of riddling etiquette. In an earlier chapter we noted the range of moves open to each of the riddling personae, the ploys whereby they may advance their own tenure and restrict that of other participants. Instructive here are the resources available to the riddler to prolong his turn, and the countermoves used by riddlee to censure undue gluttony. Two levels of rules appeared to be in effect: one level restricted to the accomplishment of viable riddle acts; another level of a more legalistic nature dealing with infractions arising out of riddling hubris. An important point was that these frameworks were flexible enough to require interpretive implementation. At every moment riddling participants found it propitious to impose creatively their own constructions of the shared etiquette on the flow of events. In this manner personal motivations were effectively facilitated and constrained by the governing conventions; at the same time, these conventions received articulation in the clash of rival strategies.

Without even dealing with the specific content of riddling, we are able to assess its importance in primary socialization. In familiarizing children with the recurrent problematic of achieving private purposes through public means, the riddling session clearly prepares them for a multitude of analogous predicaments constituting perhaps the backbone of social existence. The artful combination of collaborative and competitive ethics, the ability to maneuver successfully within a partially defined social nexus, these are the very building blocks of social intercourse. Scholars have seen riddling as a model of interrogation, which it is, but in broader terms it models the great majority of life experiences. For only rarely do we encounter situations either fully determined or entirely lacking social definition. Generally speaking, our social lives engage us in precisely the dialectic of individual and society, of etiquette and strategy, that we find so admirably reflected in riddling sessions.

In discussing socialization and children's riddling, we have confined ourselves to the skills and understandings allowing people to act in concert to create social constructions such as the riddling session. But underlying these actions is a substratum of knowledge determining the particular content of this particular social construction. In taking up the unique content of riddling (as opposed to other, structurally analogous social constructions) we will enter the realm of enculturation as I have defined that term above. In making the transition between socialization and enculturation, we should stress the complementarity of one to the other. In regard to riddling, the socialization provided in this social arena is instrumental toward the refinement and mastery of incipient cultural competence. By the same token, the knowledge acquired through enculturation finds its expression through the channels of social intercourse. The social skills acquired through socialization and the conceptual skills acquired through enculturation are thus mutually dependent.

## ENCULTURATION

Pooling understandings garnered from a group of related academic disciplines, we might define enculturation as the process insuring that members of a given society acquire substantially the same basic perceptual schemata. This latter term is taken from cognitive psychology, especially the work of Ulric Neisser, whose thinking we will pause over for a moment here. Neisser envisions a perceptual cycle moving from schema, which directs exploration, to available information about the experiential world, which in turn modifies the initial schema. He defines the crucial term here as follows: "A schema is that portion of the entire perceptual cycle which is internal to the perceiver, modifiable by experience, and somehow specific to what is being perceived" (Neisser 1976:54). While these cognitive schemata are necessarily rooted in experience of the world, they also derive in part from innate genetic capacities, and eventually they acquire a certain stability and partial independence from immediate sensory data. Neisser notes that perceptual schemata serve as anticipations of likely or possible perceptual constellations, stored within the perceiver and activated by the appropriate cues originating in the experiential world or in the individual psyche itself. This separation of schemata from immediate sensory experience has a developmental disposition:

> At first, the child can only talk about things that he is actually perceiving and doing or that he anticipates in the immediate future. Perceptual schemata are firmly anchored to available information, and so are words. Later in development he learns to break the perceptual cycle, detaching his anticipations from the stimulus information that originally instigated and confirmed them, and enlisting them in other schemata for other reasons. (Neisser 1976:171)

It should not prove too controversial to stipulate at this point that Neisser's perceptual schemata are essentially the individual-based manifestation of what we have been referring to as cognitive or conceptual orders. All that remains to establish this correlation is to account for the cultural imprint on them, to grant them a social value. Neisser himself raises this question near the end of his book: "Schemata are developed by experience; everyone's experiences are different; therefore we must all be very different from one another. Since every person's perceptual history is unique we should all have unique cognitive structures, and the differences between us can only increase as we grow older and become more individualized" (Neisser 1976: 187). But there are, as he goes on to observe, certain factors mitigating against this psychological argument for solipsism. For one thing, we all begin with the same basic biological inheritance. Second, in broad terms, our experiences of the world do have a certain commonality. And finally, most significant from our point of view, we are born into a cultural milieu that regulates the development of schemata through a variety of formal and informal social channels. It is this third factor, least developed by Neisser, which ties in most directly to our own purposes. For I would construe the various formats of children's play, including that of riddling, as indispensable adjuncts to this social monitoring of schemata formation. In these settings children attend to proposed orderings of their peers and expose their own sense of conceptual order to the scrutiny of peer-group associates. Riddling sessions amply illustrate this process of schemata calibration at work.

The effect of this excursion into cognitive psychology is one of grounding our notion of cognitive orders in the individual and collective experience. Through constant exposure to the perceptual cycle, the individual eventually gains a detachable anticipatory handle on the flux of experience. These perceptual schemata are rooted in commerce with the experiential world, but they transcend experience in several ways. For one thing, they are stored in the individual psyche and can be brought under conscious scrutiny even in the absence of the appropriate sensory cues. For another, they have accommodated themselves to the community world view, conveyed to the individual through a variety of interactional formats. Virtually every social event witnessed or participated in has the capacity to mold the individual's developing schemata in accordance with collective attitudes and values. Finally, the perceptual schemata derive in part from the biological inheritance common to all members of the species. Certain innate capacities define the limits of perception and the schematization of perception. The end product of this fascinating interplay of genetic apparatus, sensory experience, and cultural patterning is the cognitive order housed in every member of a given society but nonetheless reflecting common scope and orientation.

A consideration of riddling and enculturation allows us to focus in on the mechanics responsible for the collective imprint on perceptual schemata. Cognitive orders are fashioned from perceptual schemata through the intervention of community models and pedagogics. Community pedagogics may be official and formal, like elementary school in our own society, or less official and formal, like the various play arenas frequented voluntarily by children. In the riddling session we have a pedagogic format that is entertaining in its own right. Children engage in riddling not to flatter any adult prerogative, but because they enjoy riddling. But this conspicuous pleasure factor should not obscure the instructional capacity of the genre.

Riddling, like many familiar artistic experiences, delights and instructs simultaneously. In this particular context, we are concerned with the contribution made by riddling toward converting individualistic perceptual schemata into socially distributed cognitive orders.

Let's first consider the descriptive routine, that collaborative effort to match attributes and objects. In learning to pose and solve descriptive routines, children are rehearsing in a public forum their incipient control over experiential flux. Items can be extracted from experience, named, catalogued, described in terms of essential properties. We note then that riddling, even in its simplest manifestation, can only proceed once perceptual schemata have begun to detach themselves from their immediate sensory cues. The descriptive routine, with its concentration on the most ubiquitous tokens of everyday experience, with its focus on the common empirical qualities of these tokens, and with its tendency to classify similar and dissimilar tokens, is an excellent instrument of enculturation. Here the children hammer out a social vocabulary, a lexicon enfranchising the concerns and orientations endemic to their social and cultural habitat. Descriptive routines thereby provide an ideal forum for the testing and adjustment of idiosyncratic perceptual schemata in the presence of socially articulated cognitive orders.

The descriptive routine facilitates the acquisition of cognitive orders in two ways: first, it accelerates the process of detachment of perceptual schemata from immediate perceptual cues; and second, it introduces a collective constraint on the elaboration of cognitive orders. What might be said of the riddle proper, with its inherently subversive tendencies? In the first place, I think we can attribute a continuation of the two mechanisms already described in descriptive routines to riddles proper. In the riddle, children continue to fashion a social vocabulary based on idiosyncratic perception but transcending this foundation in its detachability from experience and in its tempering to community standards. However, riddles are not mere rehearsals of cognitive orders; often enough they parade the cognitive orders only to violate or rearrange them. It is essentially the block element, that deliberate grain of confusion or incongruity, that differentiates the riddle from the descriptive routine.

As we observed in an earlier chapter, several modes of cognitive reversal appear in riddles. A good many riddles focus attention on inconsistencies in the linguistic code: a single label may apply to more than one referent. The word "mustang," for example, may refer to a member of the horse family, or to a fashionable automobile. Clearly this sort of linguistic duplicity is inimical to the formulation of the social vocabulary we have been speaking of. How can we label and define our shared categories of experience if our medium of communication is playing us tricks of this kind? Other reversals involve reference to counterfactual entities, such as the red rockeater, which transcend our actual experience of the world. If cognitive categories are ultimately translations of perceptual experience, what sense can we make of these liminal creatures never actually encountered in experience? Finally, some riddle reversals draw our attention to real world paradox and anomaly, which constitute a threat to the entire notion of cognitive orders based on experience. In a series of riddles centering on the notion of identity, we found a profound challenge to the commonsense notion that the objects we label and perceive as recurrent in our experience actually belong to a superordinate class of objects possessing a common identity. In these and other manifestations, riddles proper appear to adopt a posture of hostility to the entire enterprise of cognitive order.

We have come now upon a major turning point in our analysis. In order to deal with the subversive character of riddles proper, apparently inimical to simple formulations of cognitive order, we have recourse to a pair of divergent, apparently irreconcilable hypotheses. According to one line of thinking, the apparent challenge to cognitive order contained in riddles proper is illusory, since the fractured orders are finally transcended at a higher level of abstraction. James Fernandez (1977) employs the term "creative transcendence" to describe this move from lower to higher levels of cognitive integration. He asserts that riddles "edify by puzzlement," and through them we gain access to an overarching order transcending more local and particular cognitive orders. Let us look at one of our riddles in this light:

A thousand lights in a dish, what is it?    *The stars in the sky.*

This riddle proposes metaphorical association between lights and stars, and their respective containers, a dish and the sky, on the basis of obvious perceptual continuities: emission or reflection of light in one case and concavity in the other. In terms of semantic field, we have a crossover between two normally discrete domains, that of the natural world (stars and sky) and manufactured items (lights and dish). Pursuing Fernandez's suggestion of cognitive integration, we could stipulate that this riddle concerns a transcendent set of relationships found in many different perceptual domains, namely the inclusion of atomistic units in an embracing concavity. Other analogues present themselves: eggs in a basket, peas in a pod, fish in a pond, etc. This riddle, with its apparent violation of cognitive orders segmenting the natural world and the manufactured product into separate domains, in actuality keys us to the existence of underlying relationships permeating all domains of experience. This analysis is congruent with an approach articulated by Elli Kongas-Maranda (1971a, b, c), in which the term "superset" corresponds to this group of ultimate principles underlying diverse experiential realms.

Another line of thinking suggests a rather different interpretation of the same material, and more importantly, attributes a strikingly different function to the genre of riddling. In advancing our second hypothesis we take at face value the apparent fracturing of cognitive order in riddles proper. Riddles do systematically confound such clarity of thought and expression as we are able to achieve. Semantic fields appropriately separated in our cognitive orders are brought into intimate association in the riddle, causing ineffable alternate taxonomies to flicker into existence. In our consideration of the familiar riddle

What has legs but cannot walk?    *A chair*.

we saw that a relationship between mobile and immobile tokens was herein countenanced, though this merely formal association proved to be less viable than the fusion of form and function contained in the conventional taxonomic dispensation. Following the present line of thought, we might adduce that metaphors of this kind are disruptive and have the effect of imputing a relative or arbitrary status to our cognitive orders.

Other sorts of riddles appear to operate along similar lines. A series of riddles focusing on the ambiguities of identity undermines some of the most fundamental principles whereby we interpret and order our experience. Recall the following instance:

> What has the head of a cat, the tail of a cat, and the fur of a cat but is not a cat?    *A kitten.*

While the lexical availability of "kitten" facilitates this routine, the actual focus lies on the formidable paradox: something (the kitten) is both A (a cat) and not A (not a cat). These and other fundamental cognitive principles are challenged in riddles, again with the effect of signalling the conventional and arbitrary status of these basic taxonomic devices. Surely riddles with their reversals are intent upon the fragmentation of cognitive order, in a concerted effort to force a reinterpretation of the ontological status of our conceptual systems.

Before we attempt to reconcile these conflicting hypotheses, or perhaps choose between them, let's take a peek at the contrasting enculturative role each of them provides for riddling. If we view riddles as conducive to the perception of an overarching order, as a means of gaining entry to a galaxy of principles and relationships contained in every perceptual domain but confined to none, then the enculturative role of riddles proper is complementary to that of the descriptive routine. The latter provides an initial grasp on the lower, more localized cognitive domains. Riddles proper then lead the cultural initiate into a more abstract conceptual domain, based on the lower orders but transcending them. In this formulation, enculturation in the riddling context is a continuous, cumulative process. One learns first to identify the building blocks (the lower-level cognitive orders) and then to assemble these blocks into appropriate larger constructions (the overarching, or higher-level orders). Children's riddling could prove instrumental at both stages of this unilinear process.

Moreover, this line of thinking affords us some insight into the distribution of riddling traditions in terms of societal types and even age levels within societies.[1] Fernandez (1977) maintains that riddling should flourish primarily in societies possessed of a sense of some coherent, overarching conceptual order. Obviously, this trait would be a necessary rather than a sufficient condition for riddling, since many societies (the Amerindian group, for example) are reportedly without major riddling traditions even though they are evidently possessed of the overarching cognitive order. Thus we can attribute the marginal status of riddling in our own society (among adults at any event) to the absence of this pervasive sense of ultimate order. The importance of riddling among children in our society might then indicate a belief in this quarter that experience does eventually become integrated into higher-level orders. Or it could derive from a child's model of reality, which does manage a coherent world view animated by a superset of integrating relationships and principles. Language acquisition studies indicate that the child's linguistic performance emanates from a coherent language model rather than from random imitation of adult performance (Brown 1975). The child's early language model is internally consistent even though it disregards or neutralizes some of the more subtle syntactic processes necessarily accounted for in adult models. Perhaps the child's incipient conceptual system, his model of reality or experience, possesses an analogous internal consistency gained at the expense of exhaustive coverage of the entire phenomenological field. A supposition of this sort, which in itself seems neither implausible nor particularly compelling, would allow us to interpret children's riddling as a quest for an overarching order to experience. Riddling then, with its reversal of conventional understandings, serves as an enculturative device pointing to a transcendent order permeating the particular domains of perception.

Our other hypothesis, that riddles proper are fragmenting rather than integrating mechanisms, provides us with quite another outlook on enculturation in riddling. In this view we encounter a profound discontinuity between the descriptive routine and the riddle proper. The latter teaches the child that these cognitive orders, built from perceptual schemata with such care, are perhaps less sturdy and durable than one might have thought. The perceptual cycle, with its strict experiential orientation, constantly provides data not readily assimilated into our cognitive systems, which necessarily reify something that is intrinsically continuous and dynamic. The riddle, by drawing our attention to linguistic and conceptual anomaly, encourages us to place a proper construction on the whole concept of cognitive orders. These emerge as tentative, temporary, imperfect versions of experience, constantly subject to modification or outright negation in the light of contradictory empirical data.

From the vantage point of enculturation, two complementary functions could be attributed to this subversion of cognitive order. In the first place, we could argue that the children are learning to adopt a flexible attitude toward reconstructions of experience and thereby acquiring a mental agility that will serve them well as they continue to encounter ambiguous situations calling for equivocation. Ian Hamnet provides a kindred rationale: "Classification is a pre-requisite of the intelligible ordering of experience, but if conceptual categories are reified, they become obstacles rather than means to a proper understanding and control of both physical and social reality. The ability to construct categories and also to transcend them is central to adaptive learning" (Hamnet 1967:385). Hamnet views riddling as ideally suited to the inculcation of a proper understanding of classification and its limits, the paradoxical need to classify and to transcend classification, in order to gain control over physical and social reality.

A second function legitimately attaching to riddles as devices of fragmentation is the invigoration of cognition. Our cognitive orders, our social vocabulary, serve us well in a great many pragmatic situations. As any child would attest, one must know the difference between an elephant and a loaf of bread in order to perform the simplest of social errands. Because they are expedient and, what is more, reassuring, the cognitive orders are taken seriously in most contexts. Here I think is one explanation of the extreme reaction to puns and double entendres cropping up in serious conversational settings: they question the efficiency of a code held in sober esteem as an instrument of communication and contemplation. It is only in the skewed environment of art and play that one may trifle with impunity with our basic codes of cognition and expression. As Morse Peckham (1967) has pointed out, the artistic setting is one that is insulated from the ordinary world by virtue of a conventional understanding that what transpires in art is one step removed from reality. Within this insulated environment, clearly marked off from everyday reality by physical barriers (the art museum, the frame around the painting, the stage, etc.) or by verbal or other conventions (the fairy tale's "Once upon a time . . . "), the artist or player (the riddler too) focuses attention on the very anomalies likely to be repressed or scorned in normal social commerce. Along with Hamnet, Peckham discerns an adaptive role to the arts, maintaining that "art is rehearsal for the orientation which makes innovation possible" (1967:314). In addition, he poses a question more pertinent to the point under discussion: "Did man create art in order to satisfy a physiologic need for a more stimulating environment than the order-directed social environment offers?" (1967:314).

I would not attempt to answer this question, which seems to me a bit too grandiose and inappropriately aimed at the environment rather than at our conceptualization of it. Instead, talking around his question, I would argue that riddles are indeed a form of art, set off from normal conversation by virtue of stylistic and semantic traits discussed in earlier chapters, and that they do breathe new life into familiar conceptual systems by reminding us of the experiential interstices not adequately addressed in these systems. We have seen that the riddle makes the familiar strange; it zeros in on the most intimate realms of experience, the body itself, the immediate home environment, and imbues these quotidian tokens with new power by drawing in unconventional associative networks in which they participate. In the process, riddles throw into question the assumed efficacy of our cognitive and communicative codes.

In an earlier chapter, I established that riddles were cultural devices geared to the exploration of the limitations of culture. By scrutinizing our cognitive orders, our verbal instruments, and even our basic perceptual guides, riddles force us to confront the inadequacy of culture as a translation of experience. There is always more to experience, more diversity, more resonance, more particularity, than can be captured in any cultural system. This is a fact that can be highly threatening, and is undoubtedly productive of ritual cleansing in some societies. Individuals who have strayed beyond the physical or cultural boundaries of a society may require ritual purification, as is the case with sinners in Christian societies, and hunters, to cite only one of many available examples, in certain tribal societies (see Harner 1972). Riddling thus evinces some affinity with ritual and with a range of aesthetic experiences geared toward contact with the extra-cultural. In the insulated context of riddling, children and others explore the limitations of culture. This observation is easily stated in terms of the culture/nature dichotomy. If nature represents the original source of our perceptual experience, and culture those orderings we impose upon it, then riddles inspect the transcendence of culture by nature. For there will always be a disparity between the wealth of experience and the poverty of schematization, and riddles allow us to peruse this disparity without divesting ourselves of our conceptual tools and orders, which after all have proven pragmatic value.

In pursuing some of the implications of our second hypothesis, we have entered into the problematic of cultural inconsistency. In a paraphrasing of Edward Sapir, we might observe that all cultures leak; that is, they present a myriad of ambiguous or incongruous facets, either at the perceptual or conceptual level. There is considerable evidence that members of culture, much like speakers of languages, tend to ignore these disturbing facets in everyday commerce (Festinger 1968). But a growing inventory of ethnographic evidence indicates that in the appropriate forum, specifically aesthetic and ritual, people confront either directly or indirectly these perceptual and conceptual anomalies. One of the clearer statements of this position is Claude Lévi-Strauss's treatment of mythology. Lévi-Strauss views myth as a kind of symposium meant to deal with some basic cultural anomaly or inconsistency. Thus, for example, he interprets the Oedipus myth as follows:

> The myth has to do with the inability, for a culture which holds the belief that mankind is autochthonous . . . to find a satisfactory transition between this theory and the knowledge that human beings are actually born from the union of man and woman. Although the problem obviously cannot be solved, the Oedipus myth provides a kind of logical tool which relates the original problem—born from one or born from two?—to the derivative problem: born from different or born from same? By a correlation of this type, the overrating of blood relations

is to the underrating of blood relations as the attempt to escape autoch-
thony is to the impossibility to succeed in it. Although experience con-
tradicts theory, social life validates cosmology by its similarity of structure. Hence cosmology is true. (Lévi-Strauss 1967:212)

Without entering into the intricacies of the argument, we surmise that
Lévi-Strauss attributes to this myth (and to myth in general) the function of exploring inconsistency between experience and conceptual
schemata through the construction of analogies or correlations. Our
second hypothesis, that riddles are devices of fragmentation, would
lead us to assign riddling to this family of cultural mechanisms dedicated to the exploration of cultural inconsistency. And our reference
to Morse Peckham's theory of art suggests that this form of exploration may have both adaptive value for the society and deep psychic
significance for the individual.

Our exposition of the two hypotheses is now complete. Each of
them has something of interest to contribute to our picture of riddling as enculturative device. In one instance we attend to riddling
as a handmaiden of order, marking off a set of archetypical relationships underlying local manifestations of order over the entire spectrum
of experiential domains. In the other, riddles are viewed as inimical
to order, and are thought to operate in such a fashion as to imply
strongly the relativity of all conceptual systems. In either view, we
find a significant enculturative role, that of completing the process of
building conceptual schemata out of the experiential base, or that of
promoting mental agility and charging with vitality the ordinary tokens
of experience. Again, each of our hypotheses entails a plausible theory
of child mentation. In one instance, the child's classificatory ambitions
are such that he anticipates an overarching order to experience and
constructs a simplified model of reality imbued with an orderliness
lacking in the more comprehensive adult models. Our second hypothesis encourages us to view the child as a cultural neophyte, closer than
the adult to the particularity of experience, less completely assimilated to cultural models of experience, and thereby endowed with an
uncanny access to the interstices of cultural systems.

The time has come to seek reconciliation of the two analytical vectors we have pursued thus far in this chapter. As a first move in this direction, let us inspect the two sets of riddles presented below:

*Set 1*

What has teeth but doesn't eat?   *A comb.*

What kind of head grows in the garden?   *A head of lettuce.*

It gots blue and white and two cherries on top.   *A police car.*

A thousand lights in a dish.   *Stars.*

*Set 2*

How do you keep a skunk from smelling?   *You hold his nose.*

What did they call Batman and Robin when they got run over?
   *Flatman and ribbon.*

I can see it and you cannot.   *The back of your head.*

It is taller sitting than standing.   *A dog.*

The first set of riddles apparently conforms to our first hypothesis: they provide a vista onto overarching order. Each of these riddles establishes a metaphorical association between items located in widely separated conceptual domains. The metaphorical association may be conventional, as in the first two items, or novel, as in the last two items. But in either case, the riddle enables us to perceive a structural affinity between items not normally conjoined in our thinking. A common anatomical principle is seen to inform diverse realms of experience. The incongruities of this first set may be said to resolve themselves at a higher level of abstraction.

The second set does not admit of a similar interpretation. Here the incongruity, whether linguistic as in the first two riddles or conceptual as in the last two, points relentlessly in the direction of inefficiency in our linguistic and conceptual codes. Try as I might, I find no hint of an overarching order implicit in these equivocations. On the contrary, the second set of riddles constitutes a challenge to the entire notion of order. Thus the duplicity of meaning attached to the word "smell," which can simultaneously take on the sense "emit an odor" and "perceive an odor," violates the principle of a one-to-one correspondence between sound and meaning in natural languages. By the same token, the peculiar status of the dog, who is in fact taller sitting than standing, violates a perceptual regularity readily formulated as a conceptual proposition: that creatures are taller in the standing position. As the riddle suggests, the data are not quite so tidy; only in the case of creatures whose vertical axis predominates will this proposition hold.

It appears, then, that our corpus of riddles differentially establishes each of our two hypotheses. Referring back to our classification of reversals in riddles, worked out in chapter 5, we can see that the two hypotheses divide our corpus into two units: those routines utilizing polysemy, or metaphor, as the means of reversal; and those utilizing homophony or perceptual and conceptual paradox as the means of reversal. Those riddles built out of metaphor, whether conventional or novel, are capable of signalling an overarching order to experience. Two items brought into metaphorical association establish a principle of commonality belonging to an archetypical set of transcendent relationships or principles. But those riddles based on accidental phonetic coincidence, or on perceptual or cognitive anomaly, deliver us into an unresolved confrontation with linguistic or conceptual inadequacy. In short, children's riddling amply illustrates both hypotheses, and evidently two kinds of learning are going on simultaneously: some riddles teach the children of an overarching order comprehending diverse realms of experience; others instruct them to beware of overly simplistic renditions of experience. Both lessons figure significantly in the process of enculturation, in the first instance rounding off the child's indoctrination into the logic of classification, and in the second, instilling in him a certain flexibility in regard to classificatory schemes.

Let us place our findings into cross-cultural perspective for a moment. While comparison among riddling traditions is fraught with all the uncertainties of any other form of ethnology, essentially stemming from the incompatibility of different linguistic and cultural systems, there appears to be considerable insight to be gained in this instance. Roger Janelli quantified the presence of metaphor in two riddling traditions, the Lozi of Africa and English oral tradition, based on the collections of D. F. Gowlett (1966) and Archer Taylor (1951) respectively. Janelli assures us that the sample he worked with from Taylor's compendium is appropriately representative of the entire corpus (Janelli 1970). To these figures I have added a few measures of my own, producing the picture in table 7.

TABLE 7. *Percentage of Riddles Incorporating Metaphor and Other Comparisons*

| Group | Percent Metaphoric | Number of Riddles | Source |
|---|---|---|---|
| Lozi | 80 | 109 | Gowlett (1966) |
| Burma | 78 | 23 | Sien and Dundes (1964) |
| English oral tradition | 53 | 35 | Taylor (1951) |
| Los Angeles high school students | 26 | 70 | Schlesinger (1960) |
| Austin chicano children | 33 | 39 | McDowell |
| Austin anglo children | 33 | 36 | McDowell |

There emerges from these figures a correlation between traditional societies and a high level of metaphorically motivated riddles. The two traditional societies included in the table above, the Lozi of Africa and the Burmese, show a notably high proportion of metaphorical riddles. Taylor's index of riddles in English oral tradition is still predominantly composed of metaphorical riddles, though the proportions of metaphorical and nonmetaphorical riddles are more nearly comparable. The sample of riddles collected from high school students in Los Angeles in 1957 reveals a remarkable drop in the proportion of metaphorical riddles, which here constitute a minority of the total riddling sample. The anglo and chicano materials collected in Austin during the period 1975–76 fall very close to the low mark established by the Los Angeles sample. In our own Austin samples, as in the Los Angeles sample, it is the riddle based on semantically unmotivated language play that has stepped in to take up the slack. Riddles based on language play account for an even 50 percent of the Los Angeles sample, 49 percent of the anglo sample from Austin, and 40 percent of our chicano sample. In spite of the vagaries of cross-cultural comparison, we appear to have hit on a significant correlation, a matching of traditional society with predominantly metaphorically composed riddling traditions, and a complementary matching of urban, industrialized society with a predominance of nonmetaphorical, especially linguistically constituted riddling traditions.

Enculturation by riddling in the modern, industrial context thus involves a rather different focus from the same process carried out in traditional society. The latter setting exhibits a conspicuous concentration on what James Fernandez calls "creative transcendence," the distillation of integrative factors operating over a range of experiential sectors. In the urban industrial scene the emphasis has shifted to concentration on the limitations of cultural systems. A substantial minority of the total riddling output still retains the traditional transcendent function, but the greater portion of the riddling corpus is now devoted to the specification of inadequacy in linguistic and conceptual systems.

The implications of this contrast in enculturation by riddling in traditional and modern societies are legion and for the most part beyond the scope of the present study. But let me suggest a few perspectives that appear to be worthy of further consideration. First, viewing riddling as an expressive model, we would expect that the contrast we have discovered here should communicate something concerning the society housing each kind of riddling tradition. The notion here, developed in a series of publications by John Roberts and various associates (see Roberts, Arth, and Bush 1959), is that play activities are modelled on scenarios and contingencies possessing cultural saliency. The corollary to this proposition is, of course, that play activities prepare individuals for roles and postures they will assume outside the play arena. While it might be tempting to view riddles as models of interrogation, the foregoing analysis allows us to bestow upon them a more lofty vocation. Riddles in the modern, industrial society serve as models of synthetic and analytic thinking. They encourage children to discover the archetypical set of commonalities binding diverse experiential realms into a single, coherent world view; and at the same time, they require children to confront the tentative status of conceptual systems, thereby fostering a flexibility of cognition evidently of some utility in a great many cultural settings. It is a significant observation (which cannot be more fully explored here) that traditional societies foster exclusively synthetic conceptualization in the riddling format, if our brief excursion into the cross-cultural data did indeed produce reliable results.[2]

In the final analysis, we are led to speculate that the familiar conditions of the contemporary urban experience, with the constant shuffling of individuals from one community to another, and with the development of a cosmopolitan culture drawn from an enormous range of concurrent and historical human experience, have created a society with a particular sort of cosmological orientation and a particular set of routine social occasions. In short, the former is characterized by the absence of a highly integrated, traditional world view; and the latter brings into prominence a set of social skills founded on extreme conceptual flexibility. It is within this specific cultural context that we must locate the riddling corpus we have examined in this study, never losing sight of its roots in quite another cultural ambience, the largely rural and agrarian societies from which the contemporary global village has only comparatively recently emerged.

# Appendix

Note: In presenting these samples I have included only a portion of the total corpus. Flawed routines and variants of included routines have been neglected, as has the major part of the extensive inventory of preriddle production. The two corpora, chicano and anglo, are segregated into separate lists. By each entry I report the age and sex of the child performing the routine, even though the latter variable did not correlate with any noticeable patterns of riddling performance. When the word "several" appears, it indicates that the routine in question was performed by more than a few children. The organization of each sample follows the analytical principles established in the various chapters of the book:

> Interrogative ludic routines
> > Descriptive routines
> > > Focusing on classification or orthodox definition
> > > Focusing on instrumentality
> > > Focusing on causality
> > Riddles proper
> > > Homophonic
> > > Conventional polysemy
> > > Radical polysemy
> > > Anomaly
> > > Catches and routines of victimization

It will be noted that the chicano sample is more finely calibrated into the precise divisions given above. The anglo sample, deriving from a secondary corpus, was not sufficiently extensive to permit an identical mode of organization. The annotations are not meant to be exhaustive, but rather to establish the general currency in oral tradition of the great majority of riddles proper performed by the children of Austin. One final point: some of the allocations of particular routines to particular categories are somewhat arbitrary, since a number of routines could find a home in one or another category with equal comfort. But reading down the columns one perceives a broad consistency of type within each category, establishing to my satisfaction the utility of the present scheme.

243

## A SAMPLING OF INTERROGATIVE LUDIC ROUTINES PERFORMED BY THE CHICANO CHILDREN

I. DESCRIPTIVE ROUTINES

*A. Focusing on classification or orthodox definition*

1. What's red?  *A rose.* (girl, 7)
2. What has four legs and a pico sticking out?  *A pig.* (boy, 5)
3. What's brown and gots a hole in it?  *A doughnut.* (boy, 7)
4. What's round and it gots a lot of jelly?  *A jelly doughnut.* (girl, 7)
5. What's square and it gots a point on the top?  *A house.* (girl, 7)
6. What's an animal que gots two big horns?  *A longhorn.* (girl, 7)
7. What's brown and black and it comes with little things and it has channels?  *A radio.* (girl, 8)
8. What's brown and its round and it gots the leaves on it?  *A tree.* (girl, 7)
9. What's brown and its round and its made out of sticks?  *A bird nest.* (girl, 7)
10. What's a big old round thing and it gots water in it?  *A swimming pool.* (girl, 8)
11. What throws water off?  *Elephants.* (girl, 7)
12. It's a little circle in your stomach.  *Belly button.* (boy, 8)
13. It's in a hole, what do you call it, in the zoo?  *A guinea pig.* (boy, 8)
14. What's in the dirt and does a hole and then it's inside the hole?  *Ant.* (boy, 7)
15. What is green and has lumps on top?  *An alligator.* (boy, 8)
16. It was a president, the seventeenth president.  *Abraham Lincoln.* (boy, 8)
17. What's the one that gives you milk and it says "moo"?  *Cow.* (girl, 7)
18. What's red and it gives water to the flowers that are planted?  *A hose.* (girl, 7)
19. What's orange and has a green thing on top?  *Lamp.* (boy, 6)
20. ¿Qué es blanco y blanco?  *Vestido de novia.* (girl, 8)
21. ¿Qué tiene una cosa aquí y que no tiene piernas y que va asina?  *Una culebra.* (boy, 8)
22. What has eight wheels and rolls?  *Roller skates.* (boy, 7)
23. What has two wheels and pedals?  *Bicycle.* (boy, 6)
24. What has four wheels, no pedals, and a steering wheel?  *A car.* (boy, 7)
25. What has four legs and can run?  *A mustang.* (boy, 6)
26. What has three wheels and pedals?  *A tricycle.* (boy, 7)
27. What has two legs, it can walk?  *A monkey.* (boy, 5)
28. What has long legs and it's hard to walk?  *A seagull.* (boy, 6)

29. What has two seats, four wheels, and they can roll?    *A car.* (boy, 7)
30. What has lots of windows and they can fly?    *Airplane.* (boy, 6)
31. What are those little clocks and it's in your car?    *A dragger.* (boy, 7)
32. What's red and white, and doesn't do nothing, and has a stick down its side, and the red and white thing is against the stick?    *A flag.* (boy, 6)

*B. Focusing on causality*

33. Why did the gato and perro fight?    *They hate each other.* (girl, 7)
34. How come a rabbit goes into a hole?    *Cause she eats carrots a lot.* (girl, 5)
35. ¿Por qué come tanto los elephants?    *They want to get strong.* (boy, 6)
36. How come the pig likes to get in the mud?    *Cause he likes to take a bath in the mud.* (girl, 6)
37. How come the rabbit eat a lot?    *Cause he wants to get fat.* (boy, 6)

*C. Focusing on instrumentality*

38. How come you have to wear your pants?    *So your underwear won't show.* (boy, 6)
39. Why do you need to wear your shirt?    *So they won't see your chi chi.* (boy, 6)
40. How come you need hair?    *To not be bald headed.* (boy, 7)
41. Why do you need a moustache?    *So you won't be a* bolillo. (boy, 8) (*bolillo* equals gringo)
42. How come you need a car?    *To drive it, stupid.* (boy, 6)

II. RIDDLES PROPER

*A. Homophony*

43. Why does the little boy put ice in his father's bed?    *He wants an iced pop.* (girl, 7)
       Ainsworth, *SFQ* 1962, #301.
44. What can you make with a banana?    *Slippers.* (boy, 8)
       Withers and Benet 1954 (121).
45. What did Dela wear?    *New jerseys.* (boy, 7).
46. Which bus crosses the ocean?    *Columbus.* (girl, 8)
       Loomis, *WF* 1949 [California, 1869].
       Ainsworth, *SFQ* 1962, #265.
47. What's black and white and red all over?    *A newspaper.* (several)
       Parsons, *JAF* 1917, #8 [North Carolina].
       Waugh, *JAF* 1918, #705 [Canada].
       Johnson, *JAF* 1921, #67 [Antigua].
       Parsons, *JAF* 1921, #44 [South Carolina].

Bacon and Parsons, *JAF* 1922 [Virginia].

Parsons, *JAF* 1925 [Bermuda].

Fauset, *JAF* 1928 [Philadelphia].

Boggs, *JAF* 1934 [North Carolina].

Taylor 1951 #1498A.

Brown 1952 [North Carolina, 1920s].

Abrahams, *KFQ* 1962 [black, Philadelphia].

Barrick, *KFQ* 1963 [common before 1910].

48. How do you keep an elephant from charging? *Take away his credit card.* (boy, 8)

Barrick, *SFQ* 1964 #67.

Abrahams and Dundes, *PR* 1969, #22.

49. How do you keep a skunk from smelling? *You cut off his nose.* (boy, 7)

Schlesinger, *WF* 1960 [Los Angeles, California].

50. What did the big firecracker say to the little firecracker? *"My pop is bigger than your pop."* (boy, 7)

Halpert, *JAF* 1943 [black, New Jersey].

Withers and Benet 1954, #132.

51. What did the rug say to the floor? *"Don't move, I've got you covered."* (boy, 7)

Withers and Benet 1954, #132.

Abrahams, *KFQ* 1962 [black, Philadelphia].

Ainsworth, *SFQ* 1962, #326.

52. What did the wall say to the other wall? *"Meet you at the corner."* (girl, 8)

Withers and Benet 1954, #132.

53. Oro no es, plata no es, ¿qué es? *Plátano.* (several)

Gatschet, *JAF* 1889 [Texas-Mexican border].

Mason, *JAF* 1916 [Puerto Rico].

Guadalupe Noguera, *JAF* 1918 [Mexico].

Recinos, *JAF* 1918 [Guatemala].

Garrido de Boggs 1955 [reports variants from Santo Domingo, Spain, Argentina, Chile, Cuba, El Salvador, New Mexico].

54. Why don't ducks fly upside down? *They quack up.* (boy, 7)

55. What's the difference of "deer" and "dear"? *One is like dear mother, and the other one's deer, animal deer.* (girl, 8)


*B. Conventional Polysemy*

56. What has legs but cannot walk? *A chair.* (girl, 7)

Parsons, *JAF* 1925, #84 [Bermuda].

Taylor 1951, #305.

57. Four feet on the floor, four feet above, what is it?   *A cat on a chair.*
    (girl, 8).
    Taylor 1951, #463.
58. What has a tongue and can't talk?   *A shoe.* (girl, 7)
    Farr, *JAF* 1935 [Tennessee].
    Taylor 1951, #296.
59. What has 82 or 83 keys and can play?   *A piano.* (boy, 7)
    Brown 1952 [North Carolina, 1920s].
60. What's a tornado?   *Mother Nature doing the twist.* (boy, 7)
61. How can you make fire with two sticks?   *Be sure one is a match.*
    (girl, 8)

*C. Radical Polysemy*

62. Ten boys wear hats on the back of the head.   *Ten fingers.* (boy, 7)
    Parsons, *JAF* 1917 [Bahamas].
    Taylor 1951, #989.
63. It gots blue and white and two cherries on top.   *A police car.* (several)
    Winslow, *KFQ* 1966.
64. How come mans always shave a lot?   *Cause grass always grows on
    them.* (girl, 7)
65. What are polka dots on your face?   *Pimples.* (boy, 8)
66. What's like a turtle, it has a shell like a turtle, and it's attached to the
    ground?   *A mushroom.* (boy, 7)
67. A thousand lights in a dish.   *Stars.* (girl, 8)
68. Una vieja larga y seca, que le escurre la manteca.   *La vela.* (several)
    Espinosa, *JAF* 1916 [New Mexico], different solution.
    Mason, *JAF* 1916, #552 [Puerto Rico].
    Garrido de Boggs 1955 [reports variants in Santo Domingo, Chile,
    Argentina].
69. The tree has only two leaves, what is it?   *A man and his ears.* (girl, 8)

*D. Anomaly*

70. What's yellow and black?   *A bus full of niggers.* (boy, 7)
71. What's up in the sky and lives in the sky?   *God.* (boy, 6)
72. What has two eyes, a mouth, and no ears?   *A fish.* (boy, 8)
73. What does kangaroos has that nobody else has?   *Baby kangaroos.*
    (boy, 6)
    Clark, *SFQ* 1961 [North Carolina], (dogs and puppies).
    Ainsworth, *SFQ* 1962, #209 (dogs and puppies).
    Barrick, *SFQ* 1964 [noted on Hollywood Palace, ABC TV, Feb,
    1964], (elephants and baby elephants).

74. Redondito redondón, no tiene tapa ni tapón.  *Un anillo.* (girl, 8)
    (Little round, big round, it has neither lid nor stopper.  *A ring.*)
       Gatschet, *JAF* 1889 [Texas-Mexican border].
       Espinosa, *JAF* 1916 [New Mexico], different solution.
75. I can see it and you cannot.  *The back of your head.* (girl, 8)
76. It is taller sitting than standing.  *A dog.* (girl, 8)
77. A riddle a riddle a hole in the middle.  *A ring.* (boy, 7)
       Withers and Benet 1954, #13.
78. You can carry it wherever you go.  *Your name.* (girl, 8)
79. What's strongest?  *Love.* (girl, 8)
80. One word riddle.  *Invisible.* (girl, 8)
81. What is it we always wants and forget when it comes to us?  *Sleep.*
    (boy, 7)
       Taylor 1951, #1576 [oral, Chicago].
82. What's darker than a crow?  *Its feathers.* (girl, 8)
       Brown 1952, #149 [North Carolina, 1920s].
       Barrick, *KFQ* 1963 [common before 1905].
83. What goes up and never comes down?  *Your age.* (girl, 8)
       Taylor 1951, #141 [the solution is "smoke"].
       Schlesinger, *WF* 1960 [Los Angeles, California].
       Abrahams, *KFQ* 1962 [black, Philadelphia].
84. What is black from the outside and white from the inside?  *Niggers.*
    (girl, 8)
85. What goes up slower and comes down faster?  *The fire.* (girl, 8)
86. What's so big and eats rocks?  *A rockeater.* (boy, 7)
       Clark, *SFQ* 1961, #101.
       Winslow, *KFQ* 1966, #92.
87. Why do elephants have flat feets?  *Because jumping over the palm
    trees.* (boy, 7)

*E. Catches and Routines of Victimization*
88. Why do birds fly south?  *It's too far to walk.* (several)
       Ainsworth, *SFQ* 1962, #371.
89. What's black and white and red all over?  *An embarrassed zebra.*
    (several)
       Ainsworth, *SFQ* 1962, #196.
       Barrick, *KFQ* 1963, #46 [Pennsylvania].
       Leventhal and Gray, *WF* 1963, #148.
90. Why did the chicken cross the road?  *To get to the other side.* (sev-
    eral)
       Waugh, *JAF* 1918 [Canada].
       Perkins, *JAF* 1922 [black, New Orleans].

Bacon and Parsons, *JAF* 1922 [Virginia].
Fauset, *JAF* 1928 [Philadelphia].
Brown 1952 [North Carolina, 1920s].
Withers and Benet 1954.
Clark, *SFQ* 1961 [North Carolina].
Barrick, *KFQ* 1963 [common before 1910].

91. What's the difference between an elephant and a loaf of bread? *I won't send you to the store for bread.* (several)
    Brown 1952 [North Carolina, 1920s].
    Barrick, *SFQ* 1964 [cites an appearance in 1903].

92. Why do jays walk all the time? *They don't.* (girl, 8)

93. How come the leaves are falling off the trees? *'Cause they saw your face and they screamed.* (boy, 8)

94. How come the trees are growing leaves? *Because they saw your pee pee and they screamed.* (boy, 6)

95. How come the leaves fall? *I can't tell you.* (boy, 6)

96. You got two shoes and one sock, what do you need? (*If riddlee responds, "Another sock," then riddler administers punch to some accessible portion of riddlee's body, usually the arm*). (several)


## A SAMPLING OF INTERROGATIVE LUDIC ROUTINES PERFORMED BY THE ANGLO CHILDREN

I. DESCRIPTIVE ROUTINES AND ASSORTED PRERIDDLES

1. What has hair and lives in the jungle? *A monkey.* (girl, 7)

2. What goes tick tick and its two arms go around? *A clock.* (girl, 6)

3. What is something you always eat? *Food.* (boy, 7)

4. What did the elephant say when he fell down? *He said, "I'm gonna go in the house, my back is hurting, feels like a frog ate it up."* (boy, 5)

5. Why did the farmer pull his coat off when he went in the water? *Those were his best clothes.* (boy, 5)

6. What is blue and white and red all over? *A book.* (boy and girl, 6)

7. What's red and blue and has white all over? *A necklace.* (boy, 5)

8. What's black and has black on the bottom? *Your shoes.* (boy, 7)

9. What comes after a snowstorm? *Snow shovels.* (girl, 6)

10. What's red? *An apple.* (girl, 5)

11. What did the Aggie say to the other Aggie? (boy, 6)

12. What did the three Aggies say to the other four Aggies? (boy, 6)

13. What did the penguin say to the live penguin? (boy, 6)

14. What did the dead penguin say to the live penguin? *"I'm dying, help me I'm dying."* (boy, 6)

15. What did the ten Aggies say to the one Aggie? *"C'mon, bust this place."* (boy, 6)
16. What did the one Aggie say to the zero Aggie? (boy, 6)
17. What did the blue whale say to the duck? *"I have 200 more inches than you are."* (boy, 6)
18. What did the whale shark say to the great white? *"I am 50,000 feet bigger than you are."* (boy, 6)
19. What did the blue whale say to the great white? *"Put up your dukes or I'll beat you up."* (boy, 6)
20. What did the baby say to the cradle? *"It's time for me to fall."* (boy, 6)
21. What did the (burping noise) say to the great white? (boy, 6)
22. What did the *uhhh* say to the great white? (boy, 6)
23. What did the burp say to the great white? *"I can make more noise than you can."* (boy, 6)
24. What did Spiderman say to Ironman? *"You don't have no brains."* (boy, 6)
25. What did the Martian say to the human? (boy, 6)
26. What did the man say to the store? (boy, 6)
27. What did Captain Marvel say when he tried to fly? *He said, "I don't want to fly."* (boy, 5)


II. RIDDLES PROPER

*A. Homophonic*

28. What is the biggest pencil in the world? *Pennsylvania with 10,000 erasers.* (boy, 6)
29. Why did the man take hay to bed? *To feed his nightmares.* (boy, 6)
    Ainsworth, *SFQ* 1962, #287.
30. What did the big chimney say to the little chimney? *"You're too young to smoke."* (boy, 6)
    Ainsworth, *SFQ* 1962, #324.
31. What did the big firecracker say to the little firecracker? *"My pop is bigger than your pop."* (girl, 7)
    Halpert, *JAF* 1943 [black, New Jersey].
    Withers and Benet 1954, #132.
32. What did the rug say to floor? *"Don't move, I've got you covered."* (several)
    Withers and Benet 1954, #132.
    Abrahams, *KFQ* 1962 [black, Philadelphia].
    Ainsworth, *SFQ* 1962, #326.
33. What did the plant say to the bug? *"Bug off."* (boy, 6)
34. Why is a barn so noisy? *Cause the cows have horns.* (boy, 7)

35. What's black and white and red all over?    *A newspaper.* (several)
    (see annotation of item 47 in the chicano corpus)
36. What did the pig say when the farmer grabbed him by the tail?    *"This is the end of me."* (several)
37. What has a trunk and a tail and walks?    *A mouse going on vacation.* (girl, 6)
38. When is a swallow at the table?    *When you drink or eat.* (boy, 7)
    Parsons, *JAF* 1925 [Bermuda].
    Withers and Benet 1954, #28.
    Ainsworth, *SFQ* 1962, #84.
39. How come you have to go to bed?    *Cause the bed won't come to you.* (several)
    Withers and Benet 1954, #31.
40. If the king sits on gold, who sits on silver?    *The Lone Ranger.* (boy, 7)
41. Where does the Lone Ranger take his junk?    *To the dump (set to the melody of the Lone Ranger theme song, Rossini's William Tell Overture).*
42. What has four wheels and flies?    *A garbage truck.* (girl, 7)
    Ainsworth, *SFQ* 1962, #191.
    Barrick, *KFQ* 1963 [Pennsylvania].
43. What did the live duck say to the other live duck?    *"Put up your dukes."* (boy, 6)

*B. Conventional Polysemy*
44. What has teeth but doesn't eat?    *A comb.* (girl, 6)
    Taylor 1951, #299.
45. If you're drowning and you have some lifesavers what do you do?    *You take a lifesaver.* (boy, 6)
    Winslow, *KFQ* 1966, #84.
46. I was locked inside a house with a piano and no key, what do you do?    *Take a key from the piano.* (boy, 7)
    Brown 1952 [North Carolina, 1920s].
47. What has four legs and never walks?    *A table.* (boy, 8)
    Parsons, *JAF* 1925, #84 [Bermuda].
    Taylor 1951, #305.
48. How can you leave a room with two legs and come back with six?    *Carrying a chair.* (girl, 8)
    Taylor 1951, #464.
49. What's the last thing you take off before you sleep?    *Your feet off the floor.* (boy, 8)
    Fauset, *JAF* 1928 [black, Philadelphia].

Abrahams, *KFQ* 1962 [black, Philadelphia—not, as he says, previously unclassified].

50. What kind of head grows in the garden?   *Lettuce.* (boy, 7)
    Taylor 1951, #31.

51. What kind of coat do you put on the house?   *A coat of paint.* (boy, 7)

52. Why does time fly so fast?   *Because so many people are trying to kill it.* (girl, 7)
    Ainsworth, *SFQ* 1962, #276.

53. Why did the boy throw the clock out the window?   *To make time fly.* (girl, 8).
    Withers and Benet 1954, #25.
    Abrahams, *KFQ* 1962 [black, Philadelphia].

54. What is the best way to raise cherries?   *With a spoon.* (boy, 7)
    Withers and Benet 1954, #11.

55. What has teeth but no face?   *A saw.* (boy, 8)
    Taylor 1951, #18.

*C. Radical Polysemy*

56. What has a thousand eyes?   *A screen.* (girl, 7)
    Parsons, *JAF* 1921 [South Carolina].
    Parsons, *JAF* 1925 [Bermuda].
    Taylor 1951, #15.

*D. Anomaly*

57. Who goes to sleep with his shoes on?   *A horse.* (boy, 7)
    Withers and Benet 1954, #69.

58. What goes up white and comes down yellow?   *An egg.* (girl, 8)
    Perkins, *JAF* 1922 [black, New Orleans].
    Bacon and Parsons, *JAF* 1922 [Virginia].
    Taylor 1951, #1550.
    Ainsworth, *SFQ* 1962, #199.

59. What travels but never moves?   *A road.* (girl, 7)
    Bacon and Parsons, *JAF* 1922 [Virginia].
    Ainsworth, *SFQ* 1962, #29.

60. How many balls of string does it take to reach the moon?   *One big one.* (boy, 8)
    Johnson, *JAF* 1921 [Antigua].
    Bacon and Parsons, *JAF* 1922 [Virginia].

61. What has a head like a cat, tail like a cat, body like a cat, but is not a cat?   *A kitten.* (girl, 8)
    Waugh, *JAF* 1918 [Canada].
    Farr, *JAF* 1935 [Tennessee].

Taylor 1951, #1403.

62. What's black and white and very dangerous?  *A crow with a submachine gun.* (girl, 7)

63. What's big and red and eats rocks?  *A big red rockeater.* (girl, 7)
    Clark, *SFQ* 1961, #101.
    Winslow, *KFQ* 1966, #92.

64. What has a long tail and round ears and it hangs by its tail?  *Pooh.* (girl, 7)

65. What is brown and has blue eyes and has one arm ripped off?  *Bigfoot.* (boy, 7)

66. What is yellow and it's the fattest brain in the world?  *A ten thousand canary.* (girl, 6)
    Ainsworth, *SFQ* 1962, #20.
    Barrick, *KFQ* 1963 [Pennsylvania].

67. What is white on the outside and green on the inside and hops?  *Frog sandwich.* (girl, 7)

68. What is purple and white and shaped like a horse?  *A horse wearing pajamas.* (boy, 7)

69. Which likes to eat cookies and it's a monster?  *Cookie Monster.* (girl, 6)


*E. Catches and Routines of Victimization*

70. Why did the chicken cross the road?  *Because Colonel Sanders was chasing him.* (girl, 6)

71. Why did the chicken cross the road?  *To get to the other side.* (several)
    (see annotation of item 90 in chicano corpus)

72. What is black and white and red?  *A skunk with a heat rash.* (girl, 6)

73. What do you do when a baby is throwing food on the floor and you don't want him to?  *Make him eat on the floor.* (boy, 6)

74. If you have two shoes and only one sock what do you need?  *Another sock (administers punch).* (boy, 7)

## 1. INTRODUCTION

1. The pioneering efforts of Barker and Wright (1951) amply illustrate the fruits of an objective stance such as I recommend here, though most research programs will not require the exhaustive detail attained by these scholars.

2. A store of folklore exhibiting this latent political consciousness, drawn from the same children responsible for our primary riddling corpus, can be found in my unpublished dissertation (McDowell 1975).

3. The Texas Children's Folklore Project was carried out during the period 1974–75, under funding from the Southwest Educational Development Laboratory originating in the National Institute of Education. The project supervisor was Professor Richard Bauman, Director of the Center for Intercultural Studies in Folklore and Ethnomusicology at the University of Texas, Austin. Archive materials assembled for the project are housed at the Center for Intercultural Studies in Folklore and Ethnomusicology at the University of Texas, Austin.

4. Elinor Keenan (1976) argues persuasively that children do not simply imitate adult models, but respond to them in often creative and unpredictable fashion.

5. The delimitation of a boundary between oral literature and ordinary conversation is problematic and deserves immediate, concerted attention. As a legacy of the Russian Formalists and the Prague Circle of Linguists, we tend to assume a threshold separating artful from artless verbalization, but the concept is laden with difficulty.

## 2. INTERROGATIVE LUDIC ROUTINES

1. The debate between theoretical linguists and sociolinguists has been a flamboyant one, the former insisting on the isolation of an ideal language model (Saussure 1959, Chomsky 1965) and the latter arguing for a language model built on actual speech usage (Hymes 1970, Labov 1970).

2. Austin's prescriptions attend to ideal cases; it is abundantly clear that social interaction enfranchises a great many theoretically infelicitous speech acts.

3. One can readily identify roots to the theory of enactment, including the fundamental proposition that collective celebration encodes and intensifies the ordinary (Durkheim 1915); the aesthetic orientation toward the everyday as the source of artistic expression (Dewey 1934); and the linguistic study of everyday and special language codes (Garvin 1964).

4. Excerpted from materials gathered for the Texas Children's Folklore Project.

5. The category of routines of victimization as delimited in this study is adumbrated in the following observation of Abrahams and Dundes (1974:136): "A joking question is an enigma in which the question simply functions as a set-up for a punch line." Danielle Roemer (1977) has produced a dissertation as part of the Texas Children's Folklore Project dealing extensively with the catch, defined as a two-party, humorous, interactional routine, strategically designed to effect the surprise and victimization of one of the participants.

## 3.   TEXTURE

1. For an early folkloristic treatment of a related concept of texture see Alan Dundes (1963).

2. The phonetic symbols used in this chapter are as follows:

*Consonants*

|          |      | Bilabial | Labio-dental | Dental | Alveo-lar | Alveo-palatal | Velar |
|----------|------|----------|--------------|--------|-----------|---------------|-------|
|          | −vd  | p        |              | t      |           |               | k     |
| Stops    | +vd  | b        |              | d      |           |               | g     |
| Affricates | −vd |        |              |        |           | č             |       |
|          | +vd  |          |              |        |           | ǰ             |       |
| Fricatives |    |          |              |        |           |               |       |
| Slit     | −vd  |          | f            | θ      |           |               |       |
|          | +vd  |          | v            | ð      |           |               |       |
| Groove   | −vd  |          |              |        | s         | š             |       |
|          | +vd  |          |              |        | z         | ž             |       |
| Lateral  |      |          |              |        | l         |               |       |
| Nasal    |      | m        |              |        | n         |               | ŋ     |
| Semivowel |     | w        |              |        | r         | y             |       |

*Vowels*

| Front | Central | Back |      |
|-------|---------|------|------|
| i     | ɨ       | u    | High |
| e     | ə       | o    | Mid  |
| æ     | a       | ɔ    | Low  |

3. A remarkable analogue to this silencing of conventional intonation in riddles has come to my attention. Isbell and Roncalla Fernandez (1977) report that in Quechua riddle games, performed in highland Peru, certain

conventional topic and comment markers (in Quechua taking the form of suffixes rather than intonation patterns as in English) are also suppressed in riddling. The authors state: "Quechua riddles are linguistically anomalous: they lack the obligatory markers of common discourse, which relegates them to the realm of ambiguity" (Isbell and Roncalla Fernandez 1977:40).

4. The image comes from Menendez-Pidal (see Colin Smith 1964:15).

## 4.  STRUCTURE

1. Tzvetan Todorov (1973) proposes the following canonic form for the riddle:

What is the name of that thing (or that being) which ... ?

Our analysis would indicate a minor adjustment in the formula, to read:

What is the name of that thing (or that being) which is, has, or does X?

Even so, we should note that this formula adequately describes only a portion of our total corpus, specifically a group of descriptive routines and those riddles proper generally referred to as true riddles. Other canonic forms, describing other segments of our corpus, suggest themselves:

What did the X say to the Y?

## 5.  CONTENT

1. See the appendix for annotations of the riddles dealt with in this study.

2. Texts of narratives exploring these realms of predatory nature and supernature, and collected from these same chicano children, can be found in my unpublished dissertation (McDowell 1975).

3. Carol Chomsky (1969) shows that acquisition of syntax continues into at least the ninth year, though the great majority of syntactic structures are mastered by age six.

## 6.  NEGOTIATION

1. One of the intriguing uses of riddling is in the context of wakes (O'Suilleabhain 1961, Abrahams 1972). Here is a citation depicting the Irish custom: "Young people often resorted to riddling among themselves, when they needed a rest between more formal games. It was only an inter-

lude, however. . . . Also, trick questions which involved the unusual use or pronunciation of certain words were tossed about on these occasions" (O'Suilleabhain 1961:32).

2. Prevarication is possible in relation to all principles of riddling etiquette. In regard to riddler's recognition of correct solutions, many routines permit of a set of logically possible solutions, rather than a single definitive solution. Riddlers may hold off acceptable offerings until the riddlees of their choice come across with a solution they can approve. In some of my dealings with the chicano children, I offered tenable solutions that were rejected in favor of solutions provided by members of the peer group.

3. Ethnographic reports from other societies echo the concept of authority invested in riddler. For example, from the African Mbere: "the Mbere riddle confers formal power on the riddler, who may not enjoy such dominance in social life" (Glazer and Gorfain 1976:199).

## 7.  SESSIONS

1. Richard Bauman, supervisor of the Texas Children's Folklore Project, describes the scenario as follows: "No video crew was visible; camera was ceiling-mounted and remote-controlled—quite unobtrusive, though the kids did know they were being video-taped" (Bauman, personal communication).

## 8.  CLASS AND ETHNIC VARIABLES

1. I toyed with the possibility of utilizing Basil Bernstein's provocative concepts of the personal and positional family types, and the extended and restricted language codes, but upon inspection found that these concepts did not readily map onto my field data. A rigorous investigation centering on these issues might well turn up systematic patterning along these lines with respect to our two communities, though I am inclined to believe that the actual situation in Austin is too complex and varied to be handled by Bernstein's models.

2. *Highlights: The Monthly Book for Children* is a widely disseminated magazine with a regularly appearing riddle page. The contents of this feature are solicited from the readership, as follows: "Send us the funniest joke or the best riddle you ever heard with your name, age, and home address. If we think it good enough, we might print it in HIGHLIGHTS." This fount of children's literature (that is, literature for, not by, children) is perhaps typical in fostering a complex interplay between folk traditions and popular literature. Among the riddles encountered in a casual scanning of back issues were several routines from our corpus, including these:

What is the last thing you take off when you go to bed? *You take your feet off the floor.* (*Highlights* 31, 1976)

What has the feet of a cat and the fur of a cat but is not a cat? *A kitten.* (*Highlights* 32, 1977).

3. Marshall McLuhan (1962) and Walter Ong (1967) explore the transformations of the world occasioned by the transition from oral to script to electronic culture. Their observations have led me to propose the following highly controversial redefinition of folklore: "Folklore studies orally determined forms of communication, both in oral cultures and as they continue to exist and interact with other forms of communication in script and electronic cultures."

## 9. ACQUISITION

1. In a recent survey, Richard Bauman (1978) draws together some of the same sources and concepts developed here. Also, Danielle Roemer (1977) portrays the acquisition of catches and narratives in terms congruent with the present discussion.

2. These excerpts are from the Texas Children's Folklore Project.

3. A recent treatment of riddle acquisition (Isbell and Roncalla Fernandez 1977) details a similar progress from phonological orientation to conceptual orientation, though the age locus is quite different from the one considered in the present study. The authors posit the following sequence:

   a. riddles based on sound correspondences;
   b. riddles based on bipolar classification, and classification due to similarity;
   c. riddles as propositional puzzles about the hypothetical and the possible. (Isbell and Roncalla Fernandez 1977:46)

The first of these categories would correspond to the homophonic group treated in the present analysis; the second to interrogative ludic routines incorporating radical polysemy; and the third to routines centered on perceptual or conceptual anomaly.

## 10. ENCULTURATION

1. The question of who riddles, both in terms of social groups and segments within social groups, is a problematic one complicated by two factors: (1) the blinding effect of Western generic categorization in application to non-Western traditions; and (2) the influence of the expectancy effect in determining whether or not an investigator notices a given genre or not.

Concerning the former complication, it is now becoming increasingly apparent that American Indian societies do in fact exhibit autochthonous riddling traditions. Charles Scott (1963) sums up the historical argument and adduces new evidence; more recent work indicates a flourishing riddling tradition in Andean Peru (Isbell and Roncalla Fernandez 1977).

Concerning the latter complication, Fine and Crane (1977) illustrate the impact of the investigators' expectations in collecting riddles from North American college students, coming to the following conclusion: "The average number of riddles collected by those who expected to collect few riddles was 13.4; by those with no expectation, 15.8; and by those with high expectancy, 19.6. Apparently the anthropological questioning process was being affected by the questioner's perceptions of what was appropriate in that situation" (Fine and Crane 1977:520). Given the vagaries here, surely it is premature to suppose, as does Elli Kongas-Maranda, that "riddles have gone the way of the bow and arrow" (1976: 128).

2. I must insist that the calculations of metaphorical content in these few riddling traditions are by no means decisive proof of the evolutionary trajectory I am proposing here. This whole operation is beset with difficulties, beginning with the collection of the material itself, and culminating in my own arrangement of it. I offer these computations for their suggestive value, in the hope that they may prove controversial enough to stimulate more adequate treatment elsewhere.

# REFERENCES

Abodunde, Titus.
1976.    The Place of the Folktale in Yoruba Folk Culture. Ms.
Abrahams, Roger.
1962.    Some Riddles from the Negro of Philadelphia. *Keystone Folklore Quarterly* 7:10–17.
1964.    *Deep Down in the Jungle: Negro Narrative Folklore from the Streets of Philadelphia.* Chicago: Aldine.
1968.    Introductory Remarks toward a Rhetorical Theory of Folklore. *Journal of American Folklore* 81:143–58.
1971.    Personal Power and Social Restraint in the Definition of Folklore. *Journal of American Folklore* 84:16–30.
1972.    The Literary Study of the Bible. *Texas Studies in Literature and Language* XIV:177–97.
1974.    Black Talking on the Streets. In Richard Bauman and Joel Sherzer (editors), *Explorations in the Ethnography of Speaking.* Cambridge: Cambridge University Press.
1977.    Toward an Enactment-Centered Theory of Folklore. In William Bascom (editor), *Frontiers of Folklore.* American Association for the Advancement of Science, Washington, D. C.
Abrahams, Roger, and Dundes, Alan.
1969.    On Elephantasy and Elephanticide. *The Psychoanalytic Review* 56:225–41.
1972.    Riddles. In Richard Dorson (editor), *Folklore and Folklife: An Introduction.* Chicago: University of Chicago Press.
Acuña, Rodolfo.
1972.    *Occupied America: The Chicano's Struggle Toward Liberation.* San Francisco: Canfield Press.
Ainsworth, Catherine.
1962.    Black and White and Said All Over. *Southern Folklore Quarterly* 26:263–95.
Ariés, Philippe.
1962.    *Centuries of Childhood: A Social History of Family Life.* New York: Vintage Books.
Aristotle.
1907.    *The Poetics.* Translated by E. S. Bouchier. Oxford: Blackwell.
Austin, J. L.
1962.    *How To Do Things With Words.* Oxford: Oxford University Press.
Babcock, Barbara.
1978.    *The Reversible World: Symbolic Inversion in Art and Society.* Ithaca: Cornell University Press.

261

Bacon, A. M., and Parsons, E. C.
  1922.   Folklore from Elizabeth City County, Virginia. *Journal of American Folklore* 35:250–327.
Barker, Roger, and Wright, Herbert.
  1951.   *One Boy's Day: A Specimen Record of Behavior.* New York: Harper.
Barrick, Mac.
  1963.   Riddles from Cumberland County [Pa.]. *Keystone Folklore Quarterly* 8:59–74.
  1964.   The Shaggy Elephant Riddle. *Southern Folklore Quarterly* 28: 266–90.
Bascom, William.
  1954.   Four Functions of Folklore. *Journal of American Folklore* 67: 333–49.
  1977.   *Frontiers of Folklore.* American Association for the Advancement of Science, Washington, D. C.
Bauman, Richard.
  1970.   The Turtles: An American Riddling Institution. *Western Folklore* 29:21–25.
  1975.   Verbal Art as Performance. *American Anthropologist* 77:290–311.
  1977.   Linguistics, Anthropology and Verbal Art: Toward a Unified Perspective with a Special Discussion of Children's Folklore. In Muriel Saville-Troike (editor), *Linguistics and Anthropology, Report of the Twenty-Eighth Annual Georgetown University Round Table on Language and Linguistics.* Washington, D. C.
Bauman, Richard, and Sherzer, Joel.
  1974.   *Explorations in the Ethnography of Speaking.* Cambridge: Cambridge University Press.
Ben-Amos, Dan.
  1976.   Solutions to Riddles. *Journal of American Folklore* 89:249–54.
Benedict, Ruth.
  1935.   *Zuni Mythology.* New York: Columbia University Press.
Bernstein, Basil.
  1958.   Some Sociological Determinants of Perception: An Inquiry into Sub-Cultural Differences. *British Journal of Sociology* 9: 159–74.
  1971.   *Class, Codes, and Control.* London: Routledge and Keegan Paul.
Bloomfield, Leonard.
  1933.   *Language.* New York: Holt, Rinehart.

Boas, Franz.
    1916.    Tsimshian Mythology. Bureau of American Ethnology, Annual Report, vol. 31.
    1925.    Stylistic Aspects of Primitive Literature. *Journal of American Folklore* 38:329–39.

Boggs, Ralph Steel.
    1934.    North Carolina White Folktales and Riddles. *Journal of American Folklore* 37:289–328.

Bolinger, Dwight.
    1965.    *Forms of English: Accent, Morpheme, Order.* Cambridge: Harvard University Press.

Brady, Margaret, and Eckhardt, Rosalind.
    1975.    *Black Girls at Play: Folkloric Perspectives on Child Development.* Southwest Educational Development Corporation: Austin.

Brown, Roger.
    1975.    *A First Language: The Early Stages.* Cambridge: Harvard University Press.

Bureau of the Census.
    1970.    Population Characteristics: Texas.

Burke, Kenneth.
    1941.    *The Philosophy of Literary Form.* Baton Rouge: Louisiana State University Press.

Burns, Thomas.
    1976.    Riddling: Occasion to Act. *Journal of American Folklore* 89:139–65.

Chafe, Wallace.
    1970.    *Meaning and the Structure of Language.* Chicago: University of Chicago Press.

Chomsky, Carol.
    1969.    *The Acquisition of Syntax in Children from 5 to 10.* Cambridge: M.I.T. Press.

Chomsky, Noam.
    1965.    *Aspects of the Theory of Syntax.* Cambridge: M.I.T. Press.
    1968.    *Language and Mind.* New York: Harcourt, Brace, and World.

Clark, Joseph.
    1961.    Riddles from North Carolina. *Southern Folklore Quarterly* 25:113–25.

Colby, Benjamin.
    1966.    The Analysis of Culture Content and the Patterning of Narrative Concern in Texts. *American Anthropologist* 68:374–88.

Dewey, John.
1934.    *Art as Experience.* New York: Capricorn Books.
Dundes, Alan.
1964.    Texture, Text, and Context. *Southern Folklore Quarterly* 28: 251–65.
1965.    *The Study of Folklore.* New York: Prentice Hall.
Durkheim, Emile.
1915.    *The Elementary Forms of the Religious Life.* Glencoe: Free Press.
Elias-Olivares, Lucia.
1975.    Language Varieties and Language Use in East Austin. Ms.
Espinosa, Aurelio.
1916.    New Mexican Spanish Folklore: Riddles. *Journal of American Folklore* 28:505–35.
Evans, David.
1976.    Riddling and the Structure of Context. *Journal of American Folklore* 89:166–88.
Farr, T. J.
1935.    Riddles and Superstitions of Middle Tennessee. *Journal of American Folklore* 48:318–36.
Fauset, Arthur.
1928.    Tales and Riddles Collected in Philadelphia. *Journal of American Folklore* 41:529–57.
Fernandez, James.
1974.    The Mission of Metaphor in Expressive Culture. *Current Anthropology* 15:119–45.
Festinger, Leon.
1964.    *Conflict, Decision, and Dissonance.* Stanford: Stanford University Press.
Fillmore, C. J.
1971.    Verbs of Judging: an Exercise in Semantic Description. In C. J. Fillmore and T. D. Langendoen (editors), *Studies in Linguistic Semantics.* New York: Holt, Rinehart.
Fine, Gary, and Crane, Beverly.
1977.    The Expectancy Effect in Anthropological Research: An Experimental Study of Riddle Collection. *American Ethnologist* 4:517–24.
Freud, Sigmund.
1963.    *Jokes and Their Relation to the Unconscious.* Translated by James Strachey. New York: Norton.
Garrido de Boggs, Edna.
1955.    *Folklore infantil de Santo Domingo.* Madrid: Ediciones Cultura Hispánica.

Garvin, Paul.
  1964.    *A Prague School Reader on Esthetics, Literary Structure, and
           Style*. Washington, D. C.: Georgetown University Press.
Gatschet, Albert.
  1889.    Popular Rimes from Mexico. *Journal of American Folklore* 2:
           48–53.
Geertz, Clifford.
  1973.    *The Interpretation of Cultures*. New York: Basic Books.
Georges, Robert, and Dundes, Alan.
  1963.    Toward a Structural Definition of the Riddle. *Journal of Ameri-
           can Folklore* 76:111–18.
Gingras, Rosario.
  1974.    Problems in the Description of Spanish-English Intra-Senten-
           tial Code-Switching. In Garland Bills (editor), *Southwest Areal
           Linguistics*. San Diego: San Diego State University.
Ginsberg, Herbert, and Opper, Sylvia.
  1969.    *Piaget's Theory of Intellectual Development: An Introduction*.
           New York: Prentice Hall.
Glazer, Jack, and Gorfain, Phyllis.
  1976.    Ambiguity and Exchange: The Double Dimension of Mbere
           Riddles. *Journal of American Folklore* 89:189–238.
Goffman, Erving.
  1971.    *Relations in Public*. New York: Harper.
Goldstein, Kenneth.
  1963.    Riddling Traditions in Northeastern Scotland. *Journal of
           American Folklore* 76:330–36.
Goodenough, Ward.
  1963.    *Cooperation in Change: An Anthropological Approach to
           Community Development*. New York: Russell Sage Founda-
           tion.
  1964.    Cultural Anthropology and Linguistics. *Monograph Series on
           Languages and Linguistics* 9:167–73.
Goodman, Mary.
  1970.    *The Culture of Childhood*. New York: Columbia University
           Press.
Gowlett, D. F.
  1966.    Some Lozi Riddles and Tongue-twisters Annotated and Ana-
           lyzed. *African Studies* 25:139–58.
Guadalupe Noguera, Eduardo.
  1918.    Adivinanzas recogidos en México. *Journal of American Folk-
           lore* 31:537–40.
Gumperz, John, and Hernandez-Chavez, Eduardo.
  1972.    Bilingualism, Bidialectalism and Classroom Interaction. In

Courtney Cazden, Vera John, and Dell Hymes (editors), *Functions of Language in the Classroom*. New York: Teachers College Press.

Halpert, Herbert.
1943.    Negro Riddles Collected in New Jersey. *Journal of American Folklore* 56:200–202.

Hamnet, Ian.
1967.    Ambiguity, Classification and Change: The Function of Riddles. *Man* 2:379–93.

Harner, Michael.
1972.    *The Jívaro: People of the Sacred Waterfalls*. New York: Doubleday.

Havranek, Bohuslav.
1964.    The Functional Differentiation of the Standard Language. In Paul Garvin, (editor and translator), *A Prague School Reader on Esthetics, Literary Structure, and Style*. Washington, D. C.: Georgetown University Press.

Hymes, Dell.
1970.    The Ethnography of Speaking. In Joshua Fishman (editor), *Readings in the Sociology of Language*. The Hague: Mouton.
1971.    On Linguistic Theory, Communicative Competence and the Education of Disadvantaged Children. In Murray Wax, Stanley Diamond, and Frederick Gearing (editors), *Anthropological Perspectives on Education*. New York: Basic Books.

Jackendoff, R.
1972.    *Semantic Interpretation in Generative Grammar*. Cambridge: M.I.T. Press.

Jacobs, Jane.
1961.    *The Death and Life of Great American Cities*. New York: Vintage Books.

Jakobson, Roman.
1960.    Linguistics and Poetics: Closing Statement. In Thomas Sebeok (editor), *Style in Language*. Cambridge: M.I.T. Press.
1966.    Grammatical Parallelism and Its Russian Facet. *Language* 42: 398–429.

Jameson, Fredric.
1972.    *The Prison-House of Language*. Princeton: Princeton University Press.

Janelli, Roger.
1970.    Form and Function: A Quantitative Approach to the Riddle. Ms.

Jefferson, Gail, and Schenkein, Jim.
1977.     Some Sequential Negotiations in Conversation: Unexpanded and Expanded Versions of Projected Action Sequences. *Sociology* 11:87–103.

Johnson, Frederick.
1921.     Folklore from the British West Indies. *Journal of American Folklore* 34:40–88.

Jones, Nicholas.
1972.     Categories of Child Interaction. In Nicholas Jones (editor), *Ethnological Studies of Child Behavior*. Cambridge: Cambridge University Press.

Keenan, Elinor.
1974.     Conversational Competence in Children. *Journal of Child Language* 1:163–83.

Kongas-Maranda, Elli.
1971a.     The Logic of Riddles. In Pierre and Elli Maranda (editors), *Structural Analysis of Oral Tradition*. Philadelphia: University of Pennsylvania Press.
1971b.     Theory and Practice of Riddle Analysis. *Journal of American Folklore* 84:51–61.
1971c.     A Tree Grows: Transformations of a Riddle Metaphor. In Pierre and Elli Maranda (editors), *Structural Models in Folklore and Transformational Essays*. The Hague: Mouton.

Labov, William.
1972.     *Language in the Inner City: Studies in the Black English Vernacular*. Philadelphia: University of Pennsylvania Press.

Layton, Monique.
1976.     Luba and Finnish Riddles: A Double Analysis. *Journal of American Folklore* 89:239–48.

Leach, Edmund.
1964.     Animal Categories and Verbal Abuse. In Eric Lennenberg (editor), *New Directions in the Study of Language*. Cambridge: M.I.T. Press.
1970.     *Claude Lévi-Strauss*. New York: Viking.

Leech, Geoffrey.
1974.     *Semantics*. Middlesex: Pelican.

Leventhal, Nancy, and Cray, Ed.
1963.     Depth Collecting from a Sixth-Grade Class. *Western Folklore* 22:159–64, 231–58.

Lévi-Strauss, Claude.
1966.     *The Savage Mind*. Chicago: University of Chicago Press.
1967.     *Structural Anthropology*. New York: Anchor.

Liebow, Elliot.
   1967.   *Tally's Corner: A Study of Negro Streetcorner Men.* Boston:
           Little, Brown.
List, George.
   1963.   The Boundaries of Speech and Song. *Ethnomusicology* 7:1–16.
Lord, Albert.
   1960.   *Singer of Tales.* Cambridge: Harvard University Press.
Loomis, C. Grant.
   1948.   Traditional American Word Play: The Conundrum. *Western
           Folklore* 8:235–47.
McDowell, John.
   1974.   Interrogative Routines in Mexican-American Children's Folk-
           lore. Working Papers in Sociolinguistics, no. 20.
   1975.   The Speech Play and Verbal Art of Chicano Children: An
           Ethnographic and Sociolinguistic Study. Ph.D. Diss., Univer-
           sity of Texas.
   1976.   Riddling and Enculturation: A Glance at the Cerebral Child.
           Working Papers in Sociolinguistics, no. 36.
McGhee, P. E.
   1976.   Children's Appreciation of Humor: A Test of the Cognitive
           Congruity Principle. *Child Development* 47:420–26.
McNeill, David.
   1970.   *The Acquisition of Language: The Study of Developmental
           Psycholinguistics.* New York: Harper and Row.
McLuhan, Marshall.
   1962.   *The Gutenberg Galaxy.* New York: Simon and Schuster.
McWilliams, Carey.
   1968.   *North from Mexico: The Spanish-Speaking People of the
           United States.* New York: Greenwood Press.
Madsen, William.
   1964.   *Mexican-Americans of South Texas.* New York: Holt, Rine-
           hart, and Winston.
Malinowski, Bronislaw.
   1961.   *Argonauts of the Western Pacific.* New York: Dutton.
Malof, Joseph.
   1970.   *A Manual of English Meters.* Bloomington: Indiana University
           Press.
Mason, J. Alden.
   1916.   Porto-Rican Folklore: Riddles. *Journal of American Folklore*
           29:423–504.
Meinig, D. W.
   1969.   *Imperial Texas.* Austin: University of Texas Press.

Mukarovsky, Jan.
1964.   Standard Language and Poetic Language. In Paul Garvin (editor and translator), *A Prague School Reader on Esthetics, Literary Structure, and Style.* Washington, D. C.: Georgetown University Press.
Neisser, Ulric.
1976.   *Cognition and Reality: Principles and Implications of Cognitive Psychology.* San Francisco: W. H. Freeman and Company.
Ong, Walter.
1967.   *The Presence of the Word: Some Prolegomena for Cultural and Religious History.* New York: Simon and Schuster.
Opie, Iona, and Opie, Peter.
1959.   *The Lore and Language of School Children.* Oxford: Oxford University Press.
O'Suilleabhain, Sean.
1961.   *Irish Wake Amusements.* Ireland.
Paredes, Américo.
1958.   *"With His Pistol in His Hand": A Border Ballad and Its Hero.* Austin: University of Texas Press.
1976.   *A Texas-Mexican Cancionero: Folksongs of the Lower Border.* Urbana: University of Illinois Press.
1977.   On Ethnographic Work Among Minority Groups: A Folklorist's Perspective. *New Scholar* 6:1–32.
Parsons, Elsie Clews.
1917.   Notes on the Folklore of Guilford County, North Carolina. *Journal of American Folklore* 30:201–207.
1921.   Folklore from Aiken, South Carolina. *Journal of American Folklore* 34:1–39.
1925.   Bermuda Folklore. *Journal of American Folklore* 38:239–66.
1934.   Folklore from Georgia. *Journal of American Folklore* 47: 386–89.
Peckham, Morse.
1967.   *Man's Rage for Chaos: Biology, Behavior, and the Arts.* New York: Shocken.
Perkins, A. E.
1922.   Riddles from Negro Schoolchildren in New Orleans, Louisiana. *Journal of American Folklore* 35:105–22.
Petsch, Robert.
1899.   *Neue Beitrage zur Kenntnis des Volkratsels.* (Palaestra 4). Berlin: Mayer and Muller.

Piaget, Jean.
  1954.    *The Construction of Reality in the Child.* Translated by M. Cook. New York: Basic Books.
  1972.    *The Child and Reality: Problems of Genetic Psychology.* New York: Viking.
Pitt, Leonard.
  1966.    *The Decline of the Californios: A Social History of the Span-ish-Speaking Californians.* Berkeley: University of California Press.
Pope, Emily.
  1975.    Questions and Answers in English. Indiana University Linguistics Club.
Prentice, N., and Fathman, R.
  1975.    Joking Riddles: A Developmental Index of Children's Humor. *Developmental Psychology* 11:210–16.
Recinos, Adrian.
  1918.    Adivinanzas recogidas en Guatemala. *Journal of American Folklore* 31:544–49.
Ribeiro, Darcy.
  1968.    *The Civilizational Process.* Washington, D. C.: Smithsonian Institution.
Roberts, John; Arth, M.; and Bush, R.
  1959.    Games in Culture. *American Anthropologist* 61:597–605.
Roemer, Danielle.
  1977.    A Social Interactional Analysis of Anglo Children's Folklore: Catches and Narratives. Ph.D. Diss., University of Texas.
Rubel, Arthur.
  1966.    *Across the Tracks: Mexican-Americans in a Texas City.* Austin: University of Texas Press.
Sanches, Mary, and Kirshenblatt-Gimblett, Barbara.
  1971.    Child Language and Children's Traditional Speech Play. Penn-Texas Working Papers in Sociolinguistics, no. 5. Revised version published in Barbara Kirshenblatt-Gimblett (editor), *Speech Play.* Philadelphia: University of Pennsylvania Press, 1976.
Sapir, Edward.
  1921.    *Language.* New York: Harcourt, Brace, and World.
Sapir, J. David, and Crocker, J. Christopher.
  1977.    *The Social Use of Metaphor.* Philadelphia: University of Pennsylvania Press.
de Saussure, Ferdinand.
  1959.    *Course in General Linguistics.* Translated by Wade Baskin. New York: McGraw-Hill.

Schlesinger, Marilyn.
1960.    Riddling Questions from Los Angeles High School Students. *Western Folklore* XIX:191–95.
Scott, Charles.
1969.    On Defining the Riddle: The Problem of a Structural Unit. *Genre* 2:129–42.
Searle, John.
1969.    *Speech Acts: An Essay in the Philosophy of Language.* Cambridge: Cambridge University Press.
Serrano Martínez, Celedonio.
1950.    Diferencias entre el corrido mexicano y el romance español. *Cuauhtémoc, Revista de Cultura y de Actualidad* 2:44–47.
Shipman, M. D.
1972.    *Childhood: A Sociological Perspective.* England: National Foundation for Educational Research.
Shultz, Thomas.
1974.    Development of the Appreciation of Riddles. *Child Development* 45:100–105.
Sien, Maung Than, and Dundes, Alan.
1964.    Twenty-Three Riddles from Central Burma. *Journal of American Folklore* 77:69–75.
Sinclair, J. McH., and Coulthard, R. M.
1975.    *Towards an Analysis of Discourse.* Oxford: Oxford University Press.
Smith, Colin.
1964.    *Spanish Ballads.* Elmsford, N.Y.: Pergamon Press.
Stross, Brian.
1973.    Social Structure and Role Allocation in Tzeltal Oral Literature. *Journal of American Folklore* 86:95–113.
Sudnow, David.
1972.    *Studies in Social Interaction.* New York: Macmillan.
Sutton-Smith, Brian.
1976.    A Developmental Structural Account of Riddles. In Barbara Kirshenblatt-Gimblett (editor), *Speech Play.* Philadelphia: University of Pennsylvania Press.
1977.    Structural Parallels Between Imagination and Folk Phenomena in Childhood. Lecture delivered to the Folklore Institute at Indiana University.
Taylor, Archer.
1951.    *English Riddles from Oral Tradition.* Berkeley: University of California Press.
1952.    (editor), *Riddles.* In The Frank C. Brown Collection of North Carolina Folklore, vol. 1. Durham.

Tedlock, Dennis.
  1971.    On the Translation of Style in Oral Narrative. *Journal of American Folklore* 84:114–33.
Todorov, Tzvetan.
  1973.    Analyse du discours: l'example des devinettes. *Journal de Psychologie Normale et Pathologique* 1,2:135–55.
Ullmann, S.
  1962.    *Semantics: An Introduction to the Science of Meaning.* Oxford: Blackwell.
Waugh, F. W.
  1918.    Canadian Folklore from Ontario. *Journal of American Folklore* 31:4–82.
Whitt, Kenneth, and Prentice, Norman.
  1977.    Cognitive Processes in the Development of Children's Enjoyment and Comprehension of Joking Riddles. *Developmental Psychology* 13:129–36.
Whyte, William.
  1943.    *Street Corner Society: The Social Structure of an Italian Slum.* Chicago: University of Chicago Press.
Williams, Thomas.
  1963.    The Form and Function of Tambunan Dusun Riddles. *Journal of American Folklore* 76:95–110.
Winslow, David.
  1966.    An Annotated Collection of Children's Lore. *Keystone Folklore Quarterly* 11:151–202.
Withers, Carl, and Benet, Sula.
  1954.    *The American Riddle Book.* New York: Abelard-Schuman.